RECONSTRUCTING THE NATIVE SOUTH

RECONSTRUCTING
THE NATIVE SOUTH

American Indian Literature and the Lost Cause

MELANIE BENSON TAYLOR

THE UNIVERSITY OF GEORGIA PRESS
Athens & London

© 2011 by the University of Georgia Press

Athens, Georgia 30602

www.ugapress.org

All rights reserved

Designed by Walton Harris

Set in 10/14 Chaparral Pro

Printed digitally in the United States of America

Library of Congress Cataloging-in-Publication Data

Benson, Melanie R., 1976–

Reconstructing the native south : American Indian literature
and the lost cause / Melanie Benson Taylor.

p. cm. — (The new southern studies)

Includes bibliographical references.

ISBN 978-0-8203-3884-2 (cloth : alk. paper) —

ISBN 978-0-8203-4066-1 (pbk. : alk. paper)

1. American literature—Indian authors—History and
criticism. 2. Indians in literature. 3. Southern States—In
literature. I. Title.

PS153.I52B465 2011

810.9'897075—dc23

2011018060

British Library Cataloging-in-Publication Data available

To Mum, Pa, Hiya, and Alan,
again and always

There are voices buried in the Mississippi mud. There are ancestors and future children buried beneath currents stirred up by pleasure boats going up and down. There are stories here made of memory.
— Joy Harjo (Creek), "New Orleans"

When a people fade into the darkness at the back end of shallow canals, they take their monsters with them.
—Roger Emile Stouff (Chitimacha), from "Back End of the Canal"

CONTENTS

ACKNOWLEDGMENTS

My first and most immediate thanks go to my incomparable colleagues in the Native American Studies program at Dartmouth College. Colin Calloway, Bruce Duthu, Sergei Kan, Dale Turner, Vera Palmer, and Deb Nichols have been unstintingly generous, warm, and inspiring in ways that I can hardly begin to enumerate. Both my scholarship and my life are incalculably enriched by their friendship and example. The many fellows and visiting scholars who have spent time in our program—particularly Joyce Szabo, Ben Madley, Chris Parsons, Elaine Brown, and Louise Erdrich—have also contributed immeasurably to the pleasure of going to work every day. Sheila Laplante deserves special thanks for being a steady and irreplaceable source of support, advice, and good humor, despite the number of hats she wears (and the number of times I call her frantically for help from the photocopy room). Generous funding from Dartmouth's Sherman Fairchild Foundation and Walter and Connie Burke has facilitated my ability to research, travel, and write freely and frequently; Associate Dean Lindsay Whaley and Dean Michael Mastunduno have granted me the luxurious gift of leave time within which to do so. Finally, I am immensely grateful to the extraordinary NADs (Native Americans at Dartmouth) and especially to the students in "Indian Killers," "Native American Literature," and my First-Year Seminars over the past two years; I have learned far more from them than they could ever learn from me.

While Dartmouth has quickly become home for me, I continue to depend on the guidance and inspiration of numerous colleagues around the globe. Friends and mentors in the New Southern Studies world continue to inspire and fuel my work in countless ways and venues; I look forward to a lifetime of future projects and gatherings with George Handley, Jack Matthews, Jon Smith, Lisa Hinrichsen, Leigh Anne Duck, David A. Davis,

Cole Hutchison, Jennifer Rae Greeson, Scott Romine, Katie McKee, Martyn Bone, Keith Cartwright, Daniel Cross Turner, and many others. For inspiring conversations and camaraderie in Native American Studies, I am grateful to Siobhan Senier, Margo Lukens, Alexandra (Sasha) Harmon, Lisa Brooks, Jesse Peters, Mae Claxton, and David Treuer. In particular, I am profoundly indebted to the pioneering work of a small but growing cadre of Native South scholars, many of whom I am honored to call friends; they include Eric Gary Anderson, Annette Trefzer, Ellen Arnold, Geary Hobson, Janet McAdams, Kirstin Squint, Malinda Maynor Lowery, Sharon Holland, Katherine Osburn, Tiya Miles, Kimberly Roppolo, Rain Goméz, and the late Jack Forbes. Finally, I owe a special debt of gratitude to Geary Hobson, Janet McAdams, and Kathryn Walkiewicz for their recent compilation of the first-ever anthology of southeastern Indian literature, *The People Who Stayed*, and especially for granting me early access to its magnificent contents. It is an understatement to say that this book would never have been possible without theirs.

Once again, the entire staff at the University of Georgia Press has made this process far more smooth and pleasant than I could have imagined. Editor Nancy Grayson, in particular, continues to be a luminous example of wisdom, professionalism, and inexhaustible kindness; this book would not exist without her support and confidence. Many others have helped it evolve in swift, capable, and inimitable ways; my sincerest thanks go to John Joerschke, Jon Davies, Beth Snead, and John McLeod for their expert assistance, advice, and patience at every step in the process. Finally, I am immensely grateful to my copyeditor, Daniel Simon, for improving the original manuscript immeasurably with his meticulous and astute eye.

Finally, my most enduring and inestimable gratitude goes to my wonderful husband, Alan, and my amazing family, Mum and Pa, Hiya and Jon, Grace and Jay. You have all entertained long-winded and one-sided conversations about this book and endured my many working weekends and interminable distractions. For your unfathomable patience, and for ceaselessly reading drafts, encouraging my hopes, and shoring up my fears, I love you all more than I can say. I hope you see yourselves in the best parts of these pages, none of which could exist without you — and in ways both simple and profound, neither would I.

RECONSTRUCTING THE NATIVE SOUTH

RECONSTRUCTING THE SOUTH

Region, Tribe, and Sovereignty in the Age of Global Capitalism

Only at the moment when Lee handed Grant his sword
was the Confederacy born.
—Robert Penn Warren, *The Legacy of the Civil War* (1961)

. . . Indians, a word that exists only with the idea of
the discovery that created the modern world . . .
—Paul Chaat Smith, *Everything You Know
about Indians Is Wrong* (2009)

At the heart of this book is a challenging claim: that the biracial U.S. South and its Native American survivors have far more in common than geographical proximity. It is not difficult to recognize the myriad ways that both groups are haunted by their own private, separate histories of sweeping loss and crippling nostalgia, but we have yet to investigate the moments when the experience, rhetoric, and effects of such histories converge in explicit and startling ways. Part of this oversight rests in persistently anachronistic notions about both groups: these narratives suppose that Indians are relics preserved in the ether of a tragic colonial past and that the South has yet to fully transcend the residues of slavery, segregation, and its biracial legacy. In the contemporary literature of the U.S. South, however, Native and non-Native southerners have arrived at a common meeting place: that very fixation on storied pasts and insurmountable loss forms a shared Lost Cause more present, prescient, and uncanny than we might imagine. No longer the tragic and anachronistic residues of Removal and extinction, the living, breathing, surviving Indian in the contemporary Southeast is, as poet Janet McAdams (Alabama Creek) argues, "indigenous *through* one's Southernness" and not simply in spite of it.[1] Exactly what this means for contemporary Native American identity, usually articulated in contradistinction to that of their colonial antagonists, is an issue that neither southern nor Native American scholars have yet been willing to broach. *Reconstructing the Native South* begins gathering together the indigenous traces in southern society as well as the "southern" influences on the region's Native groups. But what will these mutual reconstructions look like after the long-standing, purposeful narratives of difference and distinction are stripped away? And why are such recognitions emerging now, more than a century and a half after Removal and the Civil War?

This a book born from my experience between these two historically polarized scholarly worlds: the murky, troubled, rapidly changing fields of both southern and Native American studies. As a practitioner of both, I have long sought ways to place them in the same conversation, either by smoking out the Indian ghosts and signifiers lurking in southern writing of the twentieth century or, conversely, by exploring southeastern Removal as a pivotal trauma haunting contemporary Native literature nationwide. In my efforts to unite these divergent critical streams, I was slow to see the distinct, revealing moments when those waters merge of their own accord—the stunning moments when Natives and southerners speak not just *about* one another but in uncanny concert, echoing one another's voices and preoccupations in kindred, unmistakable intimacy. To be sure, these moments are not always harmonious or uplifting; rather, they bear the scars of a long history of colonial aggression, dispossession, appropriation, competition, and segregation, and this book is keen to expose those injurious and divisive projects as well. But bridging the colonial gulf are a number of common themes concerning land, theft, deprivation, isolation, narcissism, and violence; taken on their own terms, they offer sober testimonies about the ravages of the postcolonial condition, the affronts of enduring racism, and the anxieties of the global economic state. Taken together, however, they stand to provide new configurations—and, quite possibly, new hope—for a generation that has grown inured to taking sides, bastardizing the other, and privatizing loss.

These affiliations are arguably more crucial now than ever. In the twenty-first-century world of advanced global capitalism, our markets and minds reach across national borders at the same time that local communities and cultures turn inward with reactionary, protective passion. Yet the competitive antagonisms and economic anxieties that tend to drive groups apart can also unite them in unexpected and sometimes unsettling ways. Indeed, in the South's shared spaces of unrecoverable loss and protracted assault from broader national and international forces, a common regional rhetoric of defeat, desire, and recompense emerges. There has been no shortage of studies devoted to southern literature's pervasive back-looking impulses and the frustrated attempts of progressive and African American southerners to move forward in the modern age. Certainly, too, the regret of American Indians over the devastating loss of precontact existence is hardly a new or surprising revelation. Yet in ways that no critic has sufficiently explained, the literature of the modern and contemporary South returns repeatedly and strategically to its Native analogues and perceived comrades in dispossession; concomitantly, the writing of the "Native South" — a body of work only recently and tentatively being acknowledged as such — also evinces an undeniably "southern" fixation on a devastating colonial past, on battered communities and sovereignty, and on antimaterial alternatives to a corrosive capitalist hegemony. This pairing may seem a counterintuitive and perhaps counterproductive yoking of colonial enemies, particularly when white southerners have a long tradition of not just erasing but usurping Indian identity for their own self-serving purposes. Yet the threads running consistently between these stories and groups insist on being noticed, and perhaps pointing us toward templates for a productive new kind of comparativism and solidarity in the age of globalization.

In what follows, I thus attempt to instantiate a new field of literary study — the Native South — at the same time that I question and complicate even the newest approaches of the New Southern Studies more broadly. In doing so, I have three key goals: first, to turn attention to the large, diverse body of literature emerging from Native Americans *in* the contemporary U.S. South, issuing from the descendants of tribes and individuals who evaded Removal and have maintained personal and communal affiliation with their southeastern homelands. Second, I suggest that such voices, while they attempt to reconstitute their indigeneity distinct from non-Native culture, ultimately betray their entanglement in more typically "southern" ideologies, discourse, and ways of forging and preserving identity and community in defensive and recuperative ways. For both cultures, parallel commitments to fierce idiosyncrasy have given way to dispositions and narratives that begin to look strikingly similar. As McAdams again observes, "The indigenous Deep South shares with the non-Native South its peculiarities, the tragic, comic world of the grotesque depicted by Faulkner and O'Connor."[2] This book explores those common "peculiarities" of that "grotesque" world, at once dreadful and comical and undeniably distinctive, inhabited not just by Faulkner and O'Connor but also by less familiar writers like Geary Hobson, Dawn Karima Pettigrew, and Janet McAdams herself. Finally, this difficult intercultural intimacy appears repeatedly to be engendered and sealed by common economic forces and anxieties issuing from a global capitalist system that both groups strive mightily to resist or deny. These are hardly crises limited to the South, but the extreme fracturing and reactionary reinventions of community on southeastern soil may be widely and startlingly revealing in ways we have hardly begun — and desperately need — to explore.

The Lost Cause(s) of the U.S. South

As Mark Fisher argues in *Capitalist Realism*, the absolute triumph of capitalism as the reigning world economic system has become a foregone conclusion, one much maligned but rarely resisted in a meaningful way. Consonant with this hegemony is a disturbing sense that human relationships, narratives, discourse, community, and sovereignty itself have become products of these forces, negotiated in and by relations of capital. Franco Berardi's recent foray into "psychopathology," *The Soul at Work* (2009), argues precisely that the new digital and frenetic environments of consumer capitalism involve and subsume our very souls — that is, the private functions of mind, language, and creativity that we regularly assume to be distinct from physical modes of labor and consumption. To insist that individual cultures remain sacrosanct beyond the reach of such forces is, at best, recklessly optimistic. *Reconstructing the Native South* attempts to demonstrate that southern communities — white, black, and Native alike — suffer both their traumatic dissolution and their triumphant reconstitution by means of economic forces; the consequent rigidity of borders between regional and tribal groups, then, must be viewed not as a function of exceptionalism so much as entanglement. The seemingly indissoluble boundaries between groups depend vitally on competitive antagonisms and material interests and hungers, ones that we must recognize and interrogate if we have any hope of moving beyond our respective prisons of absolute difference.

This is a difficult argument to make in either neo-Confederate or Native American circles. On the first score, a fervent but ultimately untenable distinction between plantation humanism and market capitalism has long fueled the myth of the southern Lost Cause; and as Bertram Wyatt-Brown suggests, the South's regional identity itself has long been founded on anticapitalist claims (183). Even now, the Civil War goes by other names in the South: to some, it was the "War of Northern Aggression"; to others, the "War for Southern Independence." These semantic choices underscore a perception among many southerners that the Civil War was a vicious attack on an honorable and righteous way of life by a greedy, ruthless intruder. Consequently, the South's antimaterial claims can be understood as attempts to distance itself from dependency on an aggressive, industrial North; in the wake of slavery and sharecropping's signal perversions of capitalism, claims to the anticapitalist idylls of the plantation economy quickly reveal themselves as deeply compromised. In an analogous way, Native Americans' insistence on anticapitalist values must be seen as an earnest attempt to recapture a prior order that, while not as obviously problematic as the South's, nonetheless evinces its connections and capitulations to a national marketplace that demands collusion or extinction. These entanglements include early trade relationships with other tribes as well as settlers; the participation of some southern Natives in agriculture and slaveholding; and new capitalist enterprises involving casinos and tourism. My aim in exposing such complicity is not to draw a false equivalence between the South's manipulations of human chattel and Natives' attempts to survive and compete in a national marketplace; nor do I want to resurrect a sham dichotomy between indigenous authenticity and modernity. Rather, my goal is to uncover the injurious ways that region, tribe, and nation fracture, suffer, and dissemble similarly under the pressures of capitalism. The sober reality underlying both southern and Native culture comprises a difficult paradox: the ability to survive and thrive as communities depends on the same economic paradigms and principles that destroyed indigenous nations and regional prosperity in the first place.

The extraordinary pressures of this ambivalence manifest themselves in self-protective schisms between cultural and racial groups that seem to grow more trenchant rather than softer over time. Put simply, the dogged and virulent racism that astonishes and frustrates progressive individuals today is often largely an ugly byproduct of economic anxieties and foreclosures. The marriage between economic conditions and racial attitudes is nothing new; indeed, the dominance of economic motivations over (or preceding) racial ones in the South's chattel economy remains a hotly contested issue in the historical literature.[3] The fictions of the contemporary South — both sociological and literary — force us to examine this confluence as it extends further into the modern age and implicates other threatening, mobile demographics such as American Indians. For a substantial portion of the South, a commitment to Lost Cause ideologies — which simply cannot be divorced from their histories of racial outrage and economic struggle — has escalated rather than diminished over time, even as the region has steadily recovered from its protracted dependency and desolation. As Gaines Foster suggests, the provocations for Lost Cause dispositions mutate depending on shifting historical circumstances: activated by moments of economic adversity, cultural invisibility, or regional assault, southerners have turned repeatedly to a fable of origins and exceptionalism to preserve a receding sense of cultural distinctiveness; certainly, too, they revisit its principles to sanction and justify the region's survival and resurgence. This Lost Cause rhetoric reached a crescendo not in the nineteenth but in fact the early decades of the twentieth century, following half a century of debilitating Reconstruction, social turmoil, and economic struggle. Not coincidentally, genealogies of southern literature frequently locate the start of the "Southern Literary Renaissance" — its pages rife with wistful antebellum nostalgia — somewhere in these difficult decades long after emancipation and just prior to the Great Depression. The project of reconstructing a sanitized past is keyed consistently to moments of economic anxiety and impoverishment, and it has long been an explicitly fictional, imaginative enterprise; the *narrative* of what the South is, was, and lost has always been a literary and mythical phenomenon.

While the Natives within the South have been comparatively quiet about their own experiences of dispossession and upheaval in the region, their stories are slowly and surely beginning to emerge under the broader institutional and political banner of a national Native American studies and literature. Also not accidentally, the surge of writing emerging from indigenous artists across the country — known as the "Native American Literary

Renaissance" — coincides with a period of intense challenge and activism: the Civil Rights era and the subsequent birth of the American Indian Movement (AIM), which brought an unprecedented level of visibility and sympathy to Native communities. The spaces opened by such movements allowed for the entry of major works of Native fiction, poetry, autobiography, and political statement into American discourse. In literature, works by N. Scott Momaday (Kiowa) and Leslie Marmon Silko (Laguna Pueblo) instantiated a new genre of literary study. Acerbic and incisive political and social commentary by Native intellectuals like Vine Deloria Jr. (Sioux) widened and transformed developing debates about "minority" rights and the decolonization of darker others around the globe. While the voices of Native America have grown increasingly prolific and assertive in the decades that followed, their conversations about Indian culture, art, and sovereignty have tended to solidify a pan-Indian and increasingly global indigenous agenda and ethos engaged in a common fight against the laws, culture, and economics of the white elite.

Thus, the transcendent issue for both southern and Native voices centers on matters of sovereignty. According to David S. Williams, "[t]he argument of the Lost Cause insists that the South fought nobly and against all odds not to preserve slavery but entirely for other reasons, such as the rights of states to govern themselves, and that southerners were forced to defend themselves against Northern aggression. When the idea of a Southern nation was defeated on the battlefield, the vision of a separate Southern people, with a distinct and noble cultural character, remained."[4] In this way, lingering support for the Confederate cause has been sanitized, with its supposedly glorious principles extracted and divorced from historical realism. Confederate battle flags continue to be flown routinely in public places and plastered on car bumpers. For Charles Reagan Wilson, the cause has evolved into a "civil religion" inspiring unequivocal faith and dedication among its devout followers. Most recently, in the early winter of 2010, the South Carolina Division of the Sons of Confederate Veterans (SCV) announced a Secession Gala commemorating the 150th anniversary of South Carolina's separation from the Union; guests arrived at the ball in period formal or prewar militia garb.[5] In response to protests by the NAACP and other civil rights groups, organizer Jeff Antley defended the event as having "nothing to do with slavery as far as I'm concerned. . . . What I'm doing is honoring the men from this state who stood up for their self-government and their rights under law. . . . The secession movement in South Carolina was a demonstration of freedom."[6] Another voice from the scv's Georgia division agreed: "All we wanted was to be left alone to govern ourselves." Michael Givens, a commander-in-chief within the organization, also contends: "Our people were only fighting to protect themselves from an invasion and for their independence."[7] The rhetoric of states' rights, patriotism, and regional sovereignty rises earnestly above the inconvenient issue of slavery and plantation avarice, which participants and defenders dismiss as an incidental and complicating factor within a more magnificent and noble cause.

Far from being a mass delusion of innocence — can so many people truly repress and dismiss such a wounding and insupportable sin of human and American history? — such utterances seem instead to suggest the ascension of a new and transformative context for framing and defending one's history and identity. In recent years, we have seen renewed and invigorated debates about the size of government and its control over states' autonomy in matters such as health care, economics, and education. For many conservatives, the content or intent of federal mandates matters far less than the principle of sovereignty that such dominion revokes. When control and authority are usurped from any society, lamentations of loss and self-righteous vindications of an a priori autonomy quickly ensue. Not incidentally, the vigor of such protests rises most sharply among the financial elite and even the working class who fear relinquishing their respective (and relative) bounties to the control of the nation and redistribution among those deemed less worthy or industrious. We see such anxieties ablaze now, when recent crises in the world economic system have promoted not solidarity but antagonism; meanwhile, global capitalism itself carves increasingly inequitable and seemingly unbridgeable wedges between classes, races, and nations.[8] At the time of this writing in 2010, the gap between rich and poor in the United States has never been greater, according to the U.S. Census Bureau; that material reality virtually ensures that the perceived borders between groups and their fictions of absolute difference will retain their functional power. Under such conditions, the ahistorical idiom of neo-Confederate honor and justification, and along with it the expurgated mantra of righteous self-rule and regional sovereignty, begin to make a skewed and disquieting sort of sense. Southern author Edward Ball, in fact, predicts that the renewed rhetoric of "states' rights" in Republican politics means "we will likely hear more from folks who cling to the whitewash explanation for secession and the Civil War" in which "the only state right the Confederate founders were interested in was the rich man's 'right' to own slaves."[9] The currency and revivification of concerns around economic control and prosperity explains in part why these belated grievances remain so persistent at this late stage in the region's apparent recovery, a full 150 years after the catastrophe of secession and war.

Surely, the appeal of sovereignty for Native communities hardly needs the added provocation of global economic crisis to be illuminated. Since the moment of colonial contact, tribes throughout the continent have struggled to maintain control over their lives and livelihoods. What, then, is the benefit of ascribing a family resemblance to the Native and the southern Lost Causes? Perhaps paradoxically, the very frequency with which the southern Lost Cause swallows the Native one is itself potentially revealing: the apt applicability of the indigenous example for southern sufferers demonstrates powerful continuities among all colonized peoples' responses to their perceived dispossession. Within a national state and a global capitalist empire that privileges and excludes along worn, corrosive lines, the notion of sovereignty, freedom, and autonomy for the suppressed becomes increasingly urgent and strenuous; and whether or not we like to admit it, the South has endured its own distinct and protracted version of colonial subjugation.[10] The fact that the Native cause and the white southern one differ radically in historical and ethical character matters little to the neo-Confederate defenders who elide their own despair seamlessly and unproblematically with Native colonial experience. One enduringly popular iteration of this ideology appears in James Ronald and Walter Donald Kennedy's *The South Was Right!* First published in 1991 and released in eighteen subsequent printings, most recently in 2008, the Mississippi brothers' manifesto deconstructs what they call the "mythology" of the Civil War. They, too, decry that "our Southern nation was invaded and conquered by a cruel and ruthless enemy who despised our people. . . . Our Southern history was perverted into a Yankee myth that is now used by our conquerors to justify their cruel oppression of our right to self-determination."[11] A later chapter titled "The Yankee Campaign of Cultural Genocide" details the systematic and continued assault on southern culture and sovereignty by northern politicians.[12] The rhetoric deployed here could easily describe the Native American experience under American invasion, its "cruel and ruthless" colonization, the ensuing manipulations and perversions of history, the squelched "self-determination," and the experience of deliberate, ongoing "cultural genocide." That the Kennedys employ such rhetoric in defense of the unregenerate South seems somewhat hysterical by contrast, but apparently not to conservative southerners nursing the wounds of defeat and dependency.

Such expressions continue seemingly unabated. In political discourse as recently as April 2010, conservative pundit Pat Buchanan indulged in strategic Indian empathy while defending Virginia governor Bob McDonnell's controversial "Confederate History Month." McDonnell's declaration dismayed many liberal politicians and caused CNN anchor Roland Martin to label such glorifications of the Confederacy "a recognition of American terrorists." To that, Buchanan counters:

> The great terrorist in that war was William Tecumseh Sherman, who violated all the known rules of war by looting, burning and pillaging on his infamous March to the Sea from Atlanta to Savannah. Sherman would later be given command of the war against the Plains Indians and advocate extermination of the Sioux.
>
> "The only good Indian is a dead Indian" is attributed both to Sherman and Gen. Phil Sheridan, who burned the Shenandoah and carried out Sherman's ruthless policy against the Indians. Both have statues and circles named for them in Washington, D.C.
>
> If Martin thinks Sherman a hero, he might study what happened to the slave women of Columbia, S.C., when "Uncle Billy's" boys in blue arrived to burn the city.[13]

Rhetorically, the maneuver is keen: by invoking the Union general's campaign to remove and exterminate the Plains Indians, Buchanan amasses enough ethical capital to yoke together colonial genocide and the invasion of the plantation South. Having done so, he turns smoothly back to the pitiable Confederate cause — even stopping to mourn tortured slave women along the way, as if they were not victims but in fact beloved matriarchs of antebellum society. By appealing to such historical convergences and manufacturing alliances among the deposed, the South has managed to headline a Lost Cause in which lesser others — Native and African Americans, specifically — play minor, supporting, and yet disappearing roles.

On the one hand, this book will suggest rather provocatively that Native and non-Native southerners find themselves pitched in a contiguous and kindred battle for tribal and regional sovereignty, respectively — a struggle exacerbated by the reigning forces and pressures of a global economic system that frays the boundaries of community by stoking the fires of individualism, competition, and antagonism. In perhaps surprising and analogous ways, this plight ensnares the cultural projects of both the biracial South and its Native inhabitants; yet it is precisely the more salient biracial history of the region that blinds us to this larger correspondence and this increasingly contemporary crisis. Put another way, the insistent focus on the South's racial and racist abominations, while critical and of enduring relevance, nonetheless obscures the larger forces of globalization and reinvigorations of regional sovereignty that come along with it. Suffering doubly under this lens are the region's Indians, who are routinely relegated either to irrelevance or to the role of tragic ally in defeat. Indeed, embedded in the South's nefarious (and repressed) uses of its "freedom" is the eviction and ensuing suppression of Native American progenitors in the southern landscape and its fertile territories. The white South's subsequent desire not just to forget but to co-opt the Indian experience entirely can therefore not be separated from broader efforts to cleanse the regional mythology of its habitual exploitations and erasures. Yet while Americans quickly detect and protest the inherent affront to African Americans in a Secession Gala, few are apt to equally indict the hypocrisies encoded in the use and appropriation of Indian allies by a regional cause responsible for uprooting, exterminating, and forever altering the region's Native peoples.

The seeming irrelevance of Native Americans to southern history, and particularly to these recent political conflagrations, has been sweepingly apparent. Indeed, the Native South is a space rarely considered an active geography within Indian country at all, even by Native scholars. On the one hand, the relative invisibility of Indian peoples in the U.S. continues to be a barrier; either erased or converted into fossils of history, the Native American exists in the cultural imagination as a befeathered, moccasined anachronism — a byproduct of colonial processes by which the original inhabitants of a territory must be co-opted and refigured in order to make the settler culture appear autochthonous.[14] Such invisibility is particularly evident in the South, though; as Mick and Ben Gidley suggest in a recent essay, "[t]he eradication of Indian tribes in the Southeast was probably more wholesale than in any other culture area,"[15] and the narratives accompanying those efforts only intensified its effects. Following Andrew Jackson's sweeping Removal efforts of the 1830s, the idea of a southeastern Indian became swiftly and virtually obsolete, emblematic of "an entire vanished way of life."[16] Today, Natives are popularly assumed to be clustered in the Southwest, in Oklahoma, on the Plains — not in the bayou- and magnolia-studded Deep South.

Yet the often surprising fact is that many Indians *do* remain in the South, either having resisted Removal or returned in later decades to reunite with families and lands left behind. But for a variety of reasons, these groups fly low on the radar of both "official" recognition and quotidian contact. Of the 564 tribes currently recognized by the federal government, only a fraction reside in southern states; many more have state recognition, and others persist in informal but highly organized and enduring communities.[17] It is true that Removal accomplished the radical diminution of tribes in the area, not simply at the moment of eviction but in the subsequent struggle to survive in a region that labored to forget its indigenous history. For the generations who survived in the South beyond Removal, preserving Native identity in the region was further fraught by the strict biracial politics of Jim Crow. Loretta Leach, a Wassamasaw Indian, grew up in 1950s South Carolina unable to admit or even inquire about her heritage: "People around us would say we were too dark to be white and too light-skinned to be black. So what were we?" she wonders. When her own children are born, she documents them officially as "white," well schooled in the lessons of her parents that "it was too hard to be Indian because you would be cast out of the community"; claiming to be black was worse, "because you might be lynched. Best not to claim anything at all. Just to be safe."[18] For many other Indians, even this feeble choice of omission was preempted by social oversight and administrative fiat: in the "paper genocide" of the South's Natives, the most notorious "murderer" was Walter Ashby Plecker, a Virginia physician who served as registrar of the state's Bureau of Vital Statistics. In this capacity, he devoted thirty-four years to "reclassifying Indian and mixed-blood Virginians" as "either black or white," using threats and coercion to train staff members to carry out his racist mission as well.[19] Despite being variously unidentified, mixed, scattered, ashamed, and uncertain of their heritage, American Indians nonetheless abound in the region, often in invigorated tribal communities but just as frequently assimilated into black or white society.[20] The romance of the Cherokee princess grandmother is more common in southern families than elsewhere in the nation, and understandably so. Certainly, many of these claims are wistful or fraudulent; but the systematic occlusion and repression of "official" identity markers suggest that many of these bloodlines may in fact be real, if distant and effectively invisible. Despite the remarkable cultural and political revitalization of many contemporary southeastern Native communities, such as the economically and culturally formidable Mississippi Choctaw, according to Tom Mould one might "visit Mississippi and . . . have no idea there is a major American Indian community here. Live in Mississippi and the Choctaw could escape you as well."[21] Their memory has been instantiated in place names and museum exhibits but rarely in appreciations of the rich, living diversity of contemporary Dixie.

How do we explain the unwillingness to engage critically with those Natives who do remain and sustain their heritage and communities, particularly at what is arguably southern studies' most progressive moment? The South's Indians simply fail to fit into the region's vexed colonial histories and Lost Cause mythology as it has long been purveyed and even attacked; it is easier and most common to see the indigenous story as a national one, with its southern chapter merely underwritten by federal Removal policies. But this narrative tells only part of the story, and it effectively — one might even say strategically — effaces both the southern colonial prologue and, more importantly, the vibrant survival coda. We have only just begun to reckon candidly with the numerous ways in which the plantation South and its Native neighbors crossed paths, bloodlines, and histories in profoundly altering and continually influential ways. *Reconstructing the Native South* deals critically with the complexities of Indian experience swallowed wholesale by the white southern Lost Cause. Recovering the core of Native community in the South is not in itself a lost cause; rather, it remains an enterprise of enduring substance and urgency. What *is* fundamentally lost, however, by both groups is the agency, control, and self-definition undone irretrievably by defeat, reconstruction, and now, the exploitative and competitive logic of market capitalism.

Reconstructing Native and Southern Studies

It would be an understatement to say that the argument advanced by *Reconstructing the Native South* challenges the prevailing trends in both Native and southern studies; yet in forcing these divergent critical streams into the same conversation, where the voices of its people have always been, we stand to push forward both fields in vital ways. Southern studies, in keeping with the progressive spirit of American studies more broadly, has been profitably transformed by the introduction of postcolonial and globalization theories and, more generally, by an awareness of the region's multiple colonial inscriptions — as variously an imperial force under plantation slavery as well as a dependent, occupied periphery. Throughout the 1990s and continuing still, a New Southern Studies exploring these critical pathways has emerged from scholars like Martyn Bone, Deborah Cohn, Leigh Anne Duck, Jennifer Rae Greeson, George Handley, Tara McPherson, Scott Romine, Jon Smith, Annette Trefzer, and others. No longer the exclusive domain of white male voices and reductively biracial histories, the South has been unveiled as the site of multiple routes within the history of American colonial settlement, immigration, and cultural and economic development. Native peoples, foreign influences, and industrial progress now figure prominently in the regional story, and the South's unique position within the nation and indeed the world at large has been acutely diagnosed and deconstructed.[22] These works advocate viewing the South as inherently transnational, born of early global forces and continuing in critical ways to reflect and interact with other nations' economies, histories, cultures, and citizens. More importantly, numerous scholars have begun to document just how long "other" southerners have been rooted there, predating and surviving the rise and collapse of the biracial plantation economy: Mexican, Chinese, and east Indian laborers tilled small crops alongside the princely cotton and tobacco acres, and they increasingly became vital components of the postslavery sharecropping system. Long assumed to be an aberration inside U.S. borders, the South is now "taking its place in a world of regions, not simply of nation-states."[23]

As a result of these broadened histories and critical purviews, the tyranny of its white elite mythologies has been dissolving rapidly. As historian Christina Snyder reminds us, "the South is more than the Confederacy. Native Americans and African Americans were just as southern as their white contemporaries, and their connections and memory and history run as deep and as true."[24] Eagerly embracing this pluralism, the vast majority of scholars working within southern studies have endeavored to give equal attention to marginalized voices within the region and the canon who redefine the very notion of "southernness." Yet while the "multicultural South" is a notion quickly gaining traction, the dominance of its black-and-white histories and voices has proven remarkably sturdy. To be sure, a handful of scholars such as Eric Gary Anderson, Ellen Arnold, and Annette Trefzer have made critical inroads in the study of Native presence in the U.S. South, and several new works are likely to emerge in the coming years. But these are exceptions within the broader conversation, where inclusion of southeastern Native histories and voices remains infrequent and largely historical, apologetic, or token in nature. Instead, the South's removal and suppression of its Native forebears functions merely as a harbinger of more visible, lasting, and haunting racial outrages to come. In the Spring 2005 special issue of *South Central Review* entitled "Rethinking Southern Literary Studies," Patricia Yaeger investigates the myriad ghosts haunting southern literature as vestiges of the region's ongoing racial trauma. We must pay attention to these tropes, she suggests, "lest we forget, in this halfway house beyond segregation, that we are still recreating, in our lives and stories, the conditions of racial haunting."[25] Yaeger locates this "return of the dispossessed" primarily in African American fiction; while these literary hauntings receive long overdue and imperative attention under Yaeger's and other critics' careful hands, they nonetheless omit and obscure the dispossession of American Indians on the same soil.[26] For reasons that echo the phenomenon of Indian invisibility nationwide, the New Southern studies has hardly begun the thorny work of summoning the South's first inhabitants and most deeply repressed ghosts.

At roughly the same time that southern studies has been struggling forward in appreciable if unfinished ways, Native American studies began to experience a reverse and inward turn. On the one hand, many writers and scholars (such as Louis Owens, Gerald Vizenor, Stuart Christie, Matthew Herman, Shari Huhndorf, Deborah Madsen, and Elvira Pulitano) have embraced the transnational, global, and hybrid models of analysis that transformed American studies and discourse more broadly, seeking a syncretic criticism to reflect the plurality of American Indians' multiple worlds, histories, and discourses. Such efforts do not deny the importance of indigenous autonomy and distinctiveness but rather attempt to buttress it. Freighted postcolonial terms like "hybridity," for instance, have often been supplanted by concepts deemed more supportive of tribal autonomy: Gerald Vizenor's idea of "transmotion," for instance, captures the reality of contemporary hybridity and mobility, but without the baggage of Western jargon to freight and discredit it. Nonetheless, even the adaptation of theoretical paradigms from the colonial center is often seen as a corrupt and corrosive form of critical imperialism. Moreover, broader trends toward multiculturalism have tended to make Native Americans less rather than more visible, lumped in with a collection of racial and ethnic others whose experiences in the U.S. have been similar in some respects but radically unique in others. Most important, no other "minority" group in America has had the distinctive experience of being unsettled, removed, forcibly assimilated, slaughtered, and undone in the land of their own origins. To insist on comparative and multicultural methodologies is to diminish those histories and obscure the particularities of Native cultures, a consequence that the Arkansas-Cherokee artist and activist Jimmie Durham has labeled outright "racism."[27]

For reasons that make perfect political and cultural sense, then, Native sovereignty maintains an exceptional status within the realm of current academic and political discourse about globalization and our multicultural and postracial futures. In this larger postcolonial context, histories of nationalism headline a dark cautionary tale about imperialism and the destructive hegemony of the nation-state; in Native studies, conversely, it remains a notion embraced as a necessary structure of survival. For many Indian critics, resisting the progressive critical trends in academia means protecting and cultivating tribal sovereignty on the ground, both political and intellectual. Critics such as Elizabeth Cook-Lynn, Robert Warrior, Jace Weaver, Craig Womack, Lisa Brooks, and others have promoted (and in Womack's case, in *Red on Red*, invented and performed) tribal-nationalist and pan-Indian modes of critical theory and interpretation.[28] Such endeavors have had immeasurable impact on protecting the integrity of American Indian nations as well as the field of Native studies, its institutional departments, and its expanding scholarly and creative organizations. Yet while it is difficult to deny their beneficial effects, tribal-nationalist efforts can also obscure rather than fortify the distinctiveness of individual communities. By generating blanket solidarity and homogeneous identity politics, pan-Indian movements institute what Gayatri Chakravorty Spivak coined "strategic essentialism" — a flattening of disparate Native groups and characteristics in the service of political unity and self-determination.

Can there be a coherent, fruitful way forward that manages to honor and preserve indigenous sovereignty at the same time that it embraces the often rich — and frequently haunting — hybridity and globalization of our contemporary world, particularly in places like the South where indigenous continuity has long been muddled by occlusion and assimilation? Critics like Womack believe that indigenous sovereignty inherently "has a profound cosmopolitanism at its core," because tribal governments necessarily "exist in complex relationships with municipal, state, and federal powers that demand constant movement between and across borders." Womack thus clarifies an important misconception about tribal nationalism as an isolationist, antimodern force; yet he nonetheless prefers to emphasize "Indian integrity" over and against the "hybrid mess" produced by multiethnic and comparative models.[29] Critics like Shari Huhndorf have challenged such hopes based on the historicity of nationalism itself, which has long tended to draw indigenous populations into global networks of exchange and competition that are deeply transformative rather than simply structural.[30] Chadwick Allen's excellent *Blood Narrative* (2002) extends such conversations by focusing not just on victimization by such forces but rather on the overlooked potential of pan-indigenous activism extending well beyond tribal and national borders.[31] While there is as yet no consensus in the field of Native studies about which direction makes the most pragmatic sense for the future and viability of indigenous peoples, the remarkable miscellany of approaches and the sometimes electric controversies between them signify that the field and its political stakes remain urgently alive and vibrantly diverse.

Of the multiple pathways toward new and ethical literary approaches to Native literatures, there are two in particular that lay a productive framework for the kind of analysis I propose here. First, the "regionalist" frame proposed by Tol Foster's "Relations and Regionality" in *Reasoning Together: The Native Critics Collective* makes possible a grounded, pragmatic perspective on the exceptional history and cultures of remnant southeastern Indians. Like the experience of many residual and partially assimilated eastern peoples more broadly, or of mixedblood or urban Indians who lack ties to reservation communities or federal recognition,[32] Native southerners' hybrid and occluded presence both within the region and the broader terrain of Native studies makes fitting them into tribal-national models particularly complex and challenging. What Foster advocates is a productive way to transcend the limitations of the tribal-nationalist frame in favor of a "relational regionalism" — one that might actually prove "in a strange way tribally specific."[33] Looking beyond the immediate borders and traditions of a particular tribal context allows us to see the powerful ways in which those outside influences are imbricated in the community's life and evolution: the region beyond the tribe's borders does not just effect change on tribal groups but is in fact changed *by* them as well. Foster warns that such revelations are neither the uncritical, glorifying regionalisms of the past nor the idealized utopias of postcolonial models: "The regional frame traces contributions and collisions between communities as those events and practices become constitutive of the communities themselves."[34] Much like Foster, Paul Lai and Lindsey Claire Smith also attempt to carve out productive new critical territory in what they call "alternative contact" zones. In a recent special issue of the journal *American Quarterly*, Lai and Smith suggest that we might adapt Mary Louise Pratt's well-circulated notion of contact zones to illustrate and theorize "contact apart from narratives of 'first contact' between Native Americans and Europeans . . . to provide further space for the generative possibilities of cross-disciplinary and cross-national discussion of Indigeneity."[35] *Reconstructing the Native South* aims to perform just this kind of cross-national, regionalist analysis in order to generate new and fruitful assessments of our present globalized state — a dizzying new horizon of boundless hybridity, contact, and affinity that paradoxically drives us further into ourselves and our private spaces of loss and longing.

In doing so, I aim to add to developing conversations about the paradoxical role of regionalism in the wake of broader globalization patterns. In *Critical Regionalism* (2007), Douglas Powell argues for a new "critical regionalist" scholarship that focuses "not on what regions are but why they are that way, on what they do as much as what has been done to them," and perhaps most important, "asks whose interests are served by a given version of region." For Powell, region is inherently a "social invention," but as such, it "supplies critical regionalism [with] a language of possibility, rooted in the landscapes of particular communities viewed in terms of their vital connectedness to other places. . . . The function of critical regionalist cultural scholarship ideally should be not only to criticize but also to plan, to envision . . . the construction of texts that can envision more just and equitable landscapes."[36] Far from being a static or reactionary concept, then, critical regionalism responds to the dynamic connectedness and pluralism of the contemporary world and ushers in the possibility of truly democratic new conceptions of community. *Reconstructing the Native South* envisions such active, inclusive new geographies of belonging while critiquing the assumptions and exclusions that normally preempt those reinventions on southern soil. Rather than retreating into local spaces and cultural camps, as the writers examined here often do, revamped regional ideologies have the power to capture the more productive lines of affiliation and solidarity made evident and imminent by the pressures of globalization. As editors Timothy R. Mahoney and Wendy J. Katz demonstrate in their collection *Regionalism and the Humanities* (2008), such renewals of localism are not anachronistic at all but rather resistant attempts to affirm "what it means to be a human" in an age where humanity itself is perpetually under assault.[37]

In the end, this book is unblinkingly realistic and grave as well as vibrantly hopeful. What I hope these cross-cultural and conjunctural new conversations might engender is a new way of understanding the coeval community forged not just in the region we call "the South" but in the vast beyond as well, in myriad alternative contact zones where Indian histories and figures have been as transformative as they have been transformed. This is a South we haven't yet seen: one in which contemporary Native and non-Native southerners alike are a product of centuries of tumultuous, antagonistic, violent, and mutually constitutive cohabitation; but perhaps unveiling the wounds of these histories and divisions can bring us to new frontiers of perception and cooperation at a time when we need fresh ideas and partnerships more than ever.

The first step in uniting these divergent cultural narratives begins with recognizing the terrific transformative power of the mythologies themselves — stories that shape and sustain each community's character as distinctive, private, and separate. Initially, these narratives tend to come from without: indeed, both Native and non-Native southerners have been routinely relegated to a state of abjection and otherness within the national imaginary. According to Edward Said's influential notion of "imagined geographies," regional spaces and communities are rendered "other" largely by outsiders anxious to repress and refract their own demons; in the process, an energetic "us" versus "them" dichotomy instantiates itself along cartographic lines and ethnic boundaries.[38] In *The Nation's Region*, Leigh Anne Duck demonstrates that the U.S. South serves a strategic function for a nation anxious to repress its own implication in the racial horrors of slavery and apartheid.[39] Similarly, the elaborate fiction of Native savagery has long been recognized as an ideological invention to keep at bay the nation's colonial evils and to confirm the righteousness of a Christian-democratic ascendancy.

Functioning thus as parallel "imagined geographies" for the national abject, both the South and Indian country have been compelled to defend their own cultural integrity and autonomy by producing still more reactionary constructions of otherness, difference, and separation from within. Those narratives often assume the potency of realism, as they begin not just to describe but to reproduce ways of thinking and being. It does little good to deny that the South remains a unique place, even if it has been complicit in its own fashioning; it is, and perhaps always will be, a place haunted and shaped by peculiar histories and forces. Similarly, entire cadres of American Indian artists and scholars remain committed to distinguishing Native Americans from other nonindigenous folks on the basis of matchless historical, cultural, and political factors. These notions are impossible to dispute; but the legacies of asserting and maintaining absolute difference tend to be far more influential and isolating than we admit. Such fictions have been especially effective in the South, where claims to cultural distinctiveness have long been deeply rooted not in historical truths so much as nostalgic re-creations. As Scott Romine recently articulated in his groundbreaking *The Real South*, the "fake" — that is, the "virtual, commodified, built, themed, invented, or otherwise artificial territoriality" of the region — eventually "becomes the real South through the intervention of narrative."[40] Similarly for American Indians, as Paul Chaat Smith attests, "the tacky, dumb stuff" invented *about* Indians by non-Natives has become "the real thing now."[41] Substituting what appears to be a "real" — if frequently "tacky" or "dumb" or invented — version of Indian identity becomes a crucial mechanism for maintaining cultural distinction in a world that equates indigeneity with anachronistic pageantry. Part of my project here will thus be unraveling the necessary fictions that we tell about ourselves in order to distinguish between tribe and enemy, friend and foe, insider and outsider. While we have been swift to defuse the white South's most damaging myths and performances, we have been notably more hesitant to deconstruct Natives' similar and no less compensatory fictions.

In the process of doing so, we must confront difficult questions: in the aftermath of Removal and colonial devastation, what remains — for either group — to be recovered? Is it acceptable to identify an Indian "Lost Cause," much as we have acknowledged the futility of the white South's tribalism and nostalgia? My goal in addressing these questions is not to forge a false harmony between historically antagonistic groups; nor is it to deny the necessity and the reality of tribal sovereignty and nationalism as it finally gains profitable traction in the South and elsewhere. Rather, my aim is to show that the divisive contours of region, tribe, and nation tend to be corrosive byproducts not just of colonial histories but, in fact, of an increasingly damaging postcolonial present; not only of the forces that once unsettled communities but the narratives that we invent in order to patch them back together; and not simply maneuvers staged from without but survival mechanisms engendered *within* fractured, imperiled communities.[42] Identifying Native writing as continuous with (rather than positioned against) the region responsible for its eviction and erasure may seem antithetical to efforts on behalf of tribal integrity and sovereignty. Yet if we ignore the echoes and the import of Lost Cause ideologies in the idiom of Native American dispossession and decolonization, we stand to miss crucial new insights about our current and collective state of global economic crisis and the reactionary, alienating measures it incites. For all regions and tribes, that recognition may be the ultimate payoff of these difficult conjunctions.

In some ways, the elision of region and tribe — as well as its repression — truly does stem from an overabundance of affinity: two distinct groups cannot simultaneously claim to be the original inhabitants and wrongfully dispossessed of the same terrain, as both Native and non-Native southerners perceived themselves to be. The struggle to own and inhabit this regional Lost Cause occupies much of chapter 1, which begins by exploring the fictions of white southerners who borrowed Native chronicles and figures to articulate and manage their own sense of regional and economic dispossession and loss. These narratives and their accompanying Indian comrades have dominated the southern story at least since the region's anomalous indignity of military defeat, occupation, and reconstruction after the Civil War.

In the post-Reconstruction decades that further taxed their economic, social, and cultural integrity, southerners began to appropriate Native experience in particularly potent ways, usurping an identity assumed to be obsolete to contain and express their own perceived victimization and dispossession. While many readers will already be familiar with Faulkner's strange and surreal Indian characters, even if we don't quite know what to do with them, most will be surprised by the unacknowledged persistence of these tropes well into the twentieth and twenty-first centuries in works by southern writers as various as Forrest Carter, Barry Hannah, Charles Frazier, and others; the mere ubiquity of these narratives, along with their violent and vengeful content, tells us volumes about the ongoing resentment southerners harbor for their loss of sovereignty. Moreover, these stories further freight Native southerners with the aura of obsolescence and invisibility. The chapter thus concludes with an examination of the indigenous efforts — often mournful, angry, or vengeful — to reappropriate a Native voice and an identity unjustly usurped and distorted in the regional narrative.

Native writers in the South labor to distinguish themselves not just from the disgruntled white elite but from the region's African Americans as well, as we will see in chapter 2. On the one hand, we must acknowledge the remarkable degree of cultural and racial mixing and familiarity between these "other" races in the antebellum South, an affinity well documented now by historians and traced out in literary and cultural terrain; their contact and camaraderie gives way to a marvelous cultural hybridity — as well as a potent, reactionary racism. While sharing histories and frequently bloodlines with their black peers, Natives needed to establish themselves as a race fundamentally apart in order to maintain viability and visibility in a region coded persistently — from both within and without — as biracial. Consequently, there arose a distinct effort to distinguish oneself from a black populace in the tortured decades of Reconstruction and Jim Crow. The particular legacy of slaveholding among some indigenous societies complicates this relationship further. While it remains useful and fashionable for black Americans to claim Native ancestry in ways analogous to the white examples in chapter 1, the likelihood of an Indian embracing such mixture is far less common — and distinctly more threatening to the fragile notion of ethnic purity demanded by federal recognition standards and internalized by tribes eager to maintain cohesion and regional presence. What results are distinct and pragmatic versions of racial essentialism and exclusion aimed soberly at sustaining sovereignty efforts not just in the South but throughout Indian country. And yet, such polarized narratives perpetuate racial essentialisms and dichotomies, and thus do little justice to the messy, imbricated, hybrid realities lived by many of its citizens. What they reveal instead are desperate desires to be seen, to be recognized, and to honor the distinct character and survival of their people in ways that converge more often than they conflict.

Chapter 3 thus explores the impetus behind these persistently divisive and racially antagonistic formations that both bind and divide various Native and non-Native communities in the South. That alienating force is the enveloping state and sublime terrors of global capitalism, a network of principles and priorities that incites competitive antagonisms and exclusions within otherwise compatible and intimate populations. For communities rendered dependent on larger financial and federal sources, as both the broader South and its Indians experienced in their respective colonizations, a primary issue is reestablishing control over one's own economic health and prospects. Just as the South was robbed of its self-rule and solvency under Reconstruction, the South's indigenous groups remain cordoned and sustained by complicated juridical relationships to the government and its resources. For both groups, the response to such reconfigurations has been to rail against the systems of their domination and exclusion: logically and persistently, then, both groups' positions take on a reactionary antimaterial, anticapitalist character. While the myth of antebellum humanism among plantation whites is easily deconstructed, the fragility of indigenous objections to capitalism is a much trickier concept. In the comparative interstices proposed by this study and its various voices, however, it becomes difficult to separate these convergent projects from the common terrain on which they toil to survive and regain sovereignty. Situating both Native and non-Native struggles in this uncomfortably close territory allows us to apprehend the totalizing power of advanced capitalism; and from there, we might begin to assemble a more inclusive, composite community of individuals engaged in a common struggle against a different, faceless enemy.

Finally, then, chapter 4 examines the possibilities represented by a broader, more intercultural sense of contemporary tribalism and community, engaged in a collective and escalating fight against the transcendent sovereignty of a global capitalist economy. Such a prospect entails explicitly troubling the fictions of difference and separatism in the South, a process that might function as an instructive microcosm for national and transnational experience. Exploding those borders — between the Native and non-Native souths, and between the South and the ideological North — is not an easy task. As numerous works by both Native and non-Native authors demonstrate, though, unearthing the South's shared stories rather than their frightened isolation might indeed be liberatory, emancipating these vitally conjoined experiences from the walled-off boundaries of cultural difference and essentialism. While several powerful Native voices contribute to this vision, including Karenne Wood, Allison Adelle Hedge Coke, Marilou Awiakta, and Janet McAdams, it is time that we circle back and appraise the possibility of non-Indian voices joining this conversation in productive ways as well. To that end, the chapter closes with the work of a Virginia writer, Belle Boggs, whose intercultural vision of the mixed community on and near the Mattaponi Indian reservation offers a disarming new panorama of loss and hope on this freshly excavated and deeply striated southern soil.

Throughout *Reconstructing the Native South*, our focus will be mainly on southeastern Native writing from a wide variety of backgrounds. Many are relatively well known in American Indian literary studies, such as the Choctaw-Cherokee author and critic Louis Owens (whose works are discussed in chapters 1, 2, and 3) and the Cherokee-Appalachian poet Marilou Awiakta (chapter 4). Other figures are less familiar, such as the Alabama Cherokee travel writer Jerry Ellis and Eastern Band of Cherokee author Dawn Karima Pettigrew (chapter 3). A few are only marginally southern, such as the Choctaw writer LeAnne Howe, who is an enrolled member of the Choctaw Nation of Oklahoma but traces her heritage back to both the Mississippi Choctaw and the Eastern Band of Cherokee in North Carolina; likewise, Stephen Graham Jones, a Blackfeet from Texas, provides a chilling vantage on southern experience and its raveling import from a place just on the region's margin. In chapter 1, Howe and Jones help to negotiate the sweeping and often violent imaginative terrain of the "vacant" South and its migratory impact on contemporary Native literature about Removal and loss nationwide; this perspective seems vital in reminding us that these southern stories and conjunctions are not peculiar or strange but widely and disturbingly continuous and affecting. In order to grasp the full and encompassing impact of the southern experience, the remainder of *Reconstructing the South* examines only those writers born in or residing in the contemporary, post-Removal South.

While I spend significant time unraveling a select number of key works, other writers are mentioned or discussed more briefly throughout each chapter. By occasionally sacrificing depth of analysis of individual works and authors, my aim is to provide as wide a panorama as possible of the rich diversity and range of southeastern Indian writing. Until now, that canon has been relatively small and largely unexamined; but the size and visibility of the field is currently being enriched vastly by the recent publication of the pivotal anthology *The People Who Stayed: Southeastern Indian Writing After Removal* (2010), edited by Geary Hobson, Janet McAdams, and Kathryn Walkiewicz. Several new and virtually unknown writers appear in its pages for the first time; I have included many of them in my discussion here as well. For as many artists as I was able to include, nonetheless, there are even more who have yet to be discussed; I can only hope that this work is the beginning of a long critical conversation just beginning to take shape at one of the most uncertain, distressing, and precarious moments in human history.

Losses in the South and in Native communities have long been tenaciously private, and methods of recuperation remain concomitantly narrow and insular. Yet the remarkable voices emerging from the contemporary Native South suggest powerfully that another kind of story and example just might be possible, and that such narratives are urgently necessary if we hope to survive — together — in the age of global capitalism.

CHAPTER ONE

RECONSTRUCTING LOSS

Native Americans, Nostalgia, and Tribalography in Southern Literature

> We have a few old mouth-to-mouth tales we exhume from old trunks and boxes and drawers of letters without salutation or signature, in which men and women who once lived and breathed are now merely initials or nicknames out of some now incomprehensible affection which sound to us like Sanskrit or Choctaw; we see dimly people, the people in whose living blood and seed we ourselves lay dormant and waiting, in this shadowy attenuation of time possessing now heroic proportions, performing their acts of simple passion and simple violence, impervious to time and inexplicable.
>
> —William Faulkner, *Absalom, Absalom!*

To read southern literature since the Civil War is to confront a world saturated with Indian characters, themes, and references and yet uncannily absent of "real" Indian survivors. These ghostly signifiers appear with particular force and frequency in the period between world wars, a precipitous moment, Annette Trefzer argues, for activating "not only such a sense of guilt but also an anxiety about regional and national identity."[1] Trefzer is the first to explore this phenomenon as a specifically *southern* preoccupation in her *Disturbing Indians: The Archaeology of Southern Fiction* (2007). In an era marked by the height of both regionalist self-identification and national belonging, Trefzer shows, the narrative of Indian dispossession "struck a chord" in the unsettled South far more potently than elsewhere in the nation.[2] Excellent critical work by scholars such as Philip Deloria, Brian Dippie, Lucy Maddox, Walter Benn Michaels, and others documents the myriad ways that Americans nationwide have engaged in Native pageantry in an effort to establish themselves as "natives" on American soil, exposing in the interstices a terrible vacancy and guilt at the core of U.S. national identity. It is no longer particularly surprising to note how frequently whites have endeavored to "play Indian" in order to "naturalize" themselves as authentic, original Americans.[3] Such strategies proved especially attractive in the South, most notably during and after its secession, Joel Martin reports, as Indian personas offered models of "warlike patriotism and rebellious nationalism, the glorification of a lost cause."[4] The fiction of the postbellum, post-Reconstruction South thus becomes increasingly inextricable from its fictions of the American Indian.

For good reason, Trefzer's focus is on a specific period within the early twentieth century, as southerners respond defensively to the pressures of national and regional assault and the invasive forces of modernization. Contemporary culture and its literature seem to be preoccupied with different and escalating concerns, particularly those associated with the pervasive hybridity, mobility, and anonymity of globalization. Under this increasingly dominant world system, preserving the exceptionalism of regions like the South begins to look like a labored, provincial, and reactionary enterprise; indeed, recent critical efforts have begun to stress the manifold ways that the South resembles — and always has — compatible colonial and postcolonial societies throughout the hemisphere and beyond. Yet despite the growing awareness that the South is neither exceptional nor permanently doomed, there continues to be an enduring tendency to mark the region as separate and distinct — and concomitant with these efforts, Native themes and characters continue to appear with alarming regularity and intimacy. Rather than functioning simply as signifiers or ghosts, contemporary Native revivifications tend to have genealogical freight. While resident Native Americans are apparently extinct, paradoxically, every third or fourth southerner asserts some degree of Cherokee heritage; indeed, no less than 40 percent of southerners claimed Native ancestry, usually in the form of a "Cherokee grandmother," according to a 1996 study by Theda Perdue and Michael Green. The quotient is "considerably more than the 22 percent who claim descent from a Confederate soldier" or the mere 2 percent who can officially declare themselves "Indian."[5] These branches of the family tree serve even more emphati-

cally to root someone as "southern," even as the reality of actual tribal identity and resilience recedes further and further from view. More disturbing is
that few critics have even noticed.

I'll Take My Stand—and My Indians, Too

When modern southerners acknowledge the region's Native roots, they generally do so to validate their own residency there in critical moments of regional
rehabilitation. Most prominently, the Nashville Agrarians, who together
penned the conservative manifesto *I'll Take My Stand* (1930), famously allied
the white South with the hardy, resistant, and sadly obsolete Indians who
had been similarly crushed by inimical federal policies and colonial-capitalist
invasions. Throughout the volume, a number of the contributors make both
tacit and explicit references to their kinship with Native Americans: primarily, they claim to share a reverential, harmonious relationship with nature,
and a proprietary custodianship of a southern landscape under industrial
assault.[6] Yet in forging this largely metaphorical alliance with their indigenous predecessors, the Agrarians also occlude and sanitize the memory of
violent settlement and Removal.[7] Seemingly without compunction or irony,
the Agrarians refer to *themselves* as "natives" and northern carpetbaggers
as "invaders."[8] Nixon's nonchalant reference to the time before "Indians de-
parted" strengthens the fiction that the Natives voluntarily stepped aside for
the South's natural and ordained succession.[9]

Southern literature has long championed this mythology, one essential
to shoring up a battered sense of regional distinctiveness and honor. In his
1940 autobiography *Lanterns on the Levee*, William Alexander Percy ("Uncle
Will" to the contemporary author Walker Percy) eulogizes his hardy ancestors
who settled the Mississippi Delta along with their African chattel, establishing wealthy plantations on those rich, fertile, delta lands. Only incidentally
does Percy mention "the *other* and very different children of God who took up
their abode beside the waters of the great river." Those "others" quickly vanished: "The Indians left not a trace except the names of rivers, plantations,
and towns, the meaning of which we have forgotten along with the pronun-
ciation."[10] We know, of course, that highly evolved Native American settlements in the Deep South and its alluvial plains had long predated European
and British settlement, and that such deeply rooted and established societies

do not simply disappear but must be forcibly and violently expelled. Illogical though it may be, the fable of Indian invisibility in the South echoes the disciplined denial of Native presence and survival nationwide. Americans acknowledge and deal (if imperfectly or hastily) with racism against *African* Americans because, at the end of the day, we applaud our national triumph over the perversions of slavery and view vestiges of discrimination as mere aberrations issuing from backward regions — a delusion that Barack Obama's "postracial" presidency has paradoxically invigorated. Confronting the legacy of Indian Removal is more difficult because no moral conflict has yet been surmounted or laid to rest; still-potent myths of American innocence and exceptionalism are fundamentally incompatible with expressions of guilt or feeble attempts at atonement. Consequently, American federal policy seems determined to suppress and legislate the Indian further and further out of existence, effectively nullifying the inconvenient presence of internal colonies with legitimate claims to sovereignty. In the South, as Joel Martin notes, we see the compulsion to erase actual Indians yet to preserve their memory in a plethora of place names like Tuscaloosa and Tallahatchee; these residues, which seem endowed with immemorial permanence, paradoxically make southern *white* civilization "seem as if it had been there forever," sanctioned and endorsed by these autochthonous signifiers.[11]

Of course, we know that the ghosts of those unjustly dispatched tend to return to haunt their killers. On the one hand, Indian ghosts betray a nation's nagging ambivalence and remorse for its sinister origins; on the other hand, they bear witness to the poignant but inevitable dispatching of simple "savagery" in the path toward "civilization" and "progress." As Renée Bergland notes, while Indian ghosts often possess Americans with supernatural guilt, they can also be transformed into useful ideological material, as "nationalist narratives continue to be hungry for resistant ones."[12] Nothing, apparently, makes a hero seem more virile than reminders of worthy and noble foes now indisputably defunct. Such earnest narratives tend to betray the anxieties of their construction, though. In his influential work *The Return of the Vanishing American* (1968), Leslie Fiedler begins with an observation that was rather novel at the time, an era predating the Native literary renaissance itself: "all of us [Americans] seem men possessed" by the soul of the Indian, he notes, and an "astonishing number of novelists have begun to write fiction in which the Indian character, whom only yesterday we were comfortably bidding farewell . . . has disconcertingly reappeared."[13] In the decades that followed, critics like Bergland took Fiedler's observations further in order to deconstruct the fragile U.S. exceptionalism lurking at the heart of its national literature. As Ojibwe author and critic David Treuer put it more recently, drawing particularly on the ghostly Native figures in William Gilmore Simms's antebellum plantation novels, American writers have long been "at pains to show Indian daily life, Indian lifeways, if only to better understand what is really going on here—Indian death."[14] At the same time that such passing is figured incessantly as fated and tragic, it also becomes spectacle: "Indian death is never private, it is always attended by larger meanings."[15] Those "larger meanings" have little to do with Indians themselves, and rather more with establishing and supporting features of the American ideological narrative that need shoring up. Such narratives have had the concomitant effect of cementing in the American imagination lasting stereotypes of stoic, mystical warriors who function as selfless allies in the erection of a new nation, who then simply disappear to make way for the "natural" progress of civilization.

Not unexpectedly, Fiedler's initial focus was primarily on the literature and cultures of the American West; in fact, he explains that southern literature is beyond the scope of his inquiry because of its primary preoccupation with the stereotypical "nigger," irremediably distinct from the western's ubiquitous "encounter with the Indian" (17–19, 21). Critical efforts since Fiedler's have expanded this geography and its imaginative consequences considerably, even while remarkably few have deemed Indian-white relations central or even relevant tropes in the southern literary canon. Notably, Treuer's reading of Simms does relocate such narratives squarely within the plantation South; and more recently, Trefzer's pivotal *Disturbing Indians* (2006) excavates the Indian ghosts plaguing southern literature in the early twentieth century. Yet as both Treuer's and Trefzer's works (along with a handful of other scholarly efforts, none of them book-length) are acutely aware, these restless indigenous spirits tend to be projections of frail white egos in crisis rather than sober reflections on the region's colonial misdeeds. Precisely because of this deflection, Indian resurfacings in modern southern literature are particularly troubling: they indicate not just an attempt to cover over the region's messy beginnings but also a self-interested need to achieve survival and amplification at any and all costs during a particularly critical period of regional recovery.

By far, the most attention to this phenomenon has settled on William Faulkner and the possible origins and purpose of his perverse Indian creations. Despite occupying relatively little terrain in either Faulkner's canon or his modern southern landscape, the Native American characters in several of his "Wilderness" stories, *Go Down Moses*, and *Requiem for a Nun* have inspired considerable scholarly output and little critical consensus.[16] At first glance, Faulkner's Indian narratives participate quite simply in the evasion of the South's long, anterior histories and in a more pervasive and personal rhetoric of doom and dispossession without local cause or complicity. Until *Requiem for a Nun* (1951), which features a brief lament for the Mississippi Choctaws' dispossession in its opening pages, Faulkner skirts the reality of Removal almost entirely, focusing instead on the intercourse of symbolic red, black, and white elements in the turbulent plantation South. Yet Native American real estate obviously underlies this world from the start in ways that he and other southerners traversed daily yet somehow repressed confronting directly. In Faulkner's mythical world, Yoknapatawpha County itself derives its name from two Chickasaw words *yaakni* (land or earth) and *pataffi / patafa* (to cut open or disembowel), together meaning "split land"; akin to the actual Yocona River in southern Lafayette county, Yoknapatawpha takes on the meaning for Faulkner of "water flowing slow through the flat land."[17] The natural processes described in the county nomenclature belie the very deliberate and violent methods by which the land was actually "split" and ravaged, torn forcibly from one population and appropriated by the covetous designs of another. In his proclaimed ownership and imaginative colonization of Yoknapatawpha, Faulkner thus becomes "sole owner and proprietor" of an indigenous landscape. In effect, he then overwrites and *uses* the Indian experience to validate the southern one. In these narratives, the white South survives and resists while the Indians must fade as ghostly testimonies of loss; the South as Faulkner knew it simply couldn't exist otherwise. Practically speaking, then, his Indians are not really Indians at all but either white or black, an elision consistent with his professed assumption that any remaining Choctaws in Mississippi had long since "vanished into the two races, either the white race or the Negro race."[18]

Nearly all of Faulkner's critics have concluded that the often ludicrous figures which Faulkner deigned to call Indians and which, when queried about their ethnographic sources, he confessed that he had simply "made . . . up," are remote from historical accuracy.[19] In Robert Dale Parker's words, these characters are, from a social-realist or historical perspective, total "nonsense."[20] Some readers have generously assumed that Faulkner simply did not have the opportunity to observe "real" Indians in Mississippi. As Duane Gage claimed, "No Indians have resided in his home county, Lafayette, since before 1860."[21] Literally, though, the eradication hypothesis is simply false; but experientially, as Tom Mould has suggested, many residents of Mississippi really don't have any idea that "there is a major American Indian community" still dwelling nearby.[22] The assumption of extinction opens the door for a liberal reimagining of Indians with metaphorical potency but no claim to authenticity: Faulkner couldn't distinguish between a Chickasaw and a Choctaw and didn't care to. For his unintentionally hybrid "Chickachoctasaw" Indians, as we might call them, he invented stilted dialogue; curiously oriental, effeminate, and sometimes grotesque features; bizarre and homicidal lusts and compulsions, which include intimations of cannibalism; and extraordinarily implausible and inconsistent genealogies. Ikkemotubbe, for example, one of the Chickasaw progenitors of these stories, is introduced as the father of a man who in previous stories was his uncle. Like so many of Faulkner's apparent "mistakes" of fact, though, these may in fact be purposeful — a way of signifying the persistently mobile spirits and implications of these restless Indian ghosts while simultaneously denying them the dignity of realistic, rooted identities in time and lineage. Faulkner's Indians do serve a distinct function in his postplantation, biracial, and painfully modernizing South — a role that has little to do with their identity as Indians, and has everything to do with the economy that supplanted them. He simply could not have represented them — nor have negotiated his modern world — in any other way.

Faulkner makes his Indians seem as alien to this new scrabbling world — and as complicit in its ascension — as the region's white elite. In the process, he projects onto these figures his own palpable ambivalence about belonging to a new social order that replicated the old in uncanny and uneven ways. His Indian characters often own plantations and slaves and behave very much like southern aristocracy. When he pitched his 1930 story "Red Leaves" to *Scribner's*, he appealed that "Few people know that Miss. Indians owned slaves, that's why I suggest you all buy it. Not because it is a good story; you can find lots of good stories. It's because I need the money."[23] Not coincidentally, he wrote both the story and the letter just a month after moving into the dilapidated plantation manor Rowan Oak, built in 1844 on land sold eight years prior by a Chickasaw chief much like Ikkemotubbe, seemingly a direct result of Jackson's Removal policies. Equally fascinated and disgusted by the seductions of the capitalist marketplace that compelled him to peddle his artistic wares, Faulkner apparently views the region's Natives not as victims but as duped participants in a corrupt and exploitative system. These primary custodians of the land commit the original sin of "selling" it to the whites in the first place when it was "not theirs to sell." Faulkner's empathy for what the Natives must have endured is overshadowed by his repugnance for the ruthless, acquisitive order that opened the field of competition and threatened his own position in it. Ikkemotubbe's real estate transactions and his thirst for gold and power earn him the name of "Doom" — an elision of "du homme" (The Man, *read*: The White Man) — and as such, he functions as a pointed signifier of the disaster wrought by the aristocratic South's acquisitive appetites and the steamroller of human lives that it crushed or converted along the way.[24]

Faulkner's Yoknapatawpha chronicles are, on the whole, consumed with exploring the all-encompassing mechanics of this doom. He seems to want the Indians' particular plight to epitomize the grotesque casualties of a pervasive postplantation mess.[25] This horror seems most alive in *Go Down, Moses* (1942), much of which centers on Isaac McCaslin's struggle to resist the incursions of industrial processes and capitalist voracity on the ravaged Mississippi wilderness. The white man can assert his noble resistance to such forces presumably because he is inspired and mentored by the mixed-blood Indian and African American Sam Fathers, illegitimate son of Ikkemotubbe (Doom) and one of his female slaves. Out of Ike and Sam's partnership, Faulkner creates a veritable trinity of the dispossessed: the contrite white southerner, the freed slave, and the tragic Chickasaw. In this scheme, the Indian Doom becomes the white master whose son and progeny is also his property. Sam is thus perceived as more negro than native; his indigeneity is more function than fact, the shadow of an exotic past meant to elevate both Ike and himself from the corrupt biracial order that haunts and plagues them both. That seems all that Faulkner — and most Americans, for that matter — can conjure up in the way of a natural, preplantation, anticommercial order, an alternative method of land stewardship and ecological balance that Faulkner yearns for even as he misunderstands, romanticizes, and stereotypes it. Not surprisingly, Ike is unable to go forward with such obsolete and impractical guides; instead, he retreats backward into a paralyzed, racist impotence, the sins of slavery still very much alive in a land haunted by other, quieter ghosts.

A fuller, more detailed examination of the complexities of Faulkner's Indian characters remains to be conducted. Elmo Howell and Lewis Dabney essayed pioneering attempts in the 1970s, and Dabney's remains the only full-length study of the subject to date; in the decades since, critics such as Trefzer and Don H. Doyle have marshaled postcolonial theory and revisionist history to probe further, and a recent special issue of *The Faulkner Journal* offered a variety of intriguing readings of these odd Indian characters.[26] Yet such interpretations nearly always place Faulkner's Indian anxieties within the biracial cosmos and concerns of the modern South. I conjure them again here as a symptom not just of the entrenched southern repression of its Indian histories and survivors, but also of the ongoing critical tendency to exacerbate such tales by viewing the South as a persistently black-and-white and antimodern space. We have the opportunity and the duty now to wade through some of the messiest terrain in all of American history, to stop asking how much Faulkner really knew about Indian history and to wonder, instead, why he and his peers could not know more or enfold them with integrity into the ongoing and forward-moving southern narratives that he otherwise confronted so brilliantly. What is more, we need to question why we as critics have been able to do little better than Faulkner in resurrecting the ghosts of the Indian past. Ike McCaslin, while meditating on the spirits of Sam Fathers's ancestors, merges them with his own progenitors and collectively embraces them all: "We want them," he exclaims. "There is plenty of room for us and for them, too."[27] Yet in its desire to share the Indians' seat, the plantation South like greedy children pushed them off the bench entirely, relegating them to the shadowy backpages of memory, of archetype, and of nostalgia. Finally, I think, we have the critical opportunity, the strong indigenous voices, and the ethical duty to behave better.

Playing in the Dark: Native American Ghosts in a Post–Civil Rights World

Faulkner might be partially excused for his historical myopia at a time of intense regional introspection and struggle when white southerners were still locked in their own narcissistic quests for position and prosperity. In terms of Native history, he was largely ignorant of the fact that resurgent tribes were steadily regaining coherence and power in his own neighborhood, and he certainly had not seen or acknowledged the effects of the Indian Reorganization Act of 1934, which restored some measure of autonomy (particularly financial) to tribes; the turbulent Civil Rights era with its Red Power subsidiary, headlined by the American Indian Movement (AIM), was still decades away. Faulkner's appropriation and invention of indigenous histories, then, can be viewed as part of a long regional tradition nearing its logical demise; but when we fast-forward to the post–Civil Rights South, the unabated prevalence of Indian ghosts and caricatures in *contemporary* southern fiction suggests an alarmingly persistent tyranny of regional ideology. In fact, the misuses of Native archetypes actually increase in frequency among late-twentieth-century writers, partly in keeping with the New Age popularity of such images and stereotypes sweeping the nation in the 1970s and after; but there has been strikingly little attention paid to these belated, evocative representations.

This critical aporia might be attributed partly to what Treuer has called "exoticized foreknowledge," the phenomenon by which Native American tropes and culture have become ready signifiers instantly legible to readers already "fully loaded with ideas, images, and notions" about Indian experience; we simply "get" the stereotype, dutifully acknowledge the national tragedy and guilt, and assume that no further interpretation can be necessary or useful.[28] These stories demand much harsher, more sustained critique, though, because they stand to illuminate a South where Indians are not irrelevant at all but foundational props in a persistently agonistic region. Much as Toni Morrison's *Playing in the Dark* (1992) revealed the African American influences at the heart of American culture, contemporary southern texts testify to a recurrent and inextricable Native American presence underwriting the southern story at every turn, both bolstering and fracturing its imperial fictions and economic and racial anxieties. Seeing this profound influence is not just a method of defusing the binary myths of southern society once and for all; it is also a way of liberating the indigenous voices lastingly colonized by this corrosive, trenchant master narrative.

One example of this pageantry proves especially illustrative precisely because, despite its utterly outrageous origins, it has failed to stir the national or regional moral compass in any appreciable way.[29] In one of the greatest literary hoaxes of all time, Alabama author Forrest Carter successfully passed off as "autobiography" his charming little book, *The Education of Little Tree* (1976). The purported memoir tells the story of a young boy orphaned at the age of five and sent to live with his grandparents in the Smoky Mountains of Tennessee. His grandmother is Cherokee and his grandfather, while white, is well-tutored in the Native "Way." Young Forrest is thus introduced to his heritage, aided by a shamanlike Cherokee called John Willow; heartwarming episodes ensue. The novel enjoyed modest but steady success until, nearly twenty years after its publication, it gained the top spot on the *New York Times* 1991 best-seller list and won the American Booksellers Book of the Year award. The revivified attention to the book ensured that the truth would finally emerge: readers discovered that Carter was not a Cherokee orphan at all. Born Asa Earl, Carter changed his first name to Forrest in honor of the Confederate general Nathan Bedford Forrest. He was well known as a white supremacist, alcoholic Klansman from Alabama whom Dan T. Carter described as "a kind of psychopath"[30] with no trace of Cherokee ancestry in his family tree.[31] Though he later denied it, as "Asa," Carter had served as a speechwriter for Alabama's prosegregationist governor George Wallace, penning some of the most indelibly racist rhetoric in American memory, such as the unforgettable lines "Segregation now! Segregation tomorrow! Segregation forever!" in Wallace's 1963 inaugural speech.[32] He cofounded *The Southerner*, a white supremacist rag; formed a White Citizens Council, but disbanded it to avoid communing with Jews, even segregationist ones; started his own "new and improved" branch of the KKK when he decided the original organization had grown "soft"; and in 1957, his cohort was linked to the brutal mutilation of an African American handyman who had reportedly talked too cavalierly about the prospect of integration.[33]

How, many wondered, could this endearing, sympathetic portrait of Native American culture emerge from a man with such brutish, intolerant views?[34] Many dismissed the incongruity as irrelevant; certainly, no compelling controversy blockaded subsequent republications of the book (stripped of its autobiographical label). It continues to be read and taught routinely in grade school classrooms across America. Even Henry Louis Gates Jr. defended *Little Tree*'s literary merits as separable from the author's less than savory biography.[35] Objections from actual Indians like Sherman Alexie

(Spokane/Coeur d'Alene) went virtually unheard: "*Little Tree* is a lovely little book," he commented, "and I sometimes wonder if it is an act of romantic atonement by a guilt-ridden white supremacist, but ultimately I think it is the racial hypocrisy of a white supremacist."[36] Alexie's view was not shared by most of mainstream America, who seemed to cling to the possibility of spiritual "redemption" for one's prior offenses, the narrative used repeatedly to defend Carter's work.[37] In 1997 director Richard Friedenberg even adapted the book for the big screen, creating a sentimental smash hit. Viewers easily detached the film version of *Little Tree* from the momentarily controversial book; even though the adaptation was largely faithful, most urged that the film be "taken on its own terms."[38] The film was nominated the next year for the prestigious Humanitas Prize — an award recognizing "[s]tories that affirm the human person, probe the meaning of life, and enlighten the use of human freedom. The stories reveal common humanity, so that love may come to permeate the human family and help liberate, enrich, and unify society."[39] While Friedenberg's film did not take home the top honor (losing out to *Good Will Hunting*), his was one of only three features nominated. Its acclaim is a worrying reminder of the ease with which Indian identity is hungrily subsumed in America; given the troubling origins of Carter's pantomime, though, these "humanitarian" depictions come to seem disturbingly consonant with white racism and nativism.

Suppressing Carter's past enables Americans to continue cloaking the dark underbelly of contemporary white liberalism, and especially the South's most laboriously tended racial fictions. Friedenberg gets away with this slippage because he works within a genre that has become commonplace in American pop culture: the New Age return to nature and spirituality, accompanied by sage Native guides. Friedenberg's prior directorial and screenplay credits include *The Life and Times of Grizzly Adams* (1974), *The Adventures of Frontier Fremont* (1976) (tagline: "The true story of one man's struggle to make the wilderness his home and the animals his friends"), and the made-for-TV version of James Fenimore Cooper's 1841 novel, *The Deerslayer* (1978). Most recently, he had written the Oscar-nominated screenplay for *A River Runs through It* (1992), an adaptation of Norman Maclean's quasi-memoir about fly-fishing and male bonding in rural Montana. Robert Redford — himself a visible activist and ally of the Native and natural worlds — directed the film. With *Little Tree*, Friedenberg works again in comfortable, seemingly universal terrain and thus manages to jettison both Carter's (and the unreconstructed South's) racist baggage, achieving instead a more encompassing American story about survival, tradition, and nature that functions as a spiritual salve. Critics like Andrew L. Urban continue to praise the film as a "journey into the healing power of mother nature, complete with its lessons of growth and survival" and declares it "balm to the burnt out film critic's soul."[40]

Clearly, it is not the Native element so much as its packaged, tragic irrelevance that the viewer finds so soothing in a "burnt out" and harsh world. Even though Little Tree's Granma and her people are apparently Cherokee holdouts in their native land, the film suggests that such groups have in fact blended into white Appalachian society; they marry, work, and interact fluidly with the other white southerners around them. In the film, Granma (Tantoo Cardinal) wears heavy country dresses and head scarves that temper her obvious indigenousness with the trappings of her Appalachian hill life. Similarly, the elder Cherokee John Willow (played by the ubiquitous Oneida actor Graham Greene) has long hair and mystical ways, but otherwise dresses in flannel shirts and country hats much like Little Tree's white Grandpa. Even Little Tree's mixed heritage invites viewers to identify their own secret desire to reunite with a long-lost Cherokee grandmother. The boy who plays Little Tree, Joseph Ashton, appears only vaguely Indian (his parents reportedly have some Cherokee ancestry); his cherubic upturned nose, wide brown eyes, and syrupy charm give him a more universal, all-American appeal. Such choices make the Indian characters seem comfortably intimate, like they could be anyone among us, and yet also, when appropriate, founts of spiritual wisdom. As one critic marveled, the film proves that "Indians are no longer the continent's indigenous people, they are . . . just like the rest of us. They like to hunt, make moonshine, gather wild herbs in season, and have a close relationship with the earth. In short, they are a lot like the hill people in the Tennessee mountains, with Indian stuff added to their lives as a kind of cultural spice."[41]

Indeed, the characterizations of Indian life in Carter's tale are so compelling because they reflect national concerns and ideologies rather than true indigenous qualities. Native values have been cannibalized in the process: in Carter's narrative, the Cherokee legacy lives on primarily in the virtues of "The Way," an indigenous code as old as the land and endorsed emphatically by natural law, with tenets regarding moderation, sustainability, and the survival of the fittest — a philosophy that echoes instead the beaten South's conviction that it will "rise again," if only it can restore reverence for the land and dominance of lesser species. In one explicitly symbolic scene, "Granpa" and Forrest watch as a slow quail is killed by a fierce hawk, which prompts Granpa to counsel: "Don't feel sad, Little Tree. It is The Way. Tal-con caught the slow and so the slow will raise no children who are also slow. . . . It is The Way. . . . When ye take the deer, do not take the best. Take the smaller and the slower and then the deer will grow stronger and always give you meat" (9). Granpa's Darwinian vision escalates quickly into a rant against greed that begins to sound transparently political: "Only Ti-bi, the bee, stores more than he can use . . . and so he is robbed by the bear, and the 'coon . . . and the Cherokee. It is so with people who store and fat themselves with more than their share. They will have it taken from them. And there will be wars over it . . . and they will make long talks, trying to hold more than their share. They will say a flag stands for their right to do this . . . and men will die because of the words and the flag . . . but they will not change the rules of The Way" (10). Cloaked in stereotypical Indian mysticism, Carter inserts his own fanatical (some might say fascist) tenets of social conservatism. These "wise" revelations in fact come to sound much more like the vengeful philosophies of Josey Wales, Carter's ex-Confederate hero and protagonist of his later novel *The Rebel Outlaw: Josey Wales*. Wales, who also happens to be part-Cherokee, is determined to find the Union soldiers who killed his family and shattered his quiet farm life in the name of "the flag."

Such sinister undertones and appropriations of Native creeds serve to neutralize any actual appreciation for the losses incurred by Indians on southern soil. Tangible cruelty toward Native Americans is figured briefly in the film when Little Tree's grandparents are caught moon-shining, and Little Tree is summarily sent away to a boarding school. Historically, such institutions attempted to Americanize Native youth, insuring a new generation of "civilized," docile citizens — "killing the Indian to save the man," as the creed went. Yet this historical campaign is cleverly downplayed, at least for Little Tree himself: he escapes the full horror and dislocation of such removal when Granpa comes to rescue him away and return him to the Smoky Mountains. Rather than being a metaphorical inversion of Cherokee Removal, Carter instead rewrites history to suit the antiestablishment desires of a vengeful white supremacist. In Little Tree's world, family, tradition, and cultural defiance routinely triumph over government intervention in ways that have largely been impossible for Indians themselves. It is easy to see why the Native American experience held so much appeal for a southern segregationist like Carter; but the "balm" it offers to white Americans' seeping national guilt is a thin salve for a deep and festering wound.

At best, such representations participate in the larger, collective amnesia about Native survival; appearing in a southern context, however, these elisions and appropriations serve and conceal the complex legacies of racism at the region's foundation. Carter's extreme racial views make his Indian pageantry far more distressing than it might otherwise be. The Mississippi writer Barry Hannah, moreover, gives us equally alarming examples of how Native precedence is actively usurped, repressed, and denied even in the contemporary South, and how such maneuvers awaken us to a crippling ambivalence and conservatism still haunting regional self-articulation. Hannah produced numerous depictions of Native American histories and figures throughout his long career, particularly in works like *Geronimo Rex* (1972), *Ray* (1980), and *Never Die* (1991); and yet, not a single scholar has attempted to explore their significance.[42] The gap is puzzling, given that Hannah's first, highly acclaimed novel is actually named after the infamous Apache warrior Geronimo, and that several of his subsequent novels play explicitly upon western settings and motifs. Stressing these nonsouthern contexts and figures, though, Hannah's works urge us to see a South erased not just of its Indians but of all colonial culpability for their absence.[43]

In order to serve a southern agenda, Hannah's Indians must hail from some other, more remote territory and reality. As romantic icons of loss and resistance, western Indians are figures with whom the southerner can identify, albeit ambivalently. "Having hated and 'removed' most literal Indians," Martin explains, "southerners fell in love with figurative ones."[44] The Indians who more regularly frequent Hannah's fiction are displaced both geographically and temporally from the contemporary South, and are thus available to invigorate his southern white male characters without the risk of regional association or conflict. The young, semiautobiographical protagonist of *Geronimo Rex*, Harry Monroe, adopts the legendary Apache warrior Geronimo as his braver, wilder, more violent alter ego; the partnership is critical for Harry during his difficult maturation, as he has been suspected of homosexuality and rejected painfully by women. Initially, he chooses books about Geronimo from his college library simply because of their similar names: "I realized that *my* last name [Monroe] could be found mixed up in it" (160). Quickly, though, we realize that he is "mixed up in" Geronimo's story more than he imagines. Harry instantly feels saddled with the burden of the books; having Geronimo's story in his possession is "like being related to some mad bore in town whom you would have to visit sooner or later" (161). Earlier in the novel, Harry remembers being told that he resembles an "Indian long-distance runner," with a stereotypically "Asian cut of face no one in the family can account for" (43). Clearly, Harry may actually be "related" to someone like Geronimo, an unaccountable disruption to his own classically white southern lineage — "French-Irishmen with memories of the Middle Ages" (43). This possibility resurfaces when Harry hears another western Indian, "Navajo Ben," lambasting American excess on a radio show broadcast out of Phoenix, Arizona: "That faraway Indian voice was unsettling to me; there was a torment in it that cut too far into me. . . . I was ready to go with him" (135). The "testimony of bruises" offered by resentful western Indians like Geronimo and Navajo Ben cuts Harry to the very core of his identity (135). These stirring figures also motivate him to action: "I was ready to go." However, rather than acknowledging his familial or regional relationship to Indian ancestors, Harry "goes" on flights of fantasy and romance that take him imaginatively out of the South.

Western Indians represent drama and romance, which southerners often invoke in order to "affix the romance of the 'frontier' to their region's narrative" and to participate symbolically in a "wild past."[45] Harry desires this wildness, though his motives are ostensibly adolescent: "What I especially liked about Geronimo," he enumerates, "was that he had cheated, lied, stolen, mutinied, usurped, killed, burned, raped, pillaged, razed, trapped, ripped, mashed, bowshot, stomped, herded, exploded, cut, stoned, revenged, prevenged, avenged" (231). In Harry's exhaustive catalog of Geronimo's crimes, we see the Indian repeating the atrocities that whites and Natives alike perpetrated in the violent collisions of western settlement. However, Harry muddies the culpability of all involved: specifically, he makes it clear that Indians like Geronimo didn't just *revenge*," they also *prevenged*" and *avenged*." Who knows, Harry seems to ask, who fired the first shot? In the midst of such confusion, juvenile fantasies about violence become viable metaphors for social action. The idea of freewheeling aggression indeed excites Harry, who begins tying a scarf around his neck and pocketing a pistol; he feels suddenly "drunk with freedom to do *anything*" (161).

Playing the Indian paradoxically frees Harry to act like a southerner. When dressing up like his Indian hero, Harry is repeatedly mistaken for a cowboy: "Ah no," he protests to his roommate Bobby Dove Fleece, "I'm an Indian, not a cowboy" (166). While Harry sounds like he might simply be explaining his Halloween costume to an uninitiated outsider, hints about his exotic heritage suggest that his "true" identity may well *be* that of a part Indian in a land of southern cowboys. However, the sharp-witted Fleece rejects the notion that one can be or play Indian in a contemporary South that is configured in primarily biracial terms: "'You talk like you want to *discover* a country, is the hopeless thing,' said Fleece, in the new tone of an impartial observer. 'You've been reading about that Indian. But, although it's true you look like Hernando DeKotex with the swamp boots, you ought to know that Mississippi has already been discovered, and that . . . it's enough of a rectangle of poor woe without you putting on that costume and pistol roaming around out of some *pageant* of gunslinging. They could use you in the United Daughters of the Confederacy as a salute-shooter at the cemetery in their birthday of the Civil War service'" (180). Fleece casts Harry as "Hernando DeKotex," a pastiche of the Spanish conquistadors led by Hernando de Soto who first colonized Mississippi and its Indian tribes; yet the allusion to menstruation (Kotex) undercuts Harry's appropriation of Geronimo as an antidote to this history of humiliation and feminization. Moreover, the reference to the United Daughters of the Confederacy conjures a specifically southern tradition of conquest and commemoration, but in sentimental, female terms.

Nonetheless, Geronimo remains integral to Harry's frustrated attempts to assert his virility. It seems to pay off when a new girlfriend delightedly dubs Harry her "Indian prince" (196) and "*Apache Valentine*" (202); in a later erotic encounter, Harry imagines that Geronimo is urging him to "[p]ush on in" (272). Sexual conquest is thus equated with colonial adventure; performing such acts in metaphorical Indian-face, Harry reveals his subversive desire to "discover" not just women but, as Fleece points out, the honor of *his* native South. Geronimo does indeed invigorate Harry Monroe's exploits, but these conquests are based upon distinctly traditional definitions of white southern manhood as patriarchal, antimaterial, and antimodern. He belittles others in order to aggrandize himself; his masculinity is occasionally dependent on African Americans deferring to him and calling him "man" (90); he repeatedly shoots things and people, and considers his pistol "the most manly thing" he could own (69); his feelings of sexual desire often turn violent, and occasionally he feels compelled to duel or "kill" for his beloved(s) (252); and he is concerned about money only when it might serve a romantic purpose, as in his desperate attempt to impress Ann Mick (52) or to support his spendthrift young wife, Prissy.

In Hannah's case, it is the white southern male ego that has been robbed of its honor, virility, and inherent worth by the tawdry, acquisitive invasion of northern forces and ideals; such self-righteous attempts at reclamation ally the southerner nominally with the Indian archetype, but in ways that then labor to conceal the hypocrisies and caverns of white privilege and the South's own colonial crimes. While locally specific and severe, Hannah's southern masculine anxieties expose larger patterns in the American male psyche, which retreats regularly to warrior fantasies as remedies for the debilitating emasculation engendered by women's rights activism and corporate life's "civilizing" influence. Coded again and again as impoverishing consequences of a base, materialistic world, these recuperations of manliness and strength use indigenous figures to achieve a higher, more transcendent power and wealth — and further impoverish the integrity and reality of Indians themselves in the wide proliferation of such narratives throughout the American consciousness. Markedly, too, they conjure up a profound violence and rage at the heart of the dispossessed, one that Hannah acknowledges in subtle but unmistakable terms. In a 1997 interview with James Lilley, Hannah claims that the western genre's prototypical "cowboys and Indians" motif strikes at the heart of humanity's "grotesque need to maim"; this suppressed "part of yourself," generally kept in check by social controls, can be cathected onto imaginative settings and fictions.[46] But which "part" of the cowboy/Indian dyad supplies or symbolizes the naturally wicked urge, the grotesque tendencies that must be restrained in and by civilization: the cowboy or the Indian, the southerner or the Native? Hannah's answer to this question is as ambivalent in interviews as it is throughout his fiction, where cowboys and Indians appear equally culpable for their violent actions. Commenting on a history of the French and Indian War in a more recent interview with Dan Williams, Hannah admits, as his character Harry earlier avers, that "I don't ever know how hostility starts, or who's to blame. . . . Indians, like all white men, have been variously cruel and enormously generous and kind. . . . Why were there massacres, and who really started the massacres?"[47] Saddled with the presumption of this historical ambiguity, Hannah's fiction symbolically redeems the South. Such narrative acts represent at best a kind of wishful amnesia; more disturbingly, they participate discursively in a southern history of repressing, dispossessing, and appropriating Native American experience.[48]

Hannah's characters do not yearn for a literal resurrection of the antebellum South, but they do in many ways mourn its demolition. As Michael Spikes has observed, there are but "few references" to the Civil War in *Geronimo Rex*;[49] the allusions Hannah does include are revealing, though, particularly in what they suggest about his interest in Indians.[50] Hannah once explained in an interview that the Civil War remained simply and powerfully emotive for southerners: "You don't have to be that bright," he told John Griffin Jones in 1980, "to be full of history. . . . It's kind of your heritage. . . . So you don't have to go to the library and read about it."[51] In keeping with Hannah's own sentiments, Harry and Fleece leave their college campus behind and drive to the Vicksburg battlefield, where Harry professes he "didn't know beans" about the battle itself but still finds himself moved and "irked" by it (217). "Jesus mercy, I was sad," he remembers; "the strange *silence*, then, is what got me — as if you walked in a dream of refracted defeat. The horror was, I could think of nothing to say. I couldn't even think of what to think" (218). Harry's remarks suggest that this contemporary southerner does not mythologize the glories of battles past; rather, he suffers the endlessly "refracted defeat" in a gloom he can neither articulate nor intellectualize. The Indian surfaces as an uncanny tool to both signify and help dispel this paralyzing shadow of "defeat." When Harry leaves Vicksburg and returns to college, "afflicted with a nervous gloom," he significantly dreams instead of "old Geronimo, peering out miserably from a cage in the zoo of American history" (221). Held captive as an "exhibit" at the World's Fair, dehumanized, and humiliated by the American government, Geronimo stands in here for the Confederate dead. Textually, "America" (that is, the North) becomes responsible for the doom of both white southerners and Indians — and in the process, conveniently absolves the South's implication in such histories.[52]

Harry thus feels compelled to avenge the colonial crimes suffered by the South and Geronimo's people simultaneously. Just pages after the Vicksburg visit, Harry returns to the school library in order to fetch more books on Geronimo; he decides to steal them instead. Inspired by the "thrill" of this petty larceny, Harry leaps out the bathroom window and strolls into the campus parking lot. There, he sees his music instructor's car, a "DeSoto" that earlier in the narrative he described as a "weak old" vehicle that "stalled out on [the teacher] perpetually" (198). Like the emasculated "DeKotex" that Fleece saw in Harry, this allegorical vessel of conquest is weak and decaying; consequently, Harry "spat at it" (231). His expectoration seems to trigger an energetic disgust for a number of other cars in the parking lot, but a closer reading reveals that he concentrates on those vehicles whose names are also associated with colonial exploration. His next target after the DeSoto is a "skyblue Cadillac. You pretentious whale, you Cadillac," he declares, just before jumping on the hood and repeatedly piercing it with his shoe heels (232). The Cadillac automobile is named after another explorer, the Frenchman Antoine Lamothe Cadillac who "discovered" an American town, Detroit, already inhabited by Michilimackinac Indian tribes, and helped convert the city into what Milo Quaife once deemed "the foremost industrial center of the earth" (x); moreover, Cadillac had southern connections as well, serving as governor of Louisiana for a short time in the early eighteenth century. But the most powerful affinity here is to Geronimo himself, who was famously forced to parade and be photographed in a brand new Cadillac convertible in 1905. In 1972 — the same year *Geronimo Rex* was published and an early moment in the dawning American Indian Movement — the "wandering cowboy poet" Michael Martin Murphey released his song "Geronimo's Cadillac" as a protest against this transcendent example of the Indian's exploitation.[53] Harry, who is himself a cowboy musician (he plays the trumpet with varying degrees of seriousness throughout the novel), performs his own protest implicitly on Geronimo's behalf by vandalizing the Cadillac in the campus parking lot, pouncing up and down on the Cadillac's "body," "weighted by the books" on Geronimo (232).

As much as Harry's actions under the guidance of Geronimo can be read as critiques of colonialism and industrial capitalism, they just as quickly serve a southern white colonial agenda as well. When Harry leaps onto a third car, it is a "Lincoln": he begins "[d]oing the spurs" until it looks "diseased . . . caved in, speckled" (232). This car's namesake is no brash European explorer or western cowboy: it is, of course, Abraham Lincoln, the American president who ended slavery and left the (white) South permanently afflicted by its loss and perceived colonization. Harry's actions conjure the image of a cowboy bringing "disease" to the indigenous inhabitants of the West, leaving them "speckled" with new and deadly afflictions like measles, and "caved in" by physical and cultural depletion. Thus, *Geronimo Rex* once again equates white southerners and Native Americans as victims of American aggression, and Harry Monroe and Geronimo converge suggestively in defense of their respective nations. Harry is pleased with the amount of physical damage he has managed to exact on the automobile: "Hundreds of dollars' worth, already," he notes satisfactorily. "My boots did their duty. The steps that cost. Five dollars a heel and toe, at least. And at that rate, I planted my boots down on the top and held my books to me, looking at the stars" (232). Harry derives this starry-eyed sense of moral superiority from the "books" about Geronimo that he "held" against his body and thus attempts to internalize. Having a copilot like Geronimo in these exploits lends sympathy and credence to his battle against authority, dominance, capitalism, and industry—all the "pretentious" and bloated spectacles refracting his own and Geronimo's suppression and inferiority.

In many ways, Hannah's depiction of this alliance amounts to a thinly fictionalized version of Forrest Carter's pantomime; both are asserted at a critical moment in the South's racial restructuring, and consequently, both point up the fragile foundations of the white male ego and the convenient patch supplied by the virile, noble, courageous Indian ally. The transcendent romance of such tales has not diminished. Take, for instance, Charles Frazier's deeply problematic novel *Thirteen Moons* (2006), the follow-up to his award-winning Civil War chronicle *Cold Mountain*. *Thirteen Moons* establishes a *quid pro quo* exchange between a white agent named Will Cooper and an Eastern Cherokee band in North Carolina. Based on the real-life figure Will Holland Thomas, Cooper is adopted into the tribe; as a lawyer and politician, the "white chief" attempts to help his adopted clan escape Removal and retain their lands. He is a wealthy landowner and slaveholder; so are some of his Cherokee peers. He fights for the Confederacy; so do his Indian friends. Cooper shuns the technologies of the modern age, like the newfangled telephone, and retreats into memories of his lost young love, a Cherokee woman; and finally, the merging of anticapitalist values, the Old South, and his Indian romance is complete. Designed to be a critique of modernism and capitalism, the novel often reads much like a defense of the antebellum South, with Native conspirators included as exculpatory accomplices. While many readers celebrated the romance at the novel's core and the humanistic fervor of the white chief, most critics derided Frazier's indulgence in "faux Native Americana," as Stephen Metcalf puts it, marshaled to cloak the fact that "the novel is a commodity disguised as an act of witness against the culture of the commodity."[54]

Not all appropriations of the Indian are so patently problematic; but most are inescapably self-serving, searching, and romantic. As I have explored elsewhere, contemporary southern writers as diverse as Walker Percy, Dorothy Allison, and Alice Walker all depict characters who retreat to "inner Indians" in an effort to shore up their psychological and emotional vacancies in the post–Civil Rights South.[55] Like Harry Monroe, Percy's protagonist Will Barrett in *The Last Gentleman* (1966) also draws on an Apache archetype as a symbol of principled virility: "What a fine thing it will be to become a man and know what to do," he thinks, "like an Apache youth who at the right time goes out into the plains alone, dreams dreams, sees visions, returns and knows he is a man. But no such time had come and he still didn't know how to live."[56] Allison's young female protagonist, a sexually and physically abused little girl named Bone, fantasizes about having a long-lost Cherokee grandfather to bequeath her a warrior spirit. She believes fervently that such a genealogical connection would explain and justify her "anger, that raw boiling rage in my stomach. Cherokee maybe, wild Indian anger maybe . . . bottomless and horrible."[57] Repeatedly, mythical Indian ancestors and allies become the faces of the "bottomless and horrible" rage of these suppressed southerners, white elite and white "trash" (as Allison's characters often acknowledge themselves) alike, whose considerable crises of identity and survival are rooted directly in the various poverties, marginalization, and abuse of contemporary southern life.

The "wild Indian" device has appeared in this context so often that it has become a veritable trope of the rebellious, angry southerner. In the opening scenes of Quentin Tarantino's 2009 blockbuster *Inglourious Basterds*, for example, an American lieutenant named Aldo Raine (played by Brad Pitt) enlists a group of Jewish American soldiers to capture and kill Nazis in the waning days of World War II. The manner of their mission is, explicitly, revenge; and strikingly, this vengeance befits a particular pattern no doubt familiar and fulfilling for American viewers: the soldiers will scalp their enemies like wild Indians. In an exaggerated Appalachian drawl, Lieutenant Raine briefs his squad: "Any and every son of a bitch we find wearin' a Nazi uniform, they're gonna die. Now, I'm the direct descendant of the mountain man Jim Bridger. That means I got a little Injun in me. And our battle plan will be that of an Apache resistance. We will be cruel to the Germans, and through our cruelty they will know who we are. . . . But I got a word of warning for all you would-be warriors. When you join my command, you take on a debit. A debit you owe me personally. Each and every man under my command owes me one hundred Nazi scalps. And I want my scalps."[58]

This economy of blood vengeance runs potently through the saga of American settlement and westward expansion. In this system, "cruelty" is a calling card, an expression of national identity, and in some cases, a paradoxical idiom of ethical redemption. In Tarantino's narrative, the thirst for revenge shifts away from national terrain — presumably past its own historical crimes — to face broader, global atrocities like the Nazi Holocaust. Notably, the ideal ambassador of this valorous vengeance is an Appalachian mountain man fired by "a little Injun" in his blood. Clearly, Tarantino plays on what has become a veritable stereotype in American popular culture: the preternaturally rancorous and ruthless southerner whose trace of Indian heritage bolsters both his dispossessed rage and a noble savagery. Not incidentally, Tarantino repeats Hannah's maneuver in *Geronimo Rex* and makes his "Injun" strategies and heritage exotic rather than local (the genealogy itself apparently remote and mythical enough to be so mutable). On the surface, Brad Pitt plays the fiery mountain man more than the "Injun," and Amerindian genocide is resurrected obliquely only to serve a more constructive twentieth-century agenda. The archetypal Indian warrior continues to provide a convenient reservoir of savage rage to service the aggrievement running thickly through the American bloodline, and in the service of colonial atrocities far from home. Goebbels and Hitler suffer especially brutal and patently revisionist send-offs, in classic Tarantino hyperbole; this wildly hyperbolic revision only deepens the unsettling irony: Indians can apparently reverse any holocaust but their own. Moreover, it is all right, even desirable, for faux-Apaches to kill Nazis; but it would be *outrageous* for "real" Indians to slay and scalp, say, white Appalachians.

Above all is the deepening sense that *Native* agency, indeed vengeance, is rendered irrelevant. Much as Hannah's revision of the oedipal narrative makes clear, *Geronimo Rex* forms the genealogical foundation for the white American male psyche — particularly in its extreme, protective, reactionary southern iterations. The savagery that we must keep at bay in order to remain human and civil finds its outlet in these disgruntled colonial shades, but the white poltergeist is alive and breathing. Such storylines continue to converge on southern soil with an alarming frequency, in the service of southern sovereignty or compatible, principled causes elsewhere (ones that incidentally make domestic atrocities and genocide seem mild by contrast). Yet the emphasis throughout is clearly not on avenging colonial crimes or honoring Native ghosts so much as invigorating the autonomy and elevating the moral authority of men whose identities are forged in a threatened age and region. Honor and patriotism are deemed causes worth fighting for, at any and all costs.

"At best," Gidley and Gidley suggest, the white southerners' adoption of such Indians constitute an attempt to embrace their "almost ancestors"[59] — attempts deeply compromised by the South's history of forcibly removing and repressing these forebears. At worst, though, these texts betray a heightening sense that real Indian traces — not the stuff of western lore — are inconvenient reminders of the region's imperial origins and frail ethical foundation. Moreover, in an age and region where economic prosperity is an embattled but imperative means to social and psychological security, Indians expose the dark side of colonial dependency. As kindred in defeat, remaining Natives are equally compatible in their perceived reliance on the federal government for sustenance. Martin postulates that the curious denial of Indian presence in the South actually has much to do with white southerners' animosity toward the stubborn remnants who resisted Removal and who, with assistance like that of the Choctaw Land Acquisition Program in 1920, received what seemed like "unnatural, even scandalous special treatment from the federal government" — a misconception that only increased as the post–Civil War South's own economic woes mounted.[60] Despite these regional struggles, generations of remnant tribes — in particular the Mississippi Choctaw in Barry Hannah's own backyard — have been steadily rebuilding tribal solvency for nearly a century; in 1971, just one year before the publication of *Geronimo Rex*, the Choctaw acquired an eighty-acre industrial park that would eventually house several manufacturing and retail plants and make them one of the largest employers in the state.

Yet like Faulkner's stories decades earlier, Hannah's novels still stubbornly refuse to acknowledge that these Indians even live — never mind thrive — in Mississippi. In fact, his works suggest precisely the opposite: the few actual southern Natives that appear in his work are overwhelmed by the numerous western types like Geronimo. The occasional Choctaws that linger on the margins of his world are bogus, diseased, or both; they appear only as abominations, rivals, and mordant threats. To Harry in *Geronimo Rex*, the remaining Choctaw in Mississippi constitute an "unnatural" and repulsive group who *still* received special treatment from the federal government in the form of free medical attention. Having graduated into a premed program at the University of Mississippi medical center, Harry is on his way to an anatomy class when he runs into a number of local Choctaws waiting on the lawn who had already "tried to collar" him the previous weekend: "The women wore dresses that looked like the flag of some crackpot nation. I'd seen two Choctaw women come in at the last minute to deliver. When they had their legs in the straddles, you could see the dye rings on their thighs which came off the dresses. Their vaginas were fossileums of old blood. Their babies came up in a rotten exhumation; then the baby was there, head full of hair, wanting to live like a son of a gun. It almost belied the germ theory of disease. The mothers did not cry out for Jesus like the Negro women. They bawled in shorter shrieks, but higher, as if in direct, private accusation against some little male toad of a god. It made my blood crawl" (281). These Indian women attempt to inhabit a "crackpot nation," the dye from their homemade "flag"-like dresses rubbing off symbolically onto their thighs, clearly the evanescent traces of what Harry sees as counterfeit claims to sovereignty. As "fossileums of old blood," their vaginas deliver only "rotten exhumations," rendering their attempts at reproduction a form of necromancy to revive an already extinct race. Still, the babies keep coming, "wanting to live like a son of a gun," negating all that Harry has learned in medical school about what should happen to diseased or decaying things.

Harry's astonished description betrays his intense fear that these grotesquely fertile Indians violate the clean (white) American nation-state that houses and supports them. Moreover, he cannot fit them into the standardized social order of the South, which became increasingly and ideologically biracial after the Civil War: the Choctaws' marginal status is confirmed when Harry tries but fails to compare them to "Negro women." They are simply something else entirely and thus need to be expelled. The Choctaws' alien matrilineal and pagan culture poses a threat not just to southern patriarchy but to its entrenched Christianity: the women's "shrieks" against some specifically "*male* toad of a god" (italics mine) make Harry's "blood crawl." Harry ultimately maintains his composure, and his privileged status as a white male, by quite literally reinscribing the Choctaws' supposedly obsequious dependency on the U.S. government. When a "squaw" hands Harry some Bureau of Indian Affairs medical aid forms so that he can authorize treatment of a sick Indian who appears to have eaten "roadkill," Harry signs them. As a mere student of medicine, he has no authority to do so; nonetheless, he tells us, "I took out my pen" — a euphemistic yet distinctly phallic gesture — and signs the forms "*Harriman Monroe, M.D.*" (282). In this performative act, Harry's superiority is confirmed, as is the Choctaws' reliance on the authority he fraudulently represents. He is not a doctor, and he is not even the type of medical student who could (or would) administer aid to these Indians: his laboratory assignment has him injecting nerve gas into dogs, after which the animals simulate temporary death. The token and empty gestures of assistance, Hannah seems to say, will do nothing to save a fraudulent race too foolish to stay away from roadkill. Denying them life and integrity in his fiction, Hannah supports his characters' refusal to recognize these Indians as viable southerners.

Later in Hannah's career, his apparent distaste for such lingering Indian monstrosities becomes far more explicit. The short story "Ride, Fly, Penetrate, Loiter" appears in Hannah's semiautobiographical collection *Captain Maximus* (1985).[61] In it, the protagonist Ned Maximus has his eye stabbed with his own filet knife by "a fake Indian named Billy Seven Fingers" whom he picks up hitchhiking "off the reservation in Neshoba County, Mississippi." The antagonism between the two characters is immediately and openly about identity politics and greed: Ned observes bitterly that the Indian is "white as me — whiter, really, because I have some Spanish" and accuses him of "gouging the Feds with thirty-second-part maximum Indian blood. . . . I had only got to the *maximum* part when he was on my face with the fish knife out of the pocket of the MG Midget" (35). With a name like "Ned Maximus," the protagonist is an updated ambassador from a Roman imperial epic; his

twentieth-century "Spanish" inheritance fits him further for the role of con-
quistador. In contrast, Billy Seven Fingers can boast only a fractional claim to
nativist authority (with his "thirty-second part maximum" blood); moreover,
his "Seven Fingers" could mean either that he is *missing* three digits, and thus
is further diminished and incomplete, or that he has a surplus of two extra
fingers on one hand. Either way, he is a walking emblem of fraud and theft: a
"seven finger discount," after all, would be even more effective than the "five
finger" variety.

After using his "maximum" designation repeatedly as a counterpoise to
the "fake" Indian's meagerness and greed, Ned reveals that the equally potent threat in this scene is Billy's "enormous sick real Indian friend" whose
comparatively large presence more demonstrably "gouges" the government
of resources, diminishes Ned's own magnitude, and makes Ned's tiny car
"seem like a toy" (36). In short, these Mississippi Indians steal, defraud,
maim, outsize, and even out-white the white southerner and his emphatically small possessions. Even more than the diseased Choctaw that Harry
spurns outside the Ole Miss medical center, these Natives continue to
threaten the white southerner at the close of the century. What is at stake
for Ned is the perception of his existence as heroic, commanding, and meaningful; these are qualities embedded in the Indian archetype but not very
well served by the two Natives that Ned confronts: "They had been drinking
Dr. Tichenor's antiseptic in Philadelphia, and I picked them up sick at five
in the morning, working on my Johnny Walker Black" (35–36). Even Ned's
drunkenness is characterized as more noble and pure than the Indians' gulp-
ing mouthwash, and specifically a brand invented by a Confederate physician (the eponymous Dr. Tichenor) who pioneered the use of antiseptics in
battlefield surgery and famously refused to share his miraculous concoction
with Union armies. Any selfishness embedded in this classically regional mythology is deftly outdone by the rapacious greed of the drunken Indians who
consume its dregs. Ned remains above the fray, transcendent and worthy:
before the stabbing, he remembers "the last thing of any note I saw with
my right eye was a Dalmatian dog run out near the road, and this was wonderful in rural Mississippi — practically a miracle — it was truth and beauty
like John Keats has it in that poem. And I wanted a dog to redeem my life
as drunks and terrible women do. But they wouldn't help me chase it. They
were too sick" (36). What the dog seemingly represents is a larger sense of

the exotic, romantic, ungraspable reality that Ned's modern South lacks; as a black-and-white hybrid, it also represents the "rare" coexistence of racial antagonists in rural Mississippi. Ned craves such a wonderful thing, but the Indians are "too sick" to pursue it. Whether it even exists to be chased at all is a looming doubt, as he conjures its presence out of a Keats poem and not out of the hard earth of rural Mississippi where it hardly seems to belong.

Whatever truth and beauty the dog represents, Ned resents the Indians for somehow ruining its potential. He lives out his own version of clarity and revelation: after the stabbing, he declares, "Now I talk white, Negro, some Elizabethan, some Apache. My dark eye pierces and writhes and brings up odd talk in me sometimes. Under the patch, it burns deep for language. I will write sometimes and my bones hurt" (38). At once an acknowledgment of the regional and psychological hybridity engendered by postslavery southern life, the fact delivered to him by Indians who serve as ugly, violent reminders, Ned's heteroglossia pointedly fails to assimilate the voice of his most intimate enemy: instead of a "Choctaw" voice, he admits only an "Apache" one. Like Harry Monroe's embrace of the storied Geronimo, Ned's own quest for masculine redemption is displaced onto a western proxy, a transference that sidesteps the inconvenience of colonial culpability. Yet there is more to it than this, when a white southerner admits a "Negro" voice before a local "Indian" one. Effectively, he dispossesses Indians from the actual area beyond a trace or memory and gives voice only to storied, vengeful substitutes like Geronimo whose burning colonial mythologies settle most intimately — and guiltlessly — in the white southerner's outraged, protective bones.

Taking Back the T(r)ail, Part 1:
Indian Givers and Sweet Vengeance

In *Red Matters*, Arnold Krupat identifies a recent metamorphosis in Native American literature, which has progressed from expressions of principled anger to more explicit projections of murderous rage and revenge. This is rage that "must be expressed," he finds, "not repressed or channeled into other possible action, and this, I think, is indeed something new, and also something frightening."[62] Krupat's evidence rests largely on one novel, Sherman Alexie's crime thriller about a Native serial murderer, *Indian Killer* (1996), but his suspicion is that such texts are emerging more and more frequently from Indian writers nationwide. Indeed, to read contemporary Native American literature is to confront texts insistently preoccupied with savage violence, murder, and suicide; these works often violently imagine the power to avenge the betrayals and thefts of colonialism or simply to end the misery of a persistently embattled existence. So far, though, critics beyond Krupat have failed to acknowledge this new and frightening genre in its entirety, in part because "real" wild Indians are more difficult to reckon with than ghostly alter egos and Halloween costumes. The vengeful Native spirit is the stuff of horror movies, which tirelessly play on the repressed fear that the ghosts of a genocidal past will return to bedevil subsequent generations. Like many similar thrillers rampant in the 1980s, even Stanley Kubrick's acclaimed *The Shining* (1980) advances a subtle commentary on America's deeply repressed imperial pasts by featuring a hotel built on a Native burial ground, despite repeated attacks by "local Indians" — a palace of leisure significantly called "The Overlook" in a patent incrimination of all the American citizens and casual viewers who would overlook the film's imperial nightmare. Indeed, the movie can be seen as a parable of the way we fail to acknowledge how deeply these colonial cruelties disturb the American narrative and family, in which Jack Nicholson ends up being the great white maniacal father and butcher of us all. Few Americans would want to curl up with a Native version of that nightmare.

Yet that is precisely the kind of story often emerging from contemporary Native America, and these narratives frequently arise from southern soil. Stephen Graham Jones, a Texas Blackfeet writer who grew up on the margins of the South, paints just such a dismal picture in his short story "Discovering America." The narrative consists of five brief encounters between an Indian protagonist and various non-Native interlocutors beginning in the U.S. South and extending west, following a symbolic path of Removal that is littered with violence. In each episode, the narrator is confronted by a different stereotype about or affront to Indian culture. As this happens variously and ineluctably at every stop of his travels — in Florida, Arkansas, Texas, and New Mexico — Jones builds for us an inexorable geography of national ignorance and bigotry patterned on the forced migration route of Indian peoples. At the southern genesis of this journey, Jones makes clear that indigenous culture has long been a virtual commodity that anyone can purchase and sport:

Because I'm Indian in Tallahassee Florida the girl behind the counter feels compelled to pull the leather strap ($1.19 per foot) around her neck, show me her
medicine pouch, how authentic it is. "Yeah," I say, "hmmm," and don't tell her
about the one-act play I'm writing, about this Indian in the gift shop at the
bottom of Carlsbad Caverns. His name isn't Curio but that's what the lady calls
him when she sighs into line with her Germanic accent and her Karl May childhood. "You should do a rain dance or something," she tells him, she's never
seen heat like this, like New Mexico. In the play she's sweating, he's sweating,
and there's uncounted tons of rock above them, all this pressure. (41)

Jones's protagonist witnesses his own story overwritten by a plot of desire
and "authenticity" seemingly on display and available for anyone's consumption; the salesgirl is virtually hanging herself already with the cheap leather
rope, her frail tie to a more spiritual and meaningful identity obviously the
very thing that will kill her. But he keeps to himself the new story he's written, set in a more explicit scene of commercial tourism, a subterranean gift
shop as dark and occluded as the truth of any marketplace above ground. In
his play, the daylight theft of Indian identity occurs allegorically: a European
woman with Karl May's spaghetti western notions of Native culture desig-
nates the Indian by a new name of her choosing, "Curio," which refers to
an object or thing considered novel, rare, or bizarre. So are contemporary
Indians rendered "curiosities" rather than human beings, their personae
packaged and sold like any cultural artifact or essence. Relief for both characters lies in a rain dance of absolution that the Indian can't or won't perform,
despite the "pressure" to give in and to relieve these emissaries of culture
and civilization.

That pressure mounts steadily throughout the story, as the protagonist
moves from place to place, encountering similar moments of misreading and
outright cruelty, his stay in each town growing shorter and shorter as his
bottled rage accumulates precipitously. In Little Rock, Arkansas, a group of
students at a party earnestly try to engage him in a conversation about spirit
animals; he feels himself inwardly "become that tall, silent Indian in Thomas
Pynchon's 'Mortality and Mercy in Vienna,' right before he goes cannibalistic
in the middle of an otherwise happening party. The working title of the play
I'm still writing is *The Time That Indian Started Killing Everybody*, and standing
there with my beer I don't revise it" (41–42). But while he doesn't revise his

murder narrative, he doesn't enact it either; and we shouldn't miss the fact that precedents for such homicidal fantasies come from non-Native fiction like Pynchon's. Everyone expects the Indian to be a killer, a belief muted only by the certainty that Indians are also an anachronism, and the general public works to safeguard that extinction. In Odessa, Texas, the narrator hitches a ride with an oilfield worker who recently returned from a stint in the protagonist's hometown, Blackfeet country in Montana. The white man "asks me if they still run over Indians up there? I turn to him and he explains the sport, even hangs a tire in the ditch to show me how it's done" (42). In Clovis, New Mexico, the attacks are still more direct. Employed at a warehouse, the protagonist works alongside other men sweeping rat droppings into piles; "when I lean over one to see what Butch is pointing at he slams his broom down, drives it all into my face. That weekend I start coughing it all up, become sure it's the hantavirus that's been killing Indians all over" (43). Such an assertion reads at first like hyperbole; but as Jones probably knows, "hanta" is the Choctaw word for "white,"[63] and thus it is the "white virus" typified by Butch's mean trick that has fatal import, manifesting in "sport" like the oil worker's chilling road game.

In every instance until this point, the "sport" or joke is at the expense of the Indian; however, in the last episode, in Carlsbad, New Mexico, the Indian gets the last laugh, and it is utterly humorless. He works with a field crew who call him "Chief"; he minds his own business and pretends not to care until "I pass one of the crew and, without looking up, he asks if I've scalped anybody today, Chief? I unplant a weed from his row, look up for the briefest moment, long enough to say it: 'Nobody you know.' He doesn't laugh, and neither do I, and then later that night in a gas station I finish the play I started writing in Florida. It starts when the clerk wipes the sweat from his forehead, says how damn hot it is. And dry. I neither nod nor don't nod, just wait for him to say it" (43). The scene shifts almost imperceptibly from a field to a store; the role of villain mutates from fieldworker to gas station attendant. The latter needn't say anything explicitly offensive, as everyone else has throughout the story, because by now the protagonist simply hears the subtext, full of rain dance requests and overtones of unequal exchange and theft, a relationship confirmed by the counter of commerce that separates them. Indeed, each antagonist throughout the story has been either a clerk or a fellow worker, which in the end amount to the same thing, as the

illusion of equality crumbles and even peer laborers loom over him and pil-
fer his humanity, his pride, his story. The original draft of his inchoate play
takes place in a subterranean shop below the Carlsbad Caverns, but an aboveground convenience store sets the scene equally well in this real-life revision,
where he finally "finishes" the script. The story he writes is indistinguishable
from the reality he lives, which follows a plot contrived long before and only
nominally in his own hand.

The gravity of murder pulls the Indian protagonist helplessly into the only
narrative he can create, and it also brings down the rain that was requested
of him: the story closes with his admission, "when the rain comes it's not
because I danced it up, but because I brought it with me" (43). Indeed, he
"brought" it from the South: "In Tallahassee, it rained all the time," he reports
just before leaving the place (41). Haunted by the histories that underwrite
and script his entire existence, those fateful narratives as pervasive and natural as rain, he descends ineluctably into the homicidal rage virtually requested
of him. He gives the people exactly what they want: and it's what they have
already imprinted on his life, suffusing the atmosphere of the South and
sending him running, but inevitably transporting its pressures wherever he
goes. In contemporary parlance, a "rainmaker" is less likely to be a medicine
man than a businessman with an exceptional talent for engendering profit
windfalls; poised at the intersection of both worlds, this protagonist fulfills
the competing narratives demanded of him, but it is frighteningly unclear
who profits from them. Instead, Jones seems to deliberately emphasize the
economic incubator for both his protagonist's violent actions and his ultimate, practical impotence.

A similar narrative of seemingly autonomic revenge comes from Louis
Owens, a Choctaw-Cherokee-Irish writer from Mississippi, in his 1996 novel
Nightland.[64] Like Jones's story, the action of Owens's takes place not in the
South but in contemporary New Mexico, where two half-Cherokee protagonists, Billy and Will, have landed via their families' multiple migrations:
Removal from the South to Indian Territory and, finally, to New Mexico.
Another friend, Mouse Melendez, descends from "a Georgia cracker who
come through here with her family and just swept my dad right off his feet"
(88). Billy's grandfather, an Eastern Cherokee named Siquani, is there also;
he claims to be an actual survivor of the Trail of Tears. Literally, this is impossible, as it would make him impossibly old in the contemporary setting of the

novel; but metaphorically, his survival is essential: "Cherokee people like that boy don't remember where they came from or how to talk right. The stories tell them of those sacred places, but they only see those places in the stories. And they stop listening. . . . The story was give to me whole by the little ones way back before the whites came, and I knew I had to come here for the story to be complete. Old people are sometimes given the gift of things like that, but only few receive the gift of changing those things" (92). This group of displaced, diasporic, mixedblood southeasterners ends up in the arid West, the place where the "story is complete" only via the living memory embodied by the Eastern Cherokee elder. Yet the prospect of changing their fate is, even in Siquani's mystical purview, uncertain. And there will be blood in their attempt, too.

In New Mexico, Billy and Will live on ranch land purchased by their now-deceased fathers — land that has literally run dry. In a reversal of Jones's ironic rainmaker parable, these Indians are unable to conjure up the rain needed to make their living; the barren earth functions as a transparent metaphor for the rewards of private property ownership that they are unable to properly cultivate or enjoy. And then salvation quite literally drops from the sky: the novel begins with a body and a suitcase of money falling to the earth, which Billy and Will witness while they're out hunting. They quickly deduce that the corpse is probably the fallout of a drug deal gone bad, jettisoned from a passing airplane. Their first instinct is to flee, to eschew involvement in such obviously lethal business — but for men whose ranches are parched and accounts nearly bankrupt, the found money (nearly a million dollars, in fact) is irresistible. They joke weakly that the "the Great Spirit" must have sent them the funds, in another ironic iteration of the "rainmaker" promise, yet their pointed sarcasm acknowledges the unproductive yield of Native tradition rather than its mystical transcendence of modern economic realities (5). So they begin to parse the more cold, hard, literal import of this reversal of fortune: "This money came from assholes and it was going to assholes," Billy reasons. "And if we turn it over to the sheriff it'll go to more assholes. The same government assholes that want to take the ranch my family put fifty years into, the same ones that'll be foreclosing on your place someday if you can't get water" (7). It's hard to resist a very literal explication of the grammar here — "this money *came from* assholes" — which means it's a waste product, a kind of manure that is, as we know, perversely vital to the health and fertility of the land. And yet in this world, the men know, it simply circulates wastefully among assholes and rarely reaches the Natives who need it to purchase water for their arid land. Someone familiar with agricultural processes — particularly in under-developed areas, as Owens certainly was — would know that when human feces are converted to fertilizer, it is called "night soil." *Nightland* — the very title of the novel — ostensibly refers to the Cherokee designation for the "West," which Siquani tells us the Cherokee have always called "Nightland" (41), as Linda Lizut Helstern confirms.[65] However, in the slippage between phrases and in his cunning play on resources as functional waste products, Owens seems to be deliberately updating that mythology in order to view the American landscape itself, situated especially in the "West" (as opposed to the lost South), as a Nightland or night soil: one vast tract of growth fed and fertilized by human excrement, by the waste of human lives. When the body and the suitcase fall together from the sky, death and dirty money together descend to earth like rain — a phenomenon that seems so utterly natural that it doesn't immediately cohere with this perverse and aberrant testimony of violence.

And yet its expansive, allegorical significance manifests quickly: when Billy and Will decide to take the money as just reward for all they have lost, breaking the chain of "assholes" and presumably putting the cash to produc-tive use, they fail to realize that they are just more assholes in the proces-sion, too; that none in America are exempt from the vitriol, the self-interest, the brutal methods of survival on the fringes of a capitalist economy; that no "Great Spirit" will come to water the lands, nor will well-intentioned "assholes" redeem it. Their boon is only the momentary illusion of salvation. Sure enough, a torrent of violence erupts almost immediately, as a helicopter comes and tries to shoot down at them. They rush home and hide the money, but the local drug dealers of course come looking. While they never find the money, after convoluted and often mystical turns in the narrative, the bad guys do manage to kill Billy, and much collateral bloodshed is incurred on both sides along the way. Significantly, we soon learn that the drug dealers aren't white: they're Indian, too. Even the corpse that falls from the sky at first only appears to be white, possibly to make optical the false assumption that rich assholes are always white; yet Will and Billy are shocked to see that he is apparently a Pueblo Indian.

Later, they have a confrontation with the Indian kingpin of these drug dealers, a university-educated Indian who explains: "I believe it's my job to rectify [History]. You might say that's how I make my living. . . . Remember those smallpox blankets they passed out to the Indians? It's very simple. I'm giving those blankets back. . . . Drugs will destroy this country. I'm returning the gift" (180, 171). In this case, the money itself is simply the return receipt, a mere signifier for his more just reward of revenge; but the kingpin won't get his money back, because Will has essentially co-opted the vengeance narrative and tried to convert it into something regenerative. He hides his half of the funds in the dry well on his property. After all the blood has been spilled and Will is the last man left standing, he opens the well to find that the money is gone but the long-dry well is now rushing with much-needed water. Ostensibly, the money has served its symbolic purpose; and its disappearance as actual currency reinforces the trope that capitalism is useful to Indians only insofar as it facilitates survival and sustenance, of both land and people, and that economies of justice and vengeance need to be pragmatic rather than simply furious and destructive. The transmutation even serves as a metaphorical reversal of Removal's desiccating effects: Will observes that "the creek that hadn't run much in a hundred years was running fast and clear *toward the southeast*" (216, emphasis added), and in the surface of the water he sees all of his southern ancestors reemerge: "a crowd of faces began to rush upward" (217). Jacquelyn Kilpatrick finds this scene typical of the trajectory of Owens's novels, which often end with the mixedblood's "return to a cultural center" in his own skin, and often far from "home."[66]

The relief of such moments is ephemeral, though. Owens reminds us that Will has had to steal from his own people — wrongheaded as they were — and dispossess them of their own hungry and misguided vengeance in order to achieve his own. Wells aren't known as wishing wells for nothing; in fact, "Will" phonetically elides with "well," especially in a southern dialect where *e*'s and *I*'s often sound similar. While the water imagery throughout the novel seems clearly linked to the Cherokee story of the Thunder Boys, and thus the presence of water an indication that thunder brings rain, the lineage of the wishing well derives from various European folktales and practices. Tossing coins into a well has long been perceived as a gesture of luck and faith. Will dumps his dirty money into the well and receives in return the very thing he hopes for: his own unified self, his long-lost ancestors, the replenishment of his land, the reversal of history altogether, rushing upward and back to a Southeast of vibrancy, coherence, and hallucinatory restitution. In a narrative where water and money are consistently correlated with waste, though, we should worry over the gap between Will's fantastical wish and the more sober reality of loss, transformation, and corruption running through the land. Simply neutralizing the threat of the vengeful Indian drug dealers or the white American forces they target does not eradicate the endless and pernicious circulation of capital and violence throughout this new world.

LeAnne Howe (Choctaw) is even more direct about the limits of theft and vengeance as a means of redemption in her powerful novel *Shell Shaker* (2001). Howe herself is a citizen of the Choctaw Nation of Oklahoma, but she traces her roots back to the Eastern Band of Cherokee as well. *Shell Shaker* centers on a present-day Choctaw family near Durant, Oklahoma, but the narrative returns incessantly and strategically toward a pre-Removal southern past tangled with the fate of the ensuing generations. The intersecting plots converge on two parallel murders: in the historical narrative, the eighteenth-century Choctaw chief Red Shoes is brutally slain by his own people for literally "trading" the community's survival to foreign invaders and becoming *Osano*, a bloodsucker, always hungering for more and better in the form of commodities and, soon, the bodies of others. In the present-day narrative, which features later generations of the same family, a new *Osano* emerges in Redford McAlester, seventh chief of the Choctaw Nation in Oklahoma and corrupt casino boss who, like Red Shoes before him, mortgages tribal sovereignty for his own avarice. Similarly, he is punished by his own people — in this case, he is fatally assaulted by his girlfriend, Auda Billy, whom he exploits both sexually and emotionally.

Howe's is a tale about the relentless haunting of history that even contemporary Indians cannot seem to shake, and like Jones and Owens, she finds the South a place of origin as well as a potential site of relief. Yet also like Jones's and Owens's, neither the rain from Tallahassee nor the quenching Thunder Boys from the old Cherokee stories can slake the thirst, hunger, and rage her contemporary protagonists face. This is not how critics have wanted to read the novel, which is praised almost universally as an illustration of resurgent tribal sovereignty and "decolonization," as Patrice Hollrah puts it.[67] P. Jane Hafen specifically applauds the way Howe "seamlessly integrates a history of desperate and gruesome struggles for survival with modern Faustian pacts with materialism and wealth."[68] Yet while most readers would like to believe that Howe's contemporary Choctaw are able to slay the demons of materialism, the novel itself fails to support such optimism. Indeed, Howe raises the specter of colonial conquest as the ultimate, defining evil only to diminish its primary influence: while European settlers did much to incite this specific wave of lust and greed, she suggests, they did not invent but merely exacerbated it. The seeds of such voracity existed already in what one character deems the "Indian commerce" of early intertribal trade relationships, in the fatal jealousies and lusts of precontact human relationships and desires.[69] These once pragmatic exercises in exchange and subsistence are heightened by the stakes of colonial competition and avarice, and the inevitable result is bloodshed *among* and not just *against* the early Choctaws. In the postcolonial iterations of this blood economy, which revolve primarily around the tribal casino, money becomes a petty vehicle for redemption and vengeance, a method of taking back and growing fat and reasserting sovereignty. "It was my dream to have all the advantages the foreigners brought into our nations without surrendering to their rules," the ghost of the slain Redford McAlester explains to his girlfriend and killer, Auda Billy; "It was the same with the casino business." To this, Auda simply replies, "I see."[70] In Auda's retort, Howe employs a rhetorical device that often cloaks a *lack* of understanding, an admission of sympathy more reluctant than sincere. Here, it seems that Auda simply does not want to admit the unpalatable: that the urge for reclamation runs deep and long, that the illusion of "having it all" is wounding and insupportable, and that — as in Owens's novel — one's own people and family and lovers might be hurt and exchanged in the process.

Auda kills Redford partially because of what he represents — a reincarnation and a generational poltergeist of an ancient lust haunting her people. A character named Divine Sarah observes, "What is in the past has not passed," echoing Faulkner's famous quotation, "The past is never dead. It isn't even past."[71] The ancient practice of blood revenge among the Choctaw returns to instigate Auda's actions, motivated by her more private and immediate cause: Redford rapes and humiliates her. Auda never acknowledges or meditates freely on her act, but throughout the novel we gather that she has acted defensively on behalf of her own wounded self as much as she has tried to protect her family and tribe from the "fate of the greedy," who return in the form of *Osano* ("to keep consuming — it's his job").[72] If anyone can function as the agents to defuse the reproduction of this destructive greed, it would be the Billy women: along with Auda, Howe gives us two sisters — one a stockbroker, and the other an actress — and their mother. All are strong, vibrant leaders in the community as well as the stock market, politics, and the theater; they have hands like men and wield guns like killers. And yet every effort to achieve agency and autonomy from corrupt forces like Redford McAlester is undermined by their thorough imbrication in the world of commerce, fragmentation, and individualism that they only faintly resist. One sister, Adair, agrees to marry her lawyer beau, an Alabama Conchatys Indian, after he describes their relationship as "a good exchange between very old, very dependable trading partners. . . . Trade hearts with me."[73] Older sister Tema has already made her trade: she is married to a white British actor named Borden, and together they appear in plays like Ibsen's *A Doll's House* and Shakespeare's *The Taming of the Shrew*. While Ibsen's drama has been read as an early feminist exploration of a wife's liberation, Shakespeare's play has been roundly critiqued for its misogyny; it is no accident that the latter play is announced in the closing pages of the book, as the evil seems expurgated from the Billy world and Tema leaves for London to begin production. These closing moments of apparent triumph are coded persistently with reminders of the women's continued subjugation to the plots, scripts, and materialism of masculine and imperial authority. By slaughtering Redford, Auda has wrought her personal revenge; but we realize, as do the protagonists in Jones's and Owens's works, that these are mere punctuations of a long colonial drama of dispossessing and repossessing loss. Auda cannot curtail but can only continue the chain of cruelty — from riverside trading to casino brokering, and from village massacres to oak-paneled office shootouts.

Like Owens and Jones again, Howe locates the final illusion of return and relief in a southern landscape. In order to bury once and for all the evil associated with Red Shoes/Redford, the Billy women's uncle and a family friend deliver McAlester's body and his suitcase of embezzled money to a final resting place in Mississippi, at the Nanih Waiya mound that holds sacred significance for the Choctaw people. Red Shoes and Redford had both professed that their material machinations were ultimately in the service of "uniting" the fractured tribe, but their own acquisitive lusts get in the way. It is left to the powerful women in the contemporary narrative to make good on this reunification, though, and so they engineer the plot to bring Redford

McAlester's body south, to be buried where the original *Osano* evil was born. At the mound, the Oklahoma and Mississippi Choctaw come together to "join hands and sing" a "miraculous beginning" into life.[74] Is this truly a "beginning," though, or just another revolution in an uncannily repetitive and cruel history? Much as Owens's Will Striker yearns for the restitution of his family and self in the waters of the well, the Billy clan and their southeastern kin gesture toward a kind of healing not yet borne out in the contemporary narratives of their writers or of the world spawned by these primal southern histories. The burial of both dollar bills and the human beings who manipulate them amount to little more than a covering-up, an earnest repression of the world we have been given. The characters who travel back to the Nanih Waiya remain there—but only because they are killed by the casino overlords who follow them in pursuit of the dirty money they have taken from Redford's stash. Indeed, the perverse agents of capitalism trail them there, for reasons that the book's historical reverberations make clear: the progenitors of the modern casino industry are ghosts haunting the mounds of the South, and until the contemporary allure and tyranny of that new world can be dispatched, every subsequent generation will join them there. Whether in Jones's revenge tale at the bottom of Carlsbad Caverns, in Owens's buried money and his wishing well of ancestors, or in Howe's homecoming to the Nanih Waiya mound—all of these authors ineluctably return to the buried histories and hungers of their people, but have no viable way to restore or relieve their gaping caverns of loss.

Taking Back the T(r)ail, Part 2: Splendid Failures

While Howe's novel fails to remake the world and recapture the Choctaw's mythical harmony and innocence, her ultimate success lies in demonstrating the power of renewal through partnership, peace, and storying itself. Howe is well known for her concept of "tribalography," which posits that American Indian literature and storytelling are foundational, and that American literature is adapting slowly to indigenous methods of narration—"not the other way around."[75] Howe's notion is an explicit revision of Morrison's thesis about African American culture in U.S. life and literature; and like Morrison, for whom the experience of slavery was pivotal in this process, Howe also locates in the early Southeast proponents of "indigenous epistemologies" and an interest "in uniting, not dividing" that should further enrich our national and political discourse.[76] It is no coincidence that both writers locate the framework for national identity and recuperation in the societies most oppressed and altered on southern soil. So far, as we have seen, the rhetoric and voice of American Indians has infiltrated southern discourse in largely nominal and self-interested ways; even when it seems impossible to recover those original traces from the anxieties and pressures of contemporary capitalist life, the effort and the confidence of the attempts may be considered splendid failures on their own terms.

In this way, we might begin to suggest ways that the southern mode of storying after immense loss and deprivation has not just co-opted but been infiltrated *by* Native rhetorics of dispossession. To mediate those losses generations after the fact is a challenge facing writers of both Native and non-Native ancestry well into the present century, as we have amply seen. But what if we begin to see the immense and private nostalgia suffusing both modes as a convergent rather than a segregated phenomenon? Certainly, the melancholy, backward-looking tendencies of southern fiction have been well documented and deconstructed, usually now by critics working from a space of ethical remove and elevation; on the contrary, we routinely celebrate the wistful reminiscences of Native authors as a crucial decolonizing methodology. What happens if we consider these impulses to be essentially the same, though — activated in both cases by profoundly present and immediate causes and deprivations for the painful longing after a lost world? Analyzing the melancholy that transformed elite white southern history and its literary tellers, historian David Anderson draws on Fred Davis's sociology of nostalgia:

> Any "untoward historic events" that tear into the fabric of a society, disrupt its taken-for-granted attitudes and practices, and cut short the very "lungs of culture" in which "people . . . breathe the air of significance" place that society's connection with its history under pressure. (8) Confronted with these "explosive upheavals," we are "driven like tumbleweed before the buffeting winds of change and upheaval." (9) Hence, the desire "to preserve [a] thread of continuity is . . . crucial. . . . [E]verything contradictory threatens to undermine what has been so patiently built up." Nostalgia looks to alleviate this condition by

exploiting "the past . . . in specially reconstructed ways." In doing so, nostalgia "cultivate[s]" an "appreciative" stance toward "former selves," it "acts to restore . . . a sense of sociohistoric continuity," and it allows "time for . . . change to be assimilated," restoring confidence and imparting meaningful links with the past. (10) In other words, nostalgia sweetens history with sentiment, its iconography of praise is constant, and it is accustomed to remember more romantically than historically.[77]

As private and narcissistic as the South's nostalgia can be, there is little to separate it — except by will or exclusion — from the consonant experience and discourse following "explosive upheaval" and change haunting their Native neighbors. What results for both is a "specially reconstructed" past aimed at preserving and sustaining communities under enormous pressure.

In one way, this forces us to reevaluate the genealogy of southern nostalgia and literary reconstruction as anything other than tribalography. This reading would satisfy new critics of the Native South, such as Eric Gary Anderson, who work to uncover the "alternative literacies" and ways of knowing and narrating that have always been foundational to and yet have rarely been acknowledged in southern literature and culture.[78] Yet I want to expand these important efforts to include a sense of both reciprocity and immediacy: these are not simply one-way bequests, nor are they linear hauntings of history. On the contrary, the rhetoric of dispossession, doom, and violence cross-pollinates the worlds and voices of these communities in compatible and overlapping ways. Rather than sustain a battle for who came first or which worldview is more influential, we need instead to see both their causes and effects as resoundingly consonant and increasingly contemporary. More troublingly, we need to acknowledge the desiccating consequences of economic seduction as a shared plight that is both indigenous and inescapable for all. The world these writers inhabit together is a South populated by ghosts, enduring vacancies of spirit and self-identification, and unrequited material and spiritual yearnings. Conjuring again Faulkner's declaration that "the past is never dead" in the South, we should also recognize Keith Basso's enormously influential work *Wisdom Sits in Places* (1996), in which he relays an Apache creed that "the country of the past . . . is never more than a narrated place-world away."[79] What writers of both groups labor to recover, in

ways more analogous and common than we would like to admit, is a reconstructed "place-world" more insular and exclusive than it ever actually was.

In an effort to refocus attention on the real story of the dispossessed
South, Native writers have frequently returned to the pivotal trauma of
Removal and the Trail of Tears; yet resurrecting that narrative proves more
complicated than merely assembling the vestiges of communal memory and
testimony. At best, the product is revisionist history that foregrounds the
broken treaties, federal transgressions of legal injunctions, and bald, rapacious greed for property and prosperity; at worst, such tales become romanticized chronicles of loss that further deflect attention from the condition of
surviving southeastern Indians. In *Pushing the Bear* (1996), Cherokee author
Diane Glancy does her best to engage that very history without allowing it
to become simply a record of extinction. At the same time, she helps us to
see the Cherokee story as vitally altered by and lastingly entangled with the
South's own uncoiling saga.

Glancy's signal achievement in *Pushing the Bear* is her use of multiple and
various narrative perspectives to chronicle the at-times unbearable steps of
the North Carolina Cherokees' removal to "Indian Territory" (present-day
Oklahoma). With remarkable evenhandedness, Glancy gives us not just
Cherokee voices but also those of white soldiers, missionaries, medics, and
bystanders. Additionally, her narrative fuses fictional re-creations with snippets of actual historical documents and testimony, and even the fictional
parts of the novel take care to employ accurate historical and cultural details, including numerous Cherokee words and phrases in order to impart
"a sense of the language." Glancy explains further that these flashes of ar-
chaic speech "can be viewed as holes in the text so the original can show
through."[80] Despite a glossary of the Sequoyah syllabary at the end, such
linguistic traces — many of them early forms no longer in use by contemporary Cherokee speakers — do indeed constitute "holes" or aporia in a cultural narrative riddled with such absences and uncertainty. Presumably, that
pervasive ambiguity is what prompts Glancy to cull her story from as many
imaginative and actual sources as possible, piecing together an approximation of the truth but allowing the fractures and gaps to exist as important
and defining elements of the southeastern Cherokee experience in general.

Try as she might to include a dizzying number of voices in her narrative,
the effect is less a sense of completion and coherence than of rupture and

distance. Rather than immerse us in the sustained consciousness of either Maritole, the woman—a wife and mother—who could be called the protagonist of the novel, or her husband, Knowbowtee, instead we are repeatedly and abruptly shuttled into too many other minds to keep track of. There is a certain breadth of observation, then, that does give us a more full and unmitigated view of the disaster enveloping this community. The Removal ordeal is thus filtered, fissured, and delivered in snapshots that often have the eloquence of poetry or the crudeness of a ledger; and yet these views rarely converge or conclude in any harmonious way. Her failure stems, at first glance, from an acknowledgment that she cannot possibly inhabit or speak for such a remote and storied past, and the issue is not one of cultural ownership or reclamation; it is one of untranslatability and communal silence. As two of the unnamed Basket Makers in her novel argue: "The trail needs stories." "No. Leave it unspoken" (153). Glancy obviously chooses, through the lens and conviction of Maritole, to "tell our story," complete with all its deferrals and silences (173).

Still, there seems to be more to it than this. Her failure to portray seamlessly and univocally this ineffable trauma seems also a testament to the lack of a uniform experience or response, which runs contrary to traditional perceptions of Native social organicism. Above all, as Jace Weaver reminds us in *That the People May Live* (1997), Native literature is committed to rendering the indigenous primacy of the community—what he dubs the practice of "communitism"—over and above that of the individual. Conversely, Glancy is unflinching about demonstrating the ways in which the North Carolina Cherokee community, like that of Howe's Choctaw, was already overcome and infected by privacy and self-interest long before Removal. Rather than providing a comprehensive, communal sweep of experience, Glancy tends to lock us within discrete minds and voices that don't always cohere. The secret and separate voices throughout the text reveal a tribe already splintered by personal views and desires, which are sometimes base and selfish. Even Maritole's husband, who seems most preoccupied with the loss of his property and prosperity, seems to have married her for purely pragmatic, economic reasons.

By soberly assessing the degree to which the theology of private ownership and narcissism dominated the southeastern Cherokee, Glancy offers a narrative "failure" that becomes one of the most significant and promising attempts to fairly assess the wreckage of an entire culture and, in the process, to prepare to see more vividly our own hybrid and still haunted contemporary reality. One of the sections offers "The Story of the Bear," which is the symbol throughout for the difficulty of the Trail: *"A long time ago the Cherokee forgot we were a tribe. We thought only of ourselves apart from others."*[81] What Glancy's text witnesses is the absolute horror of a community fractured long before the trauma of Removal. What she does succeed at brilliantly is giving us snapshots of that hybridity already in progress in the roots and rituals of southern settlement and economic development. "I knew this wasn't going to be a good Indian / bad white man story," she professes; "You know there has to be both sides in each."[82] Rather than manufacture an illusion of an innocent culture uncontaminated by European civilization until the fateful cataclysm of Removal, Glancy shows us that the Cherokee had been living, working, and emulating their white neighbors in North Carolina for decades. As Amy Elias notes, *Pushing the Bear* "depends upon an alternative text that has not been allowed to be spoken . . . because the Cherokee identity it references is not, and never was, a static iconographic identity but a fluid, historical, and inclusive one." Her process of recuperation, then, is inherently multiple and tempered by a sober postcolonial vantage; her project is openly to "create a new mode of being, a new world, not recuperate a lost one." [83]

Glancy accomplishes for southeastern Cherokee literature something like what Faulkner achieved so influentially in southern storytelling: an insistence on multiple voices and personae to reconstruct a version of the past that has emotional freight as well as accuracy. As she explains to an interviewer, "I started off *Pushing the Bear* with one voice, and it wasn't enough. I had to go back and add her husband and everybody who had traveled with them on the Trail of Tears."[84] Here Glancy repeats almost exactly the language used famously by Faulkner to describe the genesis of his own first polyvocal narrative, *The Sound and the Fury* (1929): "I tried first to tell it with one brother, and that wasn't enough. That was Section One. I tried it with another brother, and that wasn't enough. That was Section Two. I tried the third brother, because Caddy was still to me too beautiful and too moving to reduce her to telling what was going on, that it would be more passionate to see her through somebody else's eyes, I thought. And that failed and I tried myself—the fourth section—to tell what happened, and I still failed."[85]

Glancy's echo of Faulkner's statements seems too explicit to be unconscious, a veritable admission of the powerful influence that Faulkner continues to hold over the region's writers. As Michael Kreyling suggests, Faulkner is *the* "Major figure" whose long shadow every southern writer must invariably confront and often repeat.[86]

Moreover, there is in Glancy's statement an explicit allusion not just to a pattern of speech or a cliché, but to an entire worldview — a desperate longing to capture a much-desired image and history just out of reach. Not coincidentally, Faulkner's statement came shortly after he declared himself to be finished forever with publishers and their expectations, sprung from the constraints of material anxieties and free to depict a world of his purest desire. While the multiple viewpoints of *The Sound and the Fury* are the closest Faulkner can come to achieving emotional verity, even that method ultimately fails him and his passionate vision. Glancy's failure thus merges with Faulkner's in perhaps an unexpected way, as compatible exercises in reconstructing parallel worlds and visions that we can only hope to re-create and approach now in the imagination and the heart's desire. By invoking one of the most well-known statements that Faulkner made about his modernist aesthetic and his southern gloom, Glancy admits that her own project will also be a splendid failure to capture a moment and a people utterly beyond her grasp.

In these imaginative acts of nostalgic reconstruction and retaliatory violence, southeastern Native writers testify repeatedly to the inaccessibility of the past under the real and present dangers and anxieties of the present. In this world, global capitalism's forces and narratives have scripted us all in roles we can't seem to refuse or rewrite; and they compel us to steal one another's stories and solvency in an earnest attempt to recover our own. As the next chapter will demonstrate, the power of the South's binary divisions and affiliations persists, as do the vestiges of a haunted history and a contemporary economy that continue to divide, exclude, and deny recompense. In the vexed intersections of a violent, advanced-capitalist South, the thefts and collisions of history bind as potently as they divide; a common tribe of the dispossessed emerges, and a peaceful repossession seems nowhere in sight. In the closing lines to her poem "News from the Imaginary Front," Alabama Creek poet Janet McAdams reminds us that in the hunger for recognition and recuperation, our failures will be legion and our victories small but sure, and they can be found only in courageous confrontation with a dark and bloody past. In words that might provide an answer to the unrelieved thirst and barrenness at the end of so many southeastern narratives, Adams writes: "I'm licking salt from the long wound of history. / The blood is sweet and my mouth's full of it. / I'm milking this body for everything it's worth."[87]

CHAPTER TWO

RED, BLACK, AND SOUTHERN

Alliances and Erasures in the Biracial South

The racial roles we play as Americans have tended to be repeated
over the course of American history; I should say, we have tended to
repeat them. And we regret this, and tell ourselves that we will start
fresh, the past will stop now, and will not hold us anymore than it
holds an innocent child. Then we repeat our race roles again.

—Scott L. Malcomson, *One Drop of Blood:*
The American Misadventure of Race

In 1991 an African American writer and director named Julie Dash released
a highly acclaimed independent film about a remote family of West African
Gullah people in the secluded Sea Islands of South Carolina.[1] Set in 1902,
Daughters of the Dust (1991) follows the Peazant family as several members of
the clan prepare to leave the isolated island community where they have lived
since arriving from West Africa as slaves; long protected from the South's
violent economic and social turmoil, they eventually feel compelled to leave
behind their simple, static existence for the opportunities and prosperity of
mainland America. In order to convey the immense cultural sea change about
to occur, Dash relies on images dense with symbolism, surreal and poetic
movements, and a magical-realist collision of fantasy and reality that dis-
turbs any conventional sense of narrative or plot development. Moreover,
her characters speak in their heavy Gullah dialect — English tinged with West
African accents and syntax — which makes the dialogue at times extremely

difficult to follow. In short, the film presents an alien world; as one reviewer puts it, "I'd wager that the portrait of turn-of-the-century African American women you get in *Daughters of the Dust* is like nothing you've ever seen before."[2] Dash followed up the film with a novel by the same title in 1997, which picks up twenty-four years later with the granddaughter of one of the migrants: Amelia, a graduate student in anthropology living in Harlem, decides to return to the island to research her family's history and meet those who remained. *Kirkus Reviews* finds the book, much like the film, an entry into an obsolete realm, "a loving tribute to a distinctive people, exotic place, and now-vanished way of life."[3]

If all this sounds familiar to scholars of *Native* American studies, that's because it is. These are Dash's people, and Dawtah Island is where her father grew up and her grandmother still lives. It's a world filled with idiosyncratic characters and strong women, which Dash maintains "still exists. The Geechee people live and thrive on the Sea Islands."[4] It is a world that Dash deliberately portrays as singular and apart, as she labors not just to "reconstruct" but to "lovingly" honor a community that has long resisted the claims and conversions of mainstream American life. As a kind of anthropologist, like her novel's protagonist, Dash's task is to resurrect a world both hers and not hers, at once thriving and obsolete. In this way, her film often resonates with Native American efforts to depict and preserve a culture and community under assault, and to present it in tones that more accurately reflect the stories and wisdom of the past rather than the narrow linearity of the present; it is autoethnography with a purpose, with artistic and cultural urgency and intent. As Ed Guerrero avers, Dash, like so many of her Native artist peers, "pointedly sets out to reconstruct, to recover a sense of black women's history, and to affirm their cultural and political space in the expanding arena of black cinematic production."[5] This kindred impulse helps explains a puzzling element of both Dash's film and her subsequent novel — one that no critic has yet been compelled to deal with, and yet one that signifies how intimately (and often troublingly) entwined are the African and Native American projects of cultural preservation and representation. In both the movie and the book, a mysterious, heavily romanticized Cherokee man on horseback appears at critical moments as a magnetic force holding one particular member of the family on the island. Clearly meant to function as an ally and a kindred spirit in their common resistance of assimilation and subjugation, the Cherokee nonetheless looks strikingly like a cliché — one that marks the black southern narrative as frequently as it does the white one; one that distances rather than unites these two similarly embattled and allied cultures; and one that raises disquieting questions about the enduring role of Jim Crow racial politics in contemporary Native and African self-determination, echoed by numerous writers and texts throughout this chapter.

"May You Draw Strength and Courage from This Land": Native Ancestors and Allies in African American Literature

Among Dash's fictional Peazant family, attitudes toward the migration to the mainland differ widely, and a general tension between modernity and primitivism runs throughout; the matriarch of the family, Nana, has emphatically resolved to stay behind. By the end of the film, she convinces a few other family members to remain on the island as well. Refusing to go forward into the corrupt, commercial society of twentieth-century America signifies a potent, profound measure of resistance not normally available to the marginalized. While the Peazants have suffered irremediably under slavery, they have also enjoyed the relative luxury of seclusion, isolation, and cultural preservation. They remain intact as a veritable "tribe" with living connections to their West African heritage and folkways, and many of the family members know that dispersing from the island will disrupt those ties permanently and irrevocably. As Dash has noted, the Sea Islands were "the region with the strongest retention of African culture";[6] leaving that oasis effectively meant losing any remaining links to histories long erased from the lives of most American blacks. Nana knows this, and that is why she stays. That is also why so many southeastern Indian tribes also elected to defy Removal mandates and remain in their homeland, the only land they knew, the earth marked by sacred sites vital to these uniquely place-centered cultures.

So when one of the younger Peazant women, Iona ("I Own Her"), is tempted to leave the island, the ideal form of persuasion comes in an indigenous package. Enter the Native American warrior, emissary of cultural preservation and traditional, anticapitalist values. When the rest of the clan tearfully boards the rowboats that will transport them and their aspirations to the mainland, Iona is suddenly swept off her feet and spirited away on horseback by her Cherokee lover. The young warrior instantly confirms our most rudimentary stereotypes of the lusty, silent Indian warrior — and he ostensibly provides for Iona and the others a living symbol of the noble primitivism and fragile cultural tradition that the Gullah family fosters and protects. "For Dash," Scott MacDonald concludes, "and for the characters in *Daughters of the Dust*, the idea of a natural Eden remains a crucial element in any recovery from the racial horrors that brought Africans to America and kept them in chains to develop the land."[7] When the Cherokee draws Iona back to the greener pastures of this "natural Eden," Dash invokes the well-rehearsed correlation between Indians and the natural world; more than that, by making him an ambassador from Eden, she implicitly denies him and his people the reality of their own colonial past and "racial horrors." He is there simply as a vehicle — quite literally — to serve and save Iona. His only other appearance in the film occurs earlier, when he delivers a letter imploring Iona to remain on the island with him. The letter translates effortlessly into Iona's own highly specific Gullah dialect; as such, we understand that his voice and language are irrelevant, and that this message of cultural continuity is intended only for the Gullah people.

Where is his family, his tribe? Somewhere off screen, in a remote and unseen part of the island? We know that Native Americans inhabited parts of the Sea Islands before they were settled by white planters and African slaves; it is widely believed that the Gullah people themselves got their name from a Spanish rendition of a Native tribal name, and that the Gullah nickname "Geechee" derives from a Creek word.[8] Yet the frozen, anachronistic, solo Cherokee warrior is, like these bits of language, the residue of a past that functions merely as parable. If his people remain on the island, we never see them or hear of them. That is, until the later novel, in which Dash decides to provide the Indian with a name and an ostensible tribe: Iona returns to visit her family with one child on her hip and two others in tow; while her relatives fawn over her and the children and ask about her husband (apparently, the absent Cherokee man with whom she now has these mixedblood babies), Iona's mother, Haagar, turns away. The narrator tells us, "Everyone on the Island knew that Haagar would never forgive Iona for choosing to stay with St. Julian Last Child, the last Cherokee to live on the Island, rather than move North with her family" (31).[9] It seems as though St. Julian is *the* Last Child, a veritable Mohican for the Sea Islands; and his decidedly Christian name further allows us to see him as no longer a vibrant warrior but instead a martyr (like St. Julian of Antioch) or worse, a legend (like the fabricated Catholic saint Julian the Hospitaller, aka Julian the Poor). While this weighty St. Julian thus embodies in every way the tragic death of his race, and even their apotheosis into legend, the "Last Childs" are in fact still around: Amelia is able to meet a group of elders from the tribe and, along with her own family, participates in a long ceremonial gathering with the "ancient people." The elders chant and sing,

> We are the Last Childs. The last free children of the Cherokee nation. We Last Childs a strong people, a stubborn people who turn our back on the white man's march and follow the way shown by our ancestors who hid from the Spanish and the white soldiers who came after them. We come from five generations and call places name Edisto, John's Island, Dafusky, Tybee, Warsaw, Ossabaw, Sapelo, and Okefenokee home. We travel by the ancient waterways, Ogeechee, Canoochee, Ocmulgee, Oconee, and the almighty Altamaha River.
>
> We have gone in many directions to seek our own way, but always we must return to this land for our renewal. Once again we are together in this season of cold to send prayer and thanks to our ancestors who brought us to this land. Let us join together to tell the story of our people, and may you draw strength and courage from this land we call "Chicora." (185)

The elders go on to sing a long song called "The Lifesong of Chicora" that celebrates the hardy resistance of the people, their attachment to Mother Earth, their stubborn will to survive and thrive in the land they call home in their own language. It is a sympathetic portrait indeed, but one gets the sense throughout that the import of the song — which is delivered in perfect English and orderly, metered verse — is really for the Peazants who, even when they "have gone in many directions to seek [their] own way," inevitably "return to this land" to be renewed. The Indians, who may in fact be Freedmen (former African chattel of Cherokee slaveholders), seem to bequeath their story and space to their West African neighbors: "May you draw strength and courage from this land," they offer; and Dash's Gullah protagonists eagerly accept the offering.

What Dash's film and novel together highlight is prevalent throughout black southern experience and literature more broadly: coexisting in common states of subjection, slavery, marginalization, violence, and dispossession, African and Native Americans had much cause to come together over ceremonial fires and lament their shared suffering and celebrate their resolute tenancy in this land, and in particular, in the region that drives them to remote, swampy, island enclaves where they can burrow together, survive, and disappear. For all the uplifting camaraderie implied by such alliances, more disturbing implications and erasures nonetheless emerge as well, particularly when Indian romance and potency figure merely as parable, a lost cause to be mourned and then used for courage, solidarity, and inspiration. Simply put, the African American employment of Native allies and histories — while obviously more kindred and sympathetic — is ultimately no less fraught than the white appropriations demonstrated in chapter 1. While such borrowings have contributed to a growing consensus about the cohesion and cross-pollination between Native and African Americans, theirs is an alliance that fractures under sustained analysis, and most acutely in these turbulent southern contexts. While the peculiar institutions of slavery and segregation did much to bring black and Indian southerners together, it did nearly as much to drive them irrevocably apart.

Until recently, the border between African and Native groups had been policed studiously by ideological inertia, which James F. Brooks describes as "the colonial incentive to keep the two peoples apart" and hence protect the white power base from a colored coalition, particularly in the hypervigilant eras of slavery and segregation. This trend resulted in discrete historical, social, and literary canons that persisted well into the twentieth century.[10] Lately, following the multicultural drift of academia and social consciousness in the post–World War II, post–Civil Rights era, the prevailing critical trend has been to celebrate the connections rather than the divisions in the Native-African experience. The affiliation between African and Native southerners is wholly intelligible: after all, what two groups had more cause to commune over their shared trauma on southern soil? Natives and African Americans have often been viewed — and have viewed themselves — as allies in the struggle against white supremacy and its assault on traditional cultural practices and communities. Likewise, scholars in both Native and African American studies have circulated compelling narratives about the cross-racial solidarity among the South's commonly oppressed, dark-skinned others. While not all of these gestures emerge directly from southern contexts, they frequently turn to explicitly southern geographies and histories in order to sketch the origins and the vexations of this kinship. This is a gesture I would like to endorse and honor, while nonetheless complicating these visions with a reminder of the very real and persistent residues of southern race-making and separating. Paradoxically, it is the southern roots of the African-Native family tree that have cultivated not just affiliation but *dis*affiliation in ways that are often far more discordant — and far more stereotypically "southern" in character and effect — than we would like to believe.

The project of harmonious reunion is made at once easier and more complicated by the pervasive fact of black-Indian miscegenation beginning with the earliest days of European colonization. Evidence of these pre-contact trade relationships and social interaction makes it nearly indisputable that both racial and cultural mixing had not already taken place by the time Columbus arrived in the so-called New World. Scholars such as Jack D. Forbes and Ivan Van Sertima believe that American Indians and Africans may have been traversing the ocean via Atlantic currents, visiting one another's settlements long before Europeans set foot on either continent.[11] As Forbes describes, the term "mulatto" was used originally to describe the Indian-African mixedbloods ordinary already in sixteenth-century colonial America.[12] Not just in the plantation South but widely throughout the North American continent, Natives were used as slaves in missions, taken prisoner in war and sold or traded into slavery, or indentured as children at so-called educational facilities.[13] While the practice of enslaving Natives was gradually disbanded (though never legally abolished in some locales),[14] the presence of mixed African-Native slave communities had quickly become so widespread throughout the plantation South that it ensured a permanent bond, both biological and cultural, between the two groups. Particularly during the plantation era, Natives and blacks often shared status as slaves or assisted one another in escaping their bondage. Many Indian communities lived in shadowy, backwoods locations beyond the borders of white society, places that offered ideal havens for fugitive slaves to disappear; such enclaves within or near Indian tribal lands became known as "maroon" societies. Racial intermixing became increasingly common, and soon these dark others shared bloodlines along with their analogous histories of marginalization and exploitation.[15] Together, blacks and Indians resisted the earliest European colonial incursions, and in the nineteenth century, they fought side by side in the Seminole Wars conducted against the U.S. Army.[16]

Since then, the notion of a "Black Indian" or African–Native American tradition has become regular enough to command serious and ongoing critical attention.[17] One of the enduring results of this hybridity, according to Jonathan Brennan and others, was the development of a distinct body of African–Native American literature with continuous traits and purposes. Focusing specifically on folklore and mythologies, scholars of southeastern literature have discovered that "African Americans have borrowed from Native American folktales and that Native Americans have borrowed from African folktales."[18] Mary Ellison agrees that it is "specifically within the area of folktales and myths that the culture of blacks and Indians seems to mingle most powerfully and most inextricably," signifying "a shared element in cultures that had much in common."[19] In a recent dissertation on syncretic black and Indian writings by Alice Walker, Sherman Alexie, and Craig Womack, Barbara S. Tracy urges readers to witness the "call and response" relationship between Native and African story-ways that can hardly be understood in isolation, one without the other.[20] As a repository for the shared plight of dispossession and "rootlessness" in the South, African-Native literature ought to be considered a unique canon unto itself, according to Brennan; indeed, a growing body of critical works has begun tracing its contours and testifying to the remarkable energy and distinctiveness of this tradition.[21] And yet Brennan is deeply aware that comparative works can accomplish only so much, and that even a canon borne from biological hybridity fractures along the fault lines of American racial politics. Literary fields, like our own academic departments, still adhere to doggedly essentialized categories for reasons that are as vital to the vibrancy of individual communities as they are inhibitive to a fully functional cross-culturalism. Most of the writers Brennan and other African-Native critics highlight — Okah Tubbee, Alice Walker, Clarence Major — will always be considered part of either the African or Native tradition, not both, even when they assert their mixedblood backgrounds.[22] Put another way: *cultural* hybridity seems the most potent force of kinship and cross-pollination — in the histories, stories, and practices that both groups share. But such connections are effectively undone — both conceptually and practically — by the *biological* notions of race and blood quantum that preoccupied the postplantation South and continue to dominate our perceptions of racial and cultural integrity and "authenticity."

To what forces do we ascribe this stubborn recalcitrance in our cultural imagination and social laws? Biracial, essentialist thinking certainly has a secure foothold in the American consciousness broadly speaking; but to trace out the roots and the trenchancy of such ideas, we need to "turn South again," to borrow Houston A. Baker's phrase.[23] Indeed, the southern context magnifies what has become a truism in national culture as well: the widespread hybridity manifest in the history, folk culture, and even literature of these two vitally imbricated peoples in fact facilitates not racial fluidity so much as divisiveness, a plain fact exacerbated by the southern context that nurtured such relationships and antagonisms. Especially under the maniacal codes of Jim Crow, the presence of enveloping mixtures posed a conceptual and a political problem that needed to be denied or remedied at all costs. White purity needed to be maintained, and therefore black peril had to be smoked out even in its most subtle, infinitesimal forms. Caught in the ruthless mechanisms of a reductively biracial system, Indians became functionally white or black depending on the civic context (each state had its own peculiar set of rules for determining racial heritage) and their own familial situation and needs. While kinship with African neighbors was often a biological and a pragmatic necessity, such relationships increasingly flattened Indians into the dominant, biracial binary. Succumbing to this system meant further erosion of any remaining cultural integrity, a fate that many tribes avoided strenuously — and often by utilizing the same racial essentialisms permeating social discourse and identity politics. Having only recently emerged from the corrosive decades of racial apartheid, the South remains a very long way from jettisoning the biracial codes of identification that have indelibly marked its social consciousness, no matter how deeply we would like to move beyond them.

To begin with, it is notable and potentially disquieting that African Americans are far more likely to assert their kinship with Natives than the reverse, and for reasons that appear more self-serving than we might expect. If white America needs Indian ancestors and allies to staunch a gaping spiritual wound, then African American artists have gravitated toward indigenous allies for more well-intentioned yet no less insular needs. And yet, when such tales of commiseration emerge from African American sources, their indigenous themes, correlatives, and sympathies are generally interpreted as mutual recognitions of solidarity. Toni Morrison's most recent novel, *A Mercy* (2008), for example, explores the painful symmetry between a Native and an African servant's shared plight, and the bond they develop in order to manage their despair.[24] Such stories expose us to the manifold, sweeping injustices that marked the long colonial history of the South; indeed, Morrison's purported intention in assembling a multiracial cast of slaves was to "remove race from slavery" and place it on a more encompassing, eclectic stage.[25] Patrick Minges attempts something similar in his collection of black Indian slave narratives culled from WPA interview archives: some of the slaves are black (with Indian masters), some are Indian (with white masters), and a good many are of mixed descent, evidence for Minges that their stories embody "the dynamic interaction of the cultures and how historical and cultural roots provided continuity within a tragic and complicated relationship with the institution of slavery."[26] And yet, in both cases, the resulting narrative is not necessarily one of commiseration and shared suffering, but the production of a racial caste system where "slave" equals "colored" and "Indian" is a spiritual salve. In *A Mercy*, the African (Florens) and Native (Lina) slavewomen cling to each other for comfort. Lina is the sole survivor of a smallpox outbreak among her people, a relic of a nearly eradicated tribe, a vanishing race unto herself; her purpose is to console and guide Florens through the despair of their shared serfdom, and as such, she becomes typical of the sage Indian who provides vital counsel and wisdom for the suffering other. Mainly through Florens's perspective, we are repeatedly reminded of Lina's primacy as both model and mentor of survival and security: "Lina smiles when she looks at me and wraps me for warmth" (8); "Lina says Sir has a clever way of getting without giving" (7); "I need Lina to say how to shelter in wilderness" (42); "Only Lina was steady, unmoved by any catastrophe as though she has seen and survived anything" (100). These are tributes, to be sure, to the strength and resiliency and nobility of a fallen people; but like Dash's "Last Child," they are also elegies to a lone survivor with dwindling cause for self-preservation that do little to animate a sense of an enduring, vibrant people. As Florens notes with both sadness and admiration, "Lina, the silent workhorse, seemed to have lost interest in everything, including feeding herself" (132). In his critique of Toni Morrison's 1997 novel *Paradise*, Craig Womack questions the nearly universal celebration of Morrison's Indian depictions as "affirmations" of Native culture — a response he places in the larger, disquieting critical trend toward "ecstasy over any mention of Native people whatsoever no matter the quality of her depictions."[27] It may seem difficult to critique representations that appear inherently well intentioned, generous, and kind; but as Womack reminds us, it is the romantic "quality" and self-serving implications of those references that matter deeply.

In Minges's collection of slave narratives, Indian ancestry is often evoked similarly as a source of wisdom, comfort, or strength, but rarely as a functional cultural presence in the lives of these ex-slaves. More often than not, Indian blood is a rumor that provides a sense of spiritual and often supernatural fortitude. Cora Gillam, a black-Indian slave of a white family in Greenville, Mississippi, regales her interviewer with tales of her wise old "full-blood" Cherokee grandmother, who tracked down her children after they had been forced into slavery because "You know the Indians could follow trails better than other kind of folks" (20). Then there was her Uncle Tom, who "seemed all Indian" mainly because he was a legendary fighter:

> That Indian in Uncle Tom made him not scared of anybody. He had a newspaper with latest war news, and gathered a crowd of slaves to read them when peace was coming. White men say it done to get uprising among slaves. A crowd of white men gather, and take Uncle Tom to jail. Twenty of them say they would beat him, each man, 'til they so tired they can't lay on one more lick. . . . The Indian in Uncle Tom rose. Strength, big extra strength, seemed to come to him. First white man what opened that door, he leaped on him and laid him out. No white men could stand against him in that Indian fighting spirit. They was scared of him. He almost tore that jailhouse down, lady. Yes, he did. . . . Then Uncle Tom join the Union Army; was in the 54th regiment, United States volunteer (colored). . . . (21)

Uncle Tom's status as a "colored" person and a slave is assured (even without the unacknowledged irony that "Uncle Tom" has become shorthand for "docile slave"); but "that Indian" in him allows for momentary flights of glory and power — incidents that have surely been embellished to the point of apocrypha, but which clearly have their roots in a system that diminished African potency and raised Indian tragedy and nobility to the level of legend. "That Indian blood" has magical, palliative properties: "I have never worn glasses in my life," Cora reports proudly: "I guess that is some more of my Indian blood telling" (25).

As Laura L. Lovett shows in "'African and Cherokee by Choice': Race and Resistance under Legalized Segregation," such resurrections of Indian ancestry were "fairly typical" in the WPA narratives where "the Indian relative has disappeared, leaving a legacy of resistance to coercion and injustice . . . imbued with whatever stereotypically Indian qualities were advantageous to the situation."[28] The strategic deployment of Indian ancestry did not end with slavery, but in fact increased with the ruthless racism of Jim Crow: many African Americans pointed to often-remote Native ancestries "to undermine the very definition of the racial category assigned them by segregation . . . [with] an alternative positive identity" laced with romance, mystique, and danger.[29] The salvation properties afforded by such a relative proliferated as well: as Honorée Fanonne Jeffers (an African-Cherokee from Georgia) writes in "Hawk Hoof Tea":

> My mother lost an eye to the butcher knife
> when she was only five or six.
> I've told this story before, but as I age, the story becomes
> a lesson, how, if a family had not been poor
> and black, a child might have been able
> to see on both sides of her face. . . .
> Then,
> there arrived Great-Grandpa Henry,
> the son of a full Cherokee
> woman whose own story got lost,
> but what we do know is Henry
> walked in the door and cured my Mama
> and her brothers and sisters.
> This story is a spiritual awakening in me,
> sure enough.[30]

Jeffers incisively demonstrates the pronounced physical consequences of being "poor and black" in the rural South, a place where violence is routine and doctors are scarce if one has "no money and her skin was not white."[31] Under such cruel conditions, it is no surprise that Great-Grandpa Henry provides medical sustenance and a vital spiritual salve as well. Jeffers understands exactly how these affiliations operate and why they are so critical to the survival of her people: "Who wouldn't want to claim a great medicine / woman and her son as blood, make him a king / beyond a small act?"[32]

The practice of resurrecting mystical Indian progenitors and saviors had become so common that in her autobiography, *Dust Tracks on a Road*, Zora Neale Hurston bitingly declared herself "the only Negro in the United States whose grandmother on the mother's side was *not* an Indian chief."[33] Hurston does, in fact, admit to having Indian ancestry, but departs consciously "from the party line in that I neither consider it an honor or a shame."[34] The "party line" indeed acknowledged the abundance of African Americans in the early twentieth century claiming Native heritage, a phenomenon Hurston would have known well: as research assistant to anthropologist Melville Herskovits, she helped conduct a 1928 study that found 27.2 percent of black Howard University students claiming indigenous ancestry.[35] Owning and using that knowledge often had less to do with maintaining Indian culture than with softening the peril, both physical and emotional, of living black in the segregated South. As early as the 1880s and continuing to this day, African Americans in New Orleans don elaborately hand-sewn, Plains Indian–inspired regalia to march each spring as "Mardi Gras Indians." Borrowing an indigenous identity and costume allowed marginalized blacks the license to celebrate the local holiday in their own way, and in the process, to "honor" the history of Indians who had helped African Americans "in escaping the tyranny of slavery"; yet what began with good and pragmatic intentions quickly devolved into an occasion for violence, as the elaborate costumes and masks — combined with the energy of the warrior spirit — allowed groups with vendettas to battle it out anonymously on the city streets. Even now, the spirit of fierce rivalry and ambient danger remains an undercurrent of the yearly event: "After Mardi Gras, you thank GOD that you made it," says Larry Bannock, president of the New Orleans Mardi Gras Council.[36]

Such precedents surely help us understand more keenly the ways by which Natives have often resisted their quasi-mythic transcendence within African American texts and contexts. Even when African-Native writers claim a legitimate portion of Indian ancestry, the fact of shared genealogy can help more than it hurts if a writer is not deemed authentically "Native" enough. Alice Walker, for instance, has insistently embraced her Cherokee heritage in her writing, often to critical scorn. Her 1979 book of poetry *Horses Make a Landscape Look More Beautiful* begins with a "Dedication" in which she acknowledges her Native lineage: "my / 'part' Cherokee / great-grandmother / Tallulah / (Grandmamma Lula) / on my mother's side / about whom only one / agreed-upon / thing / is known: / her hair was so long / she could sit on it" (ll. 5–16). Walker seems in full control of the irony with which she renders her "part"-Cherokee grandmother in quotation marks, a cliché of the African American South; and yet she is also at pains to verify the striking physical presence and Indianness of this remote Cherokee ancestor, about whom nothing definitive is known except her long, flowing, Pocahontas-worthy hair. Never one to shy away from difficult topics — her writings are among the most explicit representations of both erotic ecstasy and emotional violence in contemporary literature — Walker appears fully aware that she is treading on sensitive cultural territory here. Yet recuperating this vital part of her heritage proves critical to her spiritual health: "To attempt to function as only one [race], when you are really two or three, leads, I believe, to psychic illness. . . . Regardless of who will or will not accept us, including, perhaps, our 'established' self, we must be completely (to the extent it is possible) who we are."[37] Walker is prepared for those who will reject her claims to indigeneity; yet who can argue with her larger point about the damaging repressions of racial essentialism?

Statements like these place us at a quandary: if an outsider claiming a Cherokee great-grandmother is seen as disrespectful to "real" Indian cultures, then does the alternative — rejecting those alliances — necessarily signify retreat into poisonous, separatist racial ideologies? Can Native American identity logically function as an exception to the larger rule? What Walker's example teaches us, and which numerous other Native texts confirm, is that an integral part of living and shaping one's identity under southern racial codes (both during and after segregation) is to grapple with such crises, and often to repeat rather than amend the corrosive essentialisms and exclusions that each group has already suffered. To write oneself an identity in the South means fundamentally having to negotiate the terms and boundaries of this conditioning, and to turn the luxury of choice in uncomfortable directions. For Walker, this entails electing to claim a place within a heritage that other Natives will choose — with equal fervency and need — to deny her. In her semiautobiographical *The Way Forward Is with a Broken Heart* (2000), which she dedicates to "the American race," Walker writes,

In Mississippi I began to crave arrowheads. It came upon me as suddenly as the desire, years before, to write poetry. I hungered for the sight of them. I ached for the feel of them in my hand. Now I think this was perhaps another beginning of the endless understanding of who I really am. . . . Craft and art and eyes steadied me, as I tottered on the journey toward my tri-racial self. Everything that was historically repressed in me has hungered to be expressed, to be recognized, to be known. . . . Indians are always in my novels because they're always on my mind. Without their presence the landscape of America seems lonely, speechless.[38]

Resurrecting this Indian grandmother and the symbols of her lost heritage is a fundamental feature of Walker's attempt to overcome her historical repression and silencing. It is not the legitimate claim to a "tri-racial" self that may be disconcerting, though, but her implicit desire to speak for the "speechless." Coincident with the yearning to write poetry is the hunger to possess the relic of a disappeared people and genealogy, as Walker mourns "how empty of Indians Mississippi was" (37); to write in this context is to raise the dead, in a sense, and to heal the ravages of a history and identity under perpetual, generational assault; but despite the gestures of community and communication and wholeness that such efforts imagine, they remain for the most part parallel utterances in a persistently segregated literary narrative.

Resisting Solidarity: Black-Indian Writers and the Legacy of Jim Crow

Within the Native-African confluence, the roots of both attachment and antagonism run deep, and they are fed by the currents of the South's long colonial and plantation histories. While there is much to be gained from embracing the hybridity of black-Indian cultures and literatures, the prevailing trend seems distressingly contrary to this recognition. On the surface, this may seem like overstatement. After all, as Brennan and others have shown in great detail, there are no shortage of texts testifying to the shared domination—and often mingled blood—of African and Native southerners who continue to find common ground, despite the darkness often buried within such genealogies. It is not my intention here to work against such partnerships or to deny the usefulness—indeed, the urgency—of thinking and moving actively beyond our persistently separatist, essentialist notions of racial identity and literary culture. Undermining such gestures, though, is an enduring emphasis on binary, essentialist thinking that seems now vitally woven *into* the cultural dispositions of both communities. When Native scholar Jack D. Forbes wrote his groundbreaking study of African and Native intersections, *Black Africans and Native Americans: Color, Race, and Caste in the Evolution of Red-Black Peoples*, he did so precisely to allow these commonly marginalized groups the opportunity to identify and negotiate their identities on their own terms rather than continue to be codified "by powerful outsiders, as well as by governments and institutions" for inimical purposes and to destructive effect.[39] However, rather than being externally imposed, racial and cultural essentialisms in our contemporary moment often now come from within—learned, perpetuated, and perverted by the unique incubator of their shared southern past.

Thus, in the trenchant biracial vacuum of the South, solidarity often becomes secondary to the more pragmatic demands of cultural self-preservation. Consequently, much of the resistance to unity in both African and Native American texts derives from an excessive concern with superficial traits and appearances. The scrupulous ocularity of Jim Crow bequeaths a lasting legacy in American society wherein race-"tainted" blood manifests and signifies in a particular and unavoidable way. The fact of Native ancestry within a predominantly African American–looking individual, even when it is genealogically close and true, can appear from the outside extraordinarily difficult to detect or claim and easy to interpret as mystical fantasy of the sort we've seen abundantly. The scrutiny and the fear cultivated by external racial measures are deeply embedded in the southern social consciousness; more than we regularly admit, though, they increasingly influenced the perception of Native identity as *racial* rather than culturally based, tribally specific, and inherently diverse. Florida Seminoles, for instance, will have vastly different histories, genetic backgrounds, and spiritual beliefs than, say, Pueblo Indians in New Mexico; and within each tribe, the variety of cultural dispositions, genealogies, and traditional practices are as various as in any community. Yet the pan-Indian flattening of difference into one Native "type" is often a protective reaction to the codifications and erasures of Jim Crow, a national phenomenon that rarely acknowledges its explicitly southern influence. Put another way, conceptions and assertions of Indian identity might become more dramatic and homogenizing—and inevitably "racist" themselves—as a countermeasure to being classified as black. Indeed, Indian identity in the South was often figured racially—usually colored, sometimes white.

Inevitably, heightened efforts to preserve a distinctive identity unwittingly reinforced similar racial codes and ideologies. As historian Claudio Saunt notes, "Though the subject is often underplayed in history books, race was a central element in the lives of southeastern Indians, not just as a marker of difference between natives and white newcomers but as a divisive and destructive force within Indian communities themselves."[40]

For black Indians, then, it can be painfully difficult to gain acceptance from fellow, skeptical Indians. In her poem "Traditional," Jennifer Lisa Vest — a mixedblood writer of black and Florida Seminole ancestry — describes the struggle of a mixed-race African-Indian to be accepted as such:

> They told her
> Her clothing
> Was not traditional enough
> For Grand Entry
> They whispered
> Looked at her sideways
> Asked her
> What kind of Indian
> Was she anyway?
> And was she on the rolls?
>
> They told her her hair
> Was too curley
> And not traditional enough
> For Grand Entry
> Her skin too dark
> Suitable only for intertribal
> Indians don't have blue eyes, they said
> Indians don't have black skin, they said. (ll. 1–18)

Vest's spare verse barely conceals her scathing critique of the "traditional" culture industry and its emphasis on the superficial characteristics and performance. What Vest wants to emphasize instead are the less visible, more potent traits that signify Native culture: "And she could dance / You should have seen her! / And she could talk story! / You should have heard her! / And she knew medicine / You should have felt her!" (ll. 19–24). Vest's catalog of indigenous qualities begins with "and" rather than "but," which is a subtle reminder that the dancer's performance may not contradict those presumptions of inauthenticity but might simply be accretive — just more superficial elements, more features of performativity, and no more or less indicative of traditional culture than blue eyes or curly hair. For despite all these things, "she still wasn't traditional enough / For those urban Indians" (ll. 25–26). Vest stops short of telling us what being "traditional enough" would mean; she simply knows that "urban Indians" engaged in pantribal powwows are not necessarily equipped to judge. The speaker of the poem receives this knowledge but doesn't share it; she doesn't even voice her presence in the poem until the last stanza, when she too comes under the gaze of those quizzical eyes:

> So when those powwow Indians looked at me sideways
> And started asking too many questions
> She said come here little girl
> Take this shawl, come and dance
> And she taught me
> How to be traditional. (ll. 27–32)

The poem ends thus, with the magnificent dancer becoming her cultural mentor, and yet an actual illustration of this lesson is omitted from the telling. Three things are left resonating: that such knowledge can be taught and learned, not simply inherited; that whatever such knowledge *is*, it is ineffable; and that even if it were something she could articulate, the speaker refuses to divulge that which may be stolen and denied her in the future.

On the one hand, Vest has a legitimate complaint about the profusion of pan-Indian, intertribal communities that rely on performance (often through powwow and other demonstrations of indigenous culture), where "tradition" may seem a manufactured tool and a political weapon that often loses its historical moorings. On the other hand, she raises a more troubling question about the increasing trend among contemporary tribes to exclude those with tenuous ancestral and cultural claims who seek recognition for some imagined spiritual (and in some cases, economic) gain, and in doing so, erode tribes' ability to maintain cultural integrity both internally and in the view of the all-important and ever-vexed federal oversight processes. Surrounded by an already diluted and suspect pool of "urban" Indians, Vest does not dismiss but in fact implicitly endorses the protective scrutiny of the tribal gaze: while she laments that the superficial performances of indigeneity automatically trump one's black skin and blue eyes in the contest for authenticity, she knows she has no choice but to dance and perform nonetheless. As the mixedblood writer Dale Marie Taylor (Cherokee-Seneca-African) writes similarly in her poem "Warrior Woman," her phenotypically black appearance makes her assertions of indigeneity seem actually "crazy" to outsiders. "This does not look right," the poem begins, taking immediate aim at the tyranny of surfaces that plagues our social consciousness (l. 1). She explains: "My friends all think I'm crazy. / A mixed blood, black, / I dream this crazy dream, this vision. A woman appears to me in my visions / dressed in white leather / beaded and painted with the / signs of her conquests" (ll. 2–8). She is "mixed blood" but the appositive phrase following immediately after clarifies what that means: "black." Her friends think she is "crazy"—period. And perhaps she wants us to think she is, too, by describing her own dream vision as "crazy." But is it mad only because it defies social logic and racial ideology—making it, therefore, not inherently crazy at all? Or is something more unsettling at work in her consciousness?

The rest of the poem suggests the latter: the embattled warrior woman in her dream vision is cloaked in leather and beads and represents every bit the romantic archetype, plucked from a Hollywood set or, worse, a Disney animation studio. She spears food and prey, captures horses ("for good"), has "hair long, shiny and black," rides "a beautiful / black mare, nostrils flaring / mane gently blowing in the soft / breezy air" (ll. 12, 13–17). She's silent, but waits and watches the speaker, "should I need / her," she guesses (ll. 19–20). The speaker implores her: "Why great ancestor spirit, do not / my people see you in me?" (ll. 29–30). The warrior woman smiles, "saying nothing," and takes the speaker's hand—and the two women ride off "together through life's changes. A lost child, a lost love, a lost friend; / we ride together drawing strength from / the thoughts of two knowing that love triumphs" (ll. 32, 35–38). Like the speaker in Vest's poem, Taylor's remains silent about the knowledge she has to impart to this frustrated descendant. And yet, is this heavily stylized, fabled white warrior woman really the missing genealogical link that she wants her people to "see" and accept? The stereotypical portrait offered by her "vision" suggests otherwise; further, we neither see nor hear what form the speaker's ancestry takes, as the warrior woman never vocally answers her question. Even on horseback with that warrior cartoon, what seems like strength and solidarity is merely a witness to unrelenting personal loss: lost children, lovers, friends. The stark isolation of this recognition makes the final, triumphant line seem heavy with the bitterness of unrequited hope. As Barbara Tracy and others have endeavored to show, the intercultural partnership between black and Native can be transformative, "a syncopation of two cultures becoming greater than their parts."[41] But in Taylor's poem, her "two" heritages galloping through life's hardships together yield little more than a "crazy" vision, a silent myth, and a companion in loss.

Despite its undercurrent of despair, Taylor's poem nonetheless labors to find in her occluded ancestry a source of strength and survival. Less common is the desire for visibly African American southerners to disavow their Native heritage; occasionally, however, they express at the very least a palpable discomfort for the origins of that indigenous blood. As poet and scholar Ron Welburn (who descends from Assateague/Gingaskin, Cherokee, and African American ancestors in Virginia) recalls, "Most of us living on the Indian-Negro color line grew up with mixed signals and coded information. Our elders had learned to protect us from the ridicule and abuse they had experienced as Indians or from which their parents had sheltered them. They instilled in us the sense that we were 'different' from our peers; but that we were Indian or of Native descent, when it was raised, was a covert issue."[42] Part of denying Indian heritage is surely to escape the "ridicule" Welburn cites, but identifying simply as "Negro" could hardly have been less wounding; implicitly, then, he seems to suggest that the "abuse" came not from whites but from fellow blacks who (for reasons left unexplored and unarticulated here) resented mixing with Indians. Perhaps a small part of this antagonism derives from the often troubled history that inevitably attended cultural collisions in the plantation South. There are disturbing annals within the black-Indian chronicle, to be sure, as Christina Snyder and other historians remind us: Indians were not just subjects and slaves like their black counterparts, but they were often masters and owners as well; confederate Indians who fought for the South during the Civil War further alienated themselves from the region's African Americans. The practice of slaveholding among antebellum Cherokees, Choctaws, Chickasaws, and Creeks has by now been well documented.[43] As Snyder points out, such habits were not necessarily introduced by white planters but were indigenous to the continent; it was the attendant racial ideologies that had to be learned. "Deeply rooted in Native history," she explains, "slavery was already present when the first Europeans and Africans arrived in the sixteenth century. . . . Not until the late eighteenth century did Southern Indians begin to graft ideas about race onto their preexisting captivity practices."[44] As Western models of economic and social function proliferated and overtook indigenous practices, so too did ideologies of racial hierarchy.

While the memory of Native slaveholding has faded, emerging now and then in textbooks and frank scholarly investigations, we cannot yet shake the residues of this past and its participation in the South's darkest chapter. Even in the twenty-first century, as Dale Marie Taylor reminds us, the vestiges of these unquiet histories live on in bloodlines mingled often by force. In her poem "We Wait," the rape of a black slave by her Cherokee master is narrated to a descendant of that trauma generations later — and the speaker implies that the telling will reproduce endlessly as long as the bloodline continues. The speaker is not the present-day, mixedblood offspring of the master's passion: rather, she is the original victim herself, a ghostly voice from history addressing as "you" the great-great-grandchild who emerges generations later in the contemporary telling. Her story is that which "waits," staring at the speaker "through these brown eyes / the eyes of our children" (ll. 1–2). What bears witness is the biological trace, the body, and the story it tells is a terrible one: a Cherokee statesman purchases "with one horse" a black slave from a white dealer (l. 7). "So I used my black shoulders, my back / for the bidding of these new masters / who seemed as much a slave to me, / pushed around by whites from land to land. . . . I joined these people, brown skinned and red / As they struggled, mixed feelings, to keep me in chains" (ll. 8–11, 16–17). Then, one dark night, wrapped in a blanket she needs to keep hidden, the woman is raped by her master.

Assimilating the dark genesis of her ancestry is the implied dilemma for the present-day receiver of this genealogical horror story, the recipient of those dark eyes and the blood of traumatic continuity and survival. Yet how do you assimilate such hate for the blood that courses through your veins? And how do you hate the abuser who paradoxically makes you free? That, indeed, is the tacit crisis for the speaker, who begins her rape narrative with the ominous admission that "my *freedom* came" along with her abuser (l. 18, emphasis added). Strikingly, she describes the ensuing rape as an act of intimacy: "large wonder / after all the beatings that I had any love left to give" (ll. 20–21). Following the initial violation ("he took as the others what he needed and left"), the man returns habitually: "He came again and again till I knew / every curve of his body and face. / Soon there was no hiding the curly headed children who / came from my body and blood" (ll. 22, 24–27). Whether "love" or rape, there seems little difference to the woman whose body is merely a vessel and a tool for the pleasure and gain of others, inured to such thefts by others who "need" what her body provides; her duty is simply to perform such services even after long days of labor and beatings, making the erotic nostalgia of her narration as disturbing as it is pathetic.

Having sex with the master apparently does liberate the woman from bondage, but it delivers her into a paradoxical kind of "freedom": when the soldiers arrive to spirit her people away to Indian Territory, she and her eleven children are taken along with the Cherokee. Her sons "walked and died with me on the Trail of Tears," yet her daughters "fled to the Tennessee hills" and survived (ll. 29, 28). While they endured in a way that the speaker does not, their fate seems little different:

> One of my daughters worked for a white man in Tennessee
> and he came to her too as her father did to me.
> Her children are her looking at you now. The strongest
> of them made strong by trust and love.
> We stare at you in the mirror that you see, in the
> mirror of your mind. We are there in you and me.
> Waiting, waiting to survive. (ll. 31–37)

The entire poem thus captures the genealogy of a mixedblood family as metaphor as much as brute fact: the collision of blood is neither peaceful nor harmonious but violent, and skin color fails to predict the charity or the evil lurking in one's heart and body. The reproduction of the family is ensured by force and theft, and survival is a product of uncanny "trust and love" — but in and for what? The ability to endure at all costs under the most dreadful conditions and losses, perhaps. Yet Taylor reminds us finally that such survival is not assured but is perpetually imminent, "waiting" for testimony and actualization. And "love" for the bedfellows in these unquiet histories, much like the "love" given by that raped ancestor generations before, can be a sentiment produced purely by circumstance, need, and faith. By posing the offspring of these terrible histories as composite faces in the mirror of the listener, a typical image for underscoring moments of self-recognition and awareness, we understand that these are histories she must come to terms with in order to comprehend and accept the fiber of her own being, that visage in the mirror "waiting" to be recognized and loved. Thus, we realize further that such histories are rooted not just in slavery or in Removal, but in the "survival" of those who remained to be raped—literally and metaphorically—by the elite southern oppressors for whom they continued to work and subject themselves. This is a specifically southern experience, one that rises out of the trauma of history to continue reproducing in uncanny, ugly repetitions into a persistently biracial twenty-first century.

And in this peculiarly vexed era, we need to confront the causes for the curious paradox of the black-Indian canon: that is, as I suggested at the outset of this chapter, such recognitions of mixture are far more likely to appear in African American works than in Native ones. At issue, it seems, is the pivotal notion of choice. For African Americans long denied the ability to assert the makeup and complexity of their heritage, this belated freedom is all important. For these very reasons, critic Sharon P. Holland embraces the term "crossblood" rather than the typical "mixedblood" to signify African-Native hybridity: "To be a mixed blood African-American is to be counted among the hundreds of thousands of African-Americans who have the knowledge of some European and/or Native ancestry, but to be a crossblood is to identify as such, to read the 'racial' categories on the U.S. census as bogus and to consistently cross the borders of ideological containment."[45] In using the more rebellious and proactive idea of the "crossblood" to liberate the African-Native from the institutionalized shackles of racial essentialism, Holland draws explicitly on Anishinaabe writer and critic Gerald Vizenor's similar use of the term: "Crossbloods are a postmodern tribal bloodline, an encounter with racialism, colonial duplicities, sentimental monogenism, and generic cultures. The encounters are comic and communal, rather than tragic and sacrificial; comedies and trickster signatures are liberations; tragedies are simulations, an invented cultural isolation. Crossbloods are communal, and their stories are splendid considerations of survivance."[46] Distinctly, both Vizenor and Holland emphasize that assertions of intercultural hybridity are vital decolonizing acts — gestures of will and agency that pointedly defy the ideological boundaries of race, especially as it has been construed and ossified in the history of the South. More recently, Scott Richard Lyons's *X-Marks: Native Signatures of Assent* examines the paucity of choice within the long trajectory of colonial history, but dwells pragmatically on the realities of Indian self-determination: "An x-mark [treaty signature] is a sign of consent in a context of coercion; it is the agreement one makes when there seems to be little choice in the matter. To the extent that little choice isn't quite the same thing as no choice, it signifies Indian agency."[47]

Here, then, is where the gulf between African and Native American histories and methods of self-determination begins to matter deeply. While black Americans were initially enslaved (sometimes by Indians) and Indians (for the most part) were considered free, that condition has essentially reversed: now, African Americans enjoy a semantic "freedom" that endows acts of choice, self-identification, and ideological resistance with increased urgency and power. Natives, on the other hand, while of course nominally free, nonetheless struggle for sovereignty not just over their communities but indeed their very identities. The federal government retains the final, monumental capacity to determine an entire tribe's existence null and void, and to demand excessive evidence of "authenticity" and continuity in cases of federal recognition. Such expectations trickle down into tribes' own internal affairs, where blood quantum requirements take on heightened importance as the biological gatekeeper for racial integrity and survival. "Choice," as Lyons admits, is often a thinly excised vestige of coercion and indoctrination; acts of "choice" such as the expulsion of black Freedmen from the Cherokee rolls indicate how deeply some tribal decisions continue to rest on the vexed racial politics that govern Indian existence. Indigenous activism based on real hopes for tribal sovereignty, and even literary-critical movements predicated on tribal nationalist politics, thus have little pragmatic space for the kind of mixture and hybridity that well-intentioned critics like Sharon Holland and even Gerald Vizenor espouse. More commonly, Natives endeavor to place clear lines of demarcation between themselves and their black kin, biological and otherwise. At the end of the day, the need to assert an *Indian* identity above all else is what matters; in the process, black ancestors and peers become increasingly obscure and obscured.

The "Last" of Everything:
Native Survival under Jim Crow

Neither homogenizing nor harmonious, race in the Southeast frequently meant elision and erasure for Indians. Southern racial codes labored to subsume the Indian into either white or black populations, imperiling Natives' cultural integrity as a group apart from either white settlers or African chattel. Gradually, the Native South became inextricably bound in not just a racial society but a biracial one that increasingly demanded alliance with either a white power structure or a black, laboring underclass. A stark binary order dominated the South long before Jim Crow institutionalized and disciplined it. According to historian Nancy Shoemaker's research, Indians began emphasizing their identity as "red" peoples in the early eighteenth century, drawing on imagery in precontact stories, precisely to distinguish themselves from both "white" and "black" monoliths; Removal and its fictions of extinction did much to ensure that "red" became a memory and a fantasy in a region long consumed by black-white issues.[48] As James Merrell reports, even as early as the nineteenth century, Catawba Indians in South Carolina had assumed white racist attitudes toward blacks as a means of safeguarding their own tenuous position, and further to distance themselves from being mistakenly interpreted as black themselves. Indeed, the practice of slavery among the tribe proliferated largely as a means of enforcing racial hierarchy between these otherwise analogous peoples, and the accompanying racism toward African Americans lingered long after slavery was abolished.[49] A similar phenomenon deteriorated interracial relationships among the Cherokee, whose ambivalent slaveholding attitudes became markedly more severe upon removal to Indian Territory and its acute new challenges to their economic and cultural survival; as Theda Perdue documents, Cherokee planters tightened control over their slave labor force, and in turn, the incidence of escape and revolt grew dramatically.[50] Under Jim Crow and the "one-drop rule," to have even a miniscule degree of African blood was to be classified as black; yet such logic not only enforced racial apartheid but also denied Indians with African heritage the opportunity to identify as anything *other* than black.[51]

For Indians who were not black at all but might easily be misidentified as such, the need to maintain racial clarity was imperative. In Geary Hobson's 2000 novella *The Last of the Ofos* (to be discussed in greater detail in chapter 3), his protagonist is the last surviving member of the "Ofo" — or Mosopelea — tribe of Louisiana. Already an occluded member of a physically vanished tribe, Thomas Darko battles further to be seen as anything besides "dark," as his name implies and predestines him, a description that could only mean "black" in the Jim Crow South. Hobson invents several situations that dramatize Darko's perilous indeterminacy in this context. He makes and runs whiskey with a gang of men — two white, and one black — all poor folks working together without regard for race, in the common effort to survive financially during the Great Depression. Within this biracial group, Darko is automatically assumed to be African American like his colleague, Benny. In one of the book's many picaresque moments, Darko and his gang have a disturbing run-in with Bonnie and Clyde. Bonnie repeatedly calls Darko a "nigger" and, after being informed that he is in fact Native, she sneers: "Oh, git out of here, nigger boy. They ain't no more Indians around anymore. Everyone knows that" (51). The presumption of extinction that "everyone knows" in the South functions here as an extreme iteration of the "vanishing race" mythos that operates on a national level. To emphasize the pervasiveness of this phenomenon, Hobson sends Darko and his crew briefly north to sell their wares in Chicago. As they enter a bar to make the transaction, the black Benny immediately moves off to the kitchen "where he seen a couple of coloreds standing around," and then their host, a man named Saltis, "look at me real close and extra-long, too, but he never said nothing" (46). One of his associates cannot hold his tongue, though:

> "What's this black dago bastard doing here?" He's talking to Saltis, but I know he mean me.
>
> "Oh, he's not a dago, Frankie," Saltis say. "Mr. Darko is a — " and he stop and look at me, then say, "What are you, sir?"
>
> "I'm Indian," I say.
>
> "Yes, Frankie. Mr. Darko is from India. He's just a customer visiting here from his home overseas."
>
> I wudn't about to correct him. . . . (47)

In this northern city, Darko's "black" otherness is apparent, but the notion of a domestic "Indian" fails even to register as a possibility. Unable to class him exactly as a "nigger," as the southern context facilitates and demands, nor as an immigrant "dago" (that is, Hispanic or Italian), these Chicago mobsters prefer to dismiss him as a visitor and "customer" from abroad. He is someone simply to do business with, and to be an economic partner in the exchange he must be something more intelligible and visible than an Ofo Indian.

Hobson's wandering protagonist thus demonstrates that Indians are effectively invisible everywhere, but his knowledge of this isolation is rooted in the swamps of Louisiana and Arkansas. As a boy, Darko's father and a Quapaw friend named Jack had been business partners running whiskey themselves: "Old Man Jack and Papa had been the only Indians in that two-camp settlement in the middle of a big cypress swamp just a mile or so from the Mississippi. I say two-camp cause that's what it was: niggers on one side and white men on the other. Papa and Jack, by agreement, stayed off by theyselves" (20). A tacit atmosphere of competition marks the "camps" posed ominously against one another, a stand-off where the Indians are tolerated as long as they remain unseen and removed. Darko's business partnership with both a white and a black man seems a reminder of how this social distance could often be transcended in the interest of economic gain and the solidarity of the working class; yet after all three get arrested for their exploits, they inevitably go their separate ways, and Darko would only occasionally "run into them" or hear of their movements over the years (60). Even a more personal relationship — a brief affair with a black woman named Melba in D.C. — cannot exceed its situational context and purpose. Darko has been searched out by an anthropologist who is anxious to study this last living speaker of a dying language, and so he ends up agreeing to relocate to Washington and work with a team of Smithsonian researchers. While there, he meets Melba, "a cook and waitress in a little restaurant close by the rooming house I lived in. Pretty soon we was keeping company. Now, I had been around black people a lot back home, but never in a close personal relationship like this" (95). But associating with Melba proves dangerous, as her ex-lover — "a crook and a real tough guy" — comes around and threatens them both, and Darko takes to "carrying my straight-razor again, and sometimes my .38" and even gets injured in a tangle on the stairs to Melba's place. The Smithsonian people are furious: "You are too valuable an artifact — uhh, a person — to be lost by such a stupid thing as a spurned boyfriend's jealous rages," one of the researchers scolds, and then informs him that "the Institution was taking out a $75,000 life insurance policy on me" (96). Far more pernicious than a simple love triangle, their relationship is marked by violence, indiscretion, and an uneasy reminder of the racial "cost" of such transgression.

When Darko tires of his role as "artifact," he decides to return home to Louisiana and asks Melba to join him:

> She say no, say too many of her family . . . was there around her in D.C. I figgered she was going to say that, so I told her that if anytime she want to come down to visit, or even stay, she is always welcome. She say she jist might do that, but I think we both knowed then that she never would.
>
> "Good-bye, Tom. You've been an awfully good friend," she say, and I think she emphasize "friend" in a real special way. Then she say, "Tom, you the lonesomest man I've ever known." (110)

Despite the intimacy he shares with Melba, Darko nonetheless maintains a clear emotional distance: he intuits her feelings for him in a way that is purely discursive and unsure ("I *think*"). Melba, surrounded by her family in D.C., acknowledges the vast loneliness that haunts Thomas Darko, the last of his tribe; but in doing so, she also implicitly recognizes the impassable gulf between them, the long geographical and racial space that they both know neither will cross permanently.

The inability of African and Native Americans to forge more enduring connections, even and especially in such conditions of intimacy and friendship, are rarely antagonistic or racist on the surface. Darko ultimately preserves his distance from black people, to be sure, but as a function of inertia rather than conscious choice. Blacks and Indians simply didn't get too "close" back home, despite constant physical proximity; likewise, the use of derogatory language to describe the other persists as an unexamined regional habit. In D.C. in 1963, Darko learns for the first time "that colored or black people don't like the word 'nigger,' what I been using all my life. I never meant no disrespect at all. I jist don't know no better till I am told" (93). Just as he negotiates and conveys his relationship with Melba through language, so too he comes to a greater understanding of race relations by way of these discursive signs. Such lessons are powerful but also essentially narratological, and moreover, they are hardly transportable back to the South, in the same way that his relationship with Melba fails to relocate. These small admissions of Darko's are a reminder that the regional status quo, while ostensibly peaceful and polite, belies the potent residues of racialized logic in its diurnal patterns of interaction and discourse. Hateful language, we know, is no less inflammatory and hurtful because it is unintended or automatic. And changing the stories we tell about our lives does not ensure that the world will shift accordingly.

Indeed, the legacy of colonialist logic did not disappear from the habits of southern society upon desegregation, but in fact proliferated in often subterranean ways as both groups struggled to achieve autonomy and prosperity after emancipation.[52] For tribes especially, and continuing well into the present century, renewed endeavors to secure political autonomy from the federal government have frequently been hampered by the perceived impurity of African American genealogies. The Oklahoma Cherokees' 2007 decision to expel from tribal rolls their Freedmen — descendants of ex-slaves who had long been considered members of the tribe — is a stark reminder that the ancillary effects of American apartheid are far-reaching and insidious.[53] Too, they frequently drive wedges between groups that might otherwise forge productive alliances: for Indians holding desperately to their frail measures of "official" cultural integrity, the cost of kinship is often simply too great. Forced to adhere to a biracial economy, Indians become either white antagonists or dark allies — no matter what kind of diversity and hybridity might have actually existed within individual families and communities.[54] The legacy of such loss cannot fail to have consequences on the ensuing Native generations who remained, struggling to identify as indigenous, and repressing the latent evidence and meaning of those other, kindred connections. As Craig Womack has admitted, citing his own literary and critical works themselves as cases in point, "If, as James Baldwin's essays suggest, white America has failed to recognize the black face staring back at it in its own mirror, this blindness seems as relevant to the red gaze as well."[55] While this claim might imply white America's reluctance to acknowledge its foundational Indian traces, it reads another way as well: the "red gaze," like the white one, fails to register the black visage staring back at it. Put another way, the kind of searching mirror moments that Dale Marie Taylor's speaker endures in "We Wait," painful as they are, occur rarely for Indian writers seeking to claim and assimilate *their* black ancestry or kinship. The decisions and choices made *for* Indians in the long decades prior to emancipation and desegregation have had consequences that cannot be reversed or called back.

Louis Owens's (Choctaw-Cherokee-Irish) 1991 novel *The Sharpest Sight* meditates further on this primal racial trauma in the Native southern narrative. The novel is set partially in Owens's childhood home near Yazoo City, Mississippi. The protagonist is a Choctaw/Cherokee/Irish man named Cole McCurtain who, along with his father, Hoey, and brother, Attis, now lives in California during the Vietnam era. The plot of the novel centers on a murder mystery involving Attis, who returns from the Vietnam War horribly altered and undone, and apparently kills his own girlfriend. Attis then goes missing, and it is presumed that the girl's family has exacted its revenge; but Cole and his father, along with a Mexican American deputy friend, are determined to uncover the truth and put Attis's body to rest. Uncle Luther, an elder relative back home in Mississippi, has intuited the drama in his dreams. Cole has not returned south since he was a child, but Hoey convinces him that the journey will have personal rewards for him as well as for Attis's unquiet spirit.

In short, Uncle Luther and the South represent the key to a cultural wellspring that Hoey and his sons have lost, long before their move out west; yet the discovery of its regional lessons will not necessarily be redemptive. Hoey explains to Cole,

> You know what it says on my birth certificate? White. I never knew it till I went in the army. I asked Uncle Luther about it and he said that because my dad was white, he figured he had a choice of what to have them put down, so he told them "white." It's funny, ain't it, to think a man can just choose like that? He was probably worried about me, because being an Indian back then was almost as bad as being a nigger. But colored people can't choose. The way people think in this country, one drop of colored blood makes a white person a nigger. But the same people think it takes a hell of a lot of Indian blood to make someone an Indian. I figure I got the same right to choose as my dad, so I chose Indian. (57–58)[56]

The "choice" available to Indians under Jim Crow seems ostensibly better than the lack of options available to African Americans, but for Hoey and his family, it is ultimately a false choice. Hoey is, of course, part white; but to be designated *only* as such on an official document means also to abnegate his Indian heritage. And since "being an Indian back then was almost as bad as being a nigger," disavowal ensured protection under the stringencies of apartheid. Hoey cites a critical paradox in American racial ideology, one where "choice" and freedom obscure the poverty of options available to minorities seeking safety and prosperity. Such dichotomous choices also remind us that federal policy has long been invested in legislating the Indian effectively out of existence, accomplishing a "paper genocide" that erases inconvenient reminders of a terrifically unjust colonial past. These measures occur nationwide, to be sure, but even more fervently in support of the South's rhetoric of extinction and nativist mythologies. As Hoey's pitiful speech demonstrates, this kind of protracted, systemic annihilation cannot be overcome by a sheer exercise of will. While Hoey celebrates his right to "choose" back his Indian birthright later in life, this feeble act of agency cannot reverse the damage already wrought on his diminished sense of indigeneity. The rest of his tribe neither knows nor accepts him anymore: "Those Choctaws down there in Mississippi don't even know I'm Indian, the ones that run that new reservation they got. Uncle Luther told me a long time ago that they started up the dances again and everything, but I don't know shit about any of that" (58). Living at a geographic remove, far out west in California, seems a choice, too — but like everything that has distanced Hoey from his heritage, this migration is merely a reification of his cultural exile.

Even at a remove, Hoey clings to his heritage and to the few relatives he has left, particularly Uncle Luther and his lover Onatima Blue Wood, both of whom are Choctaw elders maintaining the frail ties to their remnant Choctaw community and eager to pass down the lessons of their culture. Nonetheless, Hoey admits that it hasn't done much good: his minimal knowledge about being Indian has come from reading books about "things that are Indian," and still he laments that he "don't know very much" (59). But as removed as Hoey feels, the effect this distance has on the ensuing generation is even more pronounced: Cole in particular wonders what this legacy means for him, whose lack of classically "Indian" features makes his being white seem more tangible than a mere accident of will: "At least somebody looking at you or my brother could tell you were Indian of some kind. I don't look like anything" (58). The true perversity of American racial codes emerges here in Cole's tacit fear that if one is neither white nor black, he isn't "anything" at all — a zero, an absence, an erasure. Hoey reassures him that "An Indian could probably tell you was Indian, but a white person might just think you're funny looking" (58). The father and son share a laugh, but Hoey continues with a more serious lesson about Indian authenticity: "Looks don't count. Indians look all kinds of ways. . . . Now what do you do with all that mess? You just got to decide who you're going to be" (58–59). Entreating his son with the luxury of choice, to "decide" his own cultural fate, he nudges the young man toward their elder, Uncle Luther: "You got a chance to listen to him now. Maybe you can learn some of the things I never learned. . . . Just watch and listen, and remember that the man don't teach only by talking" (59).

Attis's missing body is in California, but Cole knows he won't be able to locate it or unravel the mysteries it harbors without returning to his ancestral source — the answer to the dark, painful mysteries and violence that demolished his brother's life and his family's integrity. Cole does seize the chance to go back home; but he needs Uncle Luther's assistance in both quests — his search for his own identity as well as the mystery of his brother's death — and significantly, it is *because* Luther remains in the South that the answers he harbors are most profound and revealing. As Hoey warns his son, we as readers must heed as well: Luther's lessons are often unspoken, disclosed simply by gesture or indirection, and they are as often implicitly about southern race relations as they are about Choctaw tradition. What we as readers intuit on Cole's first night in Luther's cabin is that a vast, unbroken web of American imperialism has fatally damaged all of them, and that this most recent iteration is vitally connected to the Mississippi Choctaws' suffering in the earliest days of American settlement. Clearly, Attis is provoked to madness and murder as a result of his traumatic tour of duty in the service of a U.S. war, a colossal irony and injury for American Indian soldiers that has become by now something of a cliché in Native literature;[57] but going home to Mississippi and to Luther helps Cole trace the roots of Attis's unraveling not just to Vietnam but all the way back to Removal. Still living in the backwoods of Yazoo County, removed from both tribe and white society, Luther says, "Even back here I heard of that new war they got. Hoey should not give two sons, not even one. It's that President Jackson" (65). Of course, "that President Jackson" could simply be the old recluse's misidentification of President Lyndon B. *John*son, the third of five U.S. presidents to preside over American involvement in the conflict and the first to send combat troops to the region, despite widespread dismay and protest. But as Hoey reminds us, Luther's messages are often covert, and this one seems an early preview of such: "*that* President Jackson" is any and every additional iteration of President Andrew Jackson, mastermind and executioner of the Removal policies designed to clear-cut the indigenous South of its inconvenient tribes; Johnson, Kennedy, Nixon — any and all are "*that*" Jackson for a "new" war and era, merely a new face for an American nation with an unbroken addiction to imperial conquest abroad and assault on Native peoples at home.

The lessons Luther specializes in, then, are the ones that yoke contemporary crises in Indian affairs back to these primal southern contexts. Within this container, necessarily, are the still-potent remnants of a divisive, essentialist, disabling biracial order. Such reminders are crucial, Owens seems to say, in a modern era in which we want so badly to detach our senses of self from the dictates and codes of a viciously separatist and ideological order. As a critic, Owens himself was committed to the notion that embracing hybridity, within both our communities and our cultural productions, are vital not just for psychic health but for the survival of our cultures and our planet; a firm believer in the "crossblood" ethics that Vizenor champions, Owens is also a practitioner of what he calls "cross-reading," a method of understanding "every thought, every attempt at utterance, every conceptual encounter" as evidence of a torsional, multiracial heteroglossia. Such counterefforts are critical, Owens knows, in a world where Native identity itself has already been colonized by and for non-Native needs and purposes: "The American Indian in the world consciousness has become not only a static artifact," he writes, "but more importantly, I think, a contested space, a place of signification to be emptied out and reinhabited by Euramerica . . . a territory to be reinhabited and remapped, its original inhabitant — the Vanishing American — having supposedly disappeared."[58] In the South, that purportedly vacant territory cleared for the erection of a plantation industry and then a biracial myth, Native southerners bear the particular burden of contesting the inscriptions of identity inflicted by their uncanny survival and ghostly half-life. More than anything, Luther's purpose in *The Sharpest Sight* seems to be reminding Cole (patently an autobiographical stand-in for Owens himself)[59] that Native identity in the modern era is fundamentally haunted by these origins, this primal South — and that his present condition cannot be divorced from the regional and conceptual *space* that persistently defines and delimits the possibilities for indigenous survival in sometimes uncanny ways.

Luther lives in a swampy enclave accessible only by boat, and so Hoey directs Cole to an African American man named Jobe who will take him across the river for a small fee. Cole easily finds "the ancient black man on the porch" of his store (a small hunting and trading outpost of sorts), and Jobe agrees to transport him to Uncle Luther's house for ten dollars. The incredibly old and "shriveled" black man functions as Cole's connection to his past and to his family, one that he can purchase for a minimal fee; but he cannot truly see where he is going, as Owens makes clear by draping the entire passage in a thick, impenetrable fog. Cole "saw not the river but the fog climbing up through the trees and bare vines toward [Jobe's] building." Jobe pockets the money Cole offers him and then, "saying nothing, walked around the side of the store into the fog. Cole had watched him disappear and then walked quickly after him, wondering if he was supposed to and afraid to walk too fast into what he couldn't see" (61). Clearly a harbinger of the inscrutable past that Cole is rushing into headlong, the fog hangs as a barrier between himself and his living ancestry in this remote region, an indication of how difficult it is to see clearly into such spaces. Jobe "disappears" into this fog, too, both an integral part of the place and another entity that Cole cannot truly see or understand. What unites the two, however, is their inability to navigate clearly into the space and the past that Luther occupies and represents: the two men, part-Native and black, climb into the boat and "back it away into the current neither of them could see" (62). Later, Uncle Luther gestures toward his old wooden pier and tells Cole, "Old Jobe can't never find this at night. Colored folks can't see at night the way Indians can, even colored folks that's part Indian, like Jobe" (73). Luther reveals that Jobe is in fact part Indian — but that small part, like Cole's fractional heritage, is not enough to allow him to see like an Indian in the darkness. Instead, Jobe paddles backward for a fee, and Cole rides blind by his side: after dropping him at Luther's place, Jobe says, "that ten dollars tells me I ain't ever laid eyes on you," and then he "slipped back into the fog" (62). Jobe's discretion makes no literal sense but does serve to heighten the mystery and foreboding of Cole's hopeful errand home: it seems clearly like something he ought not to be doing; a secret that Jobe will protect and keep, owing to their kindred marginality to this world; a trust that can be purchased for ten dollars, a figure that figuratively speaks to the black man; and finally, a reminder of their mutual blindness and invisibility, a fact that money cannot remedy but will in fact indemnify.

The exchange of ten dollars in fact proves to be the thing that Cole and Jobe have most in common — and the thing that most sets them apart. Money is the fatal instrument ensuring that Jobe "ain't ever laid eyes on" the world that Cole enters, one that Jobe has just as much right to access but knows the peril of penetrating. More subtly, Owens reminds us that such admissions cannot simply be purchased, despite how routinely Indian identity in the twentieth century becomes a commodity or a fashion accessory available for widespread consumption. Why should it be different for Cole, a "funny looking" white man, than it is for a black man with similarly occluded Native ancestry? Again, the distinction is choice: Cole's whiteness allows him to "decide" who he wants to be in this post–Jim Crow world, while Jobe's liberty as a mixedblood is apparently less flexible. Sure enough, Cole is welcomed instantly back into the fold of Uncle Luther's realm: with Luther, he returns to see his childhood home; he is reminded of the Indian name Luther gave him as a young boy ("Little-chief-warrior Red") (74–75); and he is instructed in the proper Choctaw way to clean Attis's bones and return them to Mississippi to rest (98). When Luther and Cole get into their canoe to cross the river, their passage is distinctly different from Cole's ride with Jobe: the fog breaks, "leaving the brown water and tall, bare trees exposed between sheets of gray" (73). Luther rows the boat just as Jobe had done, but apparently with more command: "Like the old black man, Uncle Luther bent deeply with each oar stroke, moving rhythmically with the slip of the boat over the swirling, dirty water. Cole looked back at the swampy forest around the cabin and thought of his father again. This had been his river, and even in Cole's lifetime his father had followed the old uncle at night in that forest" (73). Both Luther and Jobe match their bodies to the rhythms of the "swirling, dirty" river that engulfs and binds them together; yet only Luther helps Cole to see it clearly, and to see his father and himself in that world. Cole repossesses for his father the knowledge and the sight that he lost — the memory of seeing and moving "at night," which no black men or part-Indians are supposed to do. Yet Cole believes in this memory fully, and he grows closer and closer to owning again what was once his father's birthright, too. Yet all the while he must know where such quests lead: the river of knowledge is dirty, laced with "the smell of death and rot" Cole remembers from his youth (62): "sharp and rancid, a blend of wet and rot and musty earth, a disturbing odor Cole had never smelled in California" (73). Only in Mississippi, it seems, does the "disturbing" stench of death and rot assault his senses; perhaps this is all, in the end, that Luther can help him to recover.

Except that Luther seems invested in deepening Cole's ties to his heritage, a project accomplished partly by stories and wisdom and partly, as Hoey indicated, by tacitly undermining Jobe's kinship according to the ingrained assumptions and divisions of the segregated South. The two men are obviously friends, neighbors, traders — and yet Luther makes sure to distance the "Indian" way of seeing and knowing from the black man's. Significantly, he does so by repeatedly invoking stories not just about Jobe's inability to see in the dark but, more frequently, the old black man's proclivity for theft. The first such tale comes when Cole announces he needs to go back to California and attempt to find his brother's remains, to which Luther responds, "Soon as you're ready. Did I tell you about that pig? Seems old man Jobe was going to visit a lady friend and not paying much attention when that pig stumbled out of the woods and he run over it. Right off, he knew whose pig it was, so he turned his car around and threw it in the trunk and drove home. Had a pig roast behind the store a couple nights ago with twenty or thirty people there. Old Jobe said, 'When a man's eating another man's pig, he better eat fast'" (95). The anecdote makes little sense in context unless we realize that Luther means it to serve as a warning against Cole's haste, his rush to settle a Choctaw dispute by old-style blood revenge without fully knowing what that means. As Luther goes on to warn, "[Hoey] thinks he must act like a Choctaw, but that's just something he made up like a card game" (97). It isn't exactly, as blood sacrifice often did secure the end to a conflict in traditional Choctaw society; but Luther is reluctant to send Cole back home, back to Hoey, until he impresses upon him the more immediate need for balance, peace, and generosity. Posed against this lesson of how to truly "act like a Choctaw" is the reminder that Jobe will never be one: he acts without "paying much attention" (and we already know that he cannot "see" like an Indian anyway), and he consumes another man's property as a matter of self-preservation.

The subtle suggestion that Jobe is selfish and dishonorable gets more explicit treatment in Owens's subsequent novel, *Bone Game* (1994), which features an older Cole McCurtain once again experiencing a crisis in California that sends him reeling back to his Mississippi relatives for aid. By then, Hoey has actually moved back to the swamp with Luther; this time, when Cole needs their help, they travel from Mississippi out to California to be with him. During the road trip, Jobe is referenced twice: first, when the men have a flat tire and no jack, Hoey assumes, "Jobe must've borrowed it and not told me. That old man always was light fingered" (83). When the story is told to Cole later in the novel, Hoey is more certain: "Jobe stole my jack. . . .

Probably traded it for a pint" (225). The book's only other mention of Jobe is apparently kinder: as Luther blows on his piping hot coffee, he tells Hoey, "Jobe pours his coffee in a saucer so it cools, then he drinks it from that saucer" (115). What Luther's comment adds to these other illustrations of Jobe's "light fingered" ways is Luther's consideration for the old black man's survival instincts, the matter-of-fact way he negotiates his own self-preservation and prosperity in a world engineered against his success and ready to burn him if he isn't careful. These are challenges and temptations that Luther understands, and in a certain way he obviously admires and respects old Jobe's resourcefulness: about the "stolen" jack, Luther only says snidely, "Well, it's good of Jobe to let you park it in his barn" (83). He downplays Jobe's questionable ethics of endurance at the same time that he distances himself and his family from their influence.

These repetitious stories across two distinct narratives indicate a prevailing concern for Luther and Hoey, transmitted next to Cole, conditioned by an environment where identity politics are inseparable from a competitive, acquisitive, biracial economy. For these Indians living in geographic isolation with increasingly frail genealogical and cultural ties, there looms a tacit anxiety that more than pigs and jacks might be stolen from these Indians, and that any attempt Jobe might make to reach further into true Indian culture would be an act of larceny. The fact that Jobe owns a store, one that Luther brings his hunting skins to in trade, complicates this relationship vitally: the two men patently exist in a relationship of exchange, commerce, and apparent equity, and yet Luther is always implicitly fearful that Jobe will get the better of the bargain, will be rewarded monetarily for his suffering in ways that the Indians will not, and that such recompense will represent theft from the Natives who share his suffering and his blood, yet not his grace. That these fears are essentially unsupported by any actual evidence is simply more proof that the divisive logic of Jim Crow and its competitive antagonisms are alive and well — and continuing to wreak silent havoc — on this remote, mixed community.

Jobe himself is not the enemy, as Luther's grumpy but basically friendly comments consistently underscore: the old black man's identity as a thief merely highlights the perverse competitiveness and practical self-interest of racial segregation, a system maintained by panic and paranoia rather than reason. Where natural ties of family and community joined Native and African Americans like Luther and Jobe, the separatist logic and self-preservationist contours of Jim Crow drove them utterly apart. Like so many Indians negotiating their identities under such codes, Luther's primary impulse becomes a reactionary, isolationist one — to maintain Indian integrity at any and all costs. This meant disassociating oneself from white identity as much as blackness — a move made more difficult for men like Cole, whose heritage derives largely from Irish and European blood. Luther tacitly teaches him about this fiction of color and the need to rescue indigeneity from that overemphasis on skin tone and its imagined attributes. In *The Sharpest Sight*, Cole gets a chance to row the boat as Jobe and Luther had done so capably and with strikingly similar rhythms of body; conversely, Cole's technique is new and clumsy, and Luther laughs as the young man "awkwardly fought the heavy, sluggish current that tried to spin the boat away" (76). In this brief image, Owens deftly allows us to see Luther and Jobe as superior and well-matched captains, both in their own ways handling the current of a dark, dirty river that threatens to capsize them both; certainly, that survival instinct owes itself to their shared legacy of suppression and marginality in the tumultuous midcentury South. Cole, emissary of the new generation, is just beginning to learn how to fight that tide, and Luther's advice reveals precisely what they are always already fighting against: "'Up there,' Uncle Luther pointed upstream with his lips and chin, 'in that deep pool is where the *oka nahullo* live. They got white skins all slippery like fish. They catch you, they turn you into one of them. That ain't a good place to be at night'" (76). In the end, avoiding the "white skins" and their monstrous desire to absorb and assimilate the Indian is the unique challenge for this family, the one that sets them apart from both their own white ancestors and their African American peers — alone, struggling against the current, yet staying afloat, on the dark and dirty Yazoo River that both menaces and sustains.

The difficult, dirty negotiations of color and culture that Owens, writing in the 1990s, sees his characters struggling against in the 1970s have their roots in the perversions of the South's shifting and ideological race relations. Yet rather than improving over time, these protectionist, separatist notions of culture seem only to have hardened under the contemporary threat of multicultural invisibility. This continues to be especially true in Native communities whose ongoing struggles for political sovereignty have been hampered by presumptions of excessive racial mixing; as Malinda Maynor Lowery explains of the Lumbee tribe in North Carolina, these struggles have resulted in pressure to "'forget' about black ancestors and kin while embracing their white relatives."[60] Across the entire Southeast, as Theda Perdue notes, Indians have long recognized that their population is proportionally minute and fragile: "Their identities and whatever cultural traditions expressed those identities were at risk if southern Natives were redefined as African American. Therefore, southern Indians scrupulously guarded their racial boundaries."[61] An unintended consequence of this protectionism is that it has served to invigorate white supremacy, both within Indian communities that embraced such ideologies openly, and in conditions where Native essentialisms more subtly authorized ideas of racial separatism and hierarchy. More distressing is the idea that Natives' contemporary struggles for sovereignty and tribal nationalism have their roots in a system where separatism is impossible to disentangle from histories of racism and subjugation. Emphases on blood quantum and genealogical purity inevitably borrow much of their rhetoric and force from the ideology of Jim Crow.[62] No matter how well-intentioned and sympathetic these new sovereignties aim to be, they cannot be divorced from their dark moorings: from their confused, marginal positions within the biracial world of southern segregation, Native Americans "transformed the racism they had learned under European tutelage into a nationalist struggle for sovereignty."[63] And throughout contemporary Native southern literature, that becomes a distressing bind: we are compelled, for very good reason, to overlook the disturbing bases and implications of a deeply ingrained sense of communal protection and separatism. Yet all too often, the triumphant reassertion of tribal tradition belies the exclusionary foundations upon which it is built.

Certainly, anyone reading Dawn Karima Pettigrew's poetic novel *The Way We Make Sense* (2002) would find the work, on the surface, a celebration of African and Native Americans' gritty survival in the South. In her hands, the South's perversions — slavery, Removal, Jim Crow, and their persistent residues — become the defining undercurrents of American Indian existence more broadly. In an effort to escape the warping environment of the South, both Native and African Americans escape and go in search of opportunity and prosperity; inexorably, though, their common fate brings them together — and back home. The protagonist, Manna, has fled from her home on the Qualla reservation in the Eastern Cherokee country of North Carolina.

By the middle of the novel, she has found an abandoned baby, and the two of them have been taken in by a Native Vietnam veteran named Silas Pipe and his nephew, a powwow grass dancer; together, the four form an unconventional but comfortable new family, drinking Kool-Aid and watching *The Lone Ranger* and *The Cosby Show* on television, a routine that becomes "their daily ritual" (91).[64] The customs of contemporary life have them observing celluloid simulacra of their own culture paired significantly with the celluloid simulacra of African American culture. Watching it all, "Silas complains about the way the world is run and his grass-dancing nephew agrees with him. After a few days, the baby begins to nod along with their assessment of the world" (91–92). Yet for all their skepticism, they continue to observe; eventually, Manna wonders whether the baby should be watching Tonto and getting "loaded down by negative stereotypes" (92). That's when Silas, himself a one-time Hollywood hopeful, explains his theory of the "economics of eating":

> Jay Silverheels got to be a millionaire talking about "kemosabe" this and "kemosabe" that. That's how we win this war. We beat the white man at his own game. Mumble and murmur and act half set back so they look the other way. When they do, throw up a casino or two and part them from their money. Sell them the cigarettes that cloud their lungs at discount prices. Finally, open an online pharmacy and sell them drugs while they wait to die. Tonto knew what he was doing. (92)

Silas's bitter plan is born of pure pragmatism, and it involves racial performance in the service of economic rather than cultural survival. His theory conjures not just Native (Jay Silverheels, the Mohawk actor — and the only actual Native — to play the role of Tonto, the Lone Ranger's simple, stoic sidekick) but also African American examples of performing popular stereotypes in order to beat whites at their own game; in his speech, one can almost hear the resounding echoes of an early scene in Ralph Ellison's *Invisible Man* (1952) where the protagonist's grandfather counsels his young black grandson to "live with your head in the lion's mouth. I want you to overcome 'em with yeses, undermine 'em with grins, agree 'em to death and destruction, let 'em swoller you until they vomit or bust wide open."[65] Yet the naïve and hopeful Manna objects to such logic, countering that "According to your theory . . . Hattie McDaniel and Stepin Fetchit were geniuses." Silas protests again: "Cinema don't have nothing to do with it, young lady. We're talking about economics here. The economics of eating" (92). Manna reminds us of two of the earliest examples of black movie actors—both of whom achieved commercial success by embodying and furthering negative stereotypes: Hattie McDaniel, who famously played the stereotypical, loyal "mammy" figure in *Gone with the Wind* (1936), and Stepin Fetchit (screen name for the 1930s actor Lincoln Perry), who revived the minstrel show's bumbling, lazy slave persona who thrives on "'putting on old massa'—break the tools, break the hoe, do anything to postpone the work that was to be done." In fact, according to Perry's biographer Mel Watkins, "the Fetchit character is actually a subversive trickster—he never got around to fetching *anything*."[66]

But why cite these black examples rather than Indian ones? Where in cinematic history, and in the Native family living room, are the Native tricksters to keep company with Jay Silverheels? Compared to their African American peers, they are relatively absent from the Hollywood canon, where Indian roles until recently were routinely filled by non-Native, ethnic-looking actors. Chris Eyre, one of the few commercially successful Native directors to date, seems acutely aware of this imbalance in his 2002 film *Skins* (the follow-up to his highly acclaimed feature film *Smoke Signals* [1998]—the first to use an all-Native cast and crew). *Skins*, which is based on a novel of the same name by Paiute author Adrian Louis, takes place on the Pine Ridge (Lakota Sioux) reservation in South Dakota and follows two brothers, Rudy and Mogie Yellow Lodge: Mogie is a Vietnam vet and an alcoholic, while Rudy is a squeaky-clean tribal cop. But Rudy's demons get the better of him, too, as he grows frustrated with his limited role in eradicating the rampant crime on the reservation and begins engaging in surreptitious acts of vigilante justice. In his missions, he disguises himself in dark clothing and smears black paint over his face—an image that immediately shocks the viewer by resurrecting the now-taboo image of minstrel show performers who similarly darkened their visages. A later scene in the film features Rudy and Mogie watching an old western on television, and Mogie commenting bitterly on the exploitation of his friend American Horse, a small-time bit actor in Hollywood. Eyre obviously wants his unflinching look at contemporary reservation life to have an impact as unsettling as those old minstrel images now are—but which remain largely invisible for the general public who prefer not to acknowledge the debilitating violence and addiction plaguing tribal communities, who watch endless westerns and their stock savage characters without an inkling of their foundational role in the misery of contemporary Native life. It seems clear to me, if extraordinarily subtle in its delivery, that Rudy's cork-blackened face announces both a common legacy of racial performance and stereotype (as the Tontos and American Horses more quietly confirm) as well as a reminder of the essential disparity between the two experiences in the selective American eye.

Returning to Pettigrew's references to Hattie McDaniel and Stepin Fetchit, we can better see how she similarly evokes contemporary Natives' simultaneous affiliation with and divergence from the African American compromised efforts to achieve visibility and success after emancipation and the protracted turmoil of Jim Crow. This kinship is a vital part of what sends Manna inevitably back home to the South, the place that unites those bound by the conscriptions of a deeply inequitable society and economy. Despite the comfort of being enfolded into a new family in New Mexico, she is never fully nourished there — she literally cannot even digest milk, possibly because it signifies motherhood, the broken cord with her own mother (which we will explore more fully in chapter 3), and her own temporary status as a mere proxy parent. Indeed, the "economics of eating" begins to seem a more applicable theory than Silas perhaps intends. What Manna can digest is cornbread — not hominy exactly, but a recipe inherited from her father and printed on the back of a hardware store receipt: and significantly, the very act of preparing and eating this southern staple launches her into communion with fellow diasporic southerners. One night, Silas invites a guest over for dinner — a black woman from Mississippi — who "ate that cornbread and actually started crying. Sat there with her eyes running, calling it 'soul food.' Silas asked her why, and she said every bite reminded her of home" (125). It reminds Manna of home, too, and of how much she and all of the South's dispossessed and demeaned souls have had to pay and exchange in order to retain the simple pleasure of belonging. It is no accident that the recipe is printed on the back of a receipt, and specifically from a store that sells the wares for building things: homes, happiness, community. It is also no coincidence that Manna shares this cornbread and all it represents with yet another fellow southerner who also happens to be a carpenter: a Lumbee Indian named Bill Lawton who lives next door to Silas. The cornbread re-

minds him of home, too, and of the mixing of races that happened both literally and spiritually there, and the ways that such mixture has always marked
the experience and the struggle of his own tribe to survive and be counted as
Indians. As Manna empathizes,

> "Everybody kind of ended up all together. So when you're looking at a Creek
> Indian, a lot of times they're red, white and black all at once."
>
> Bill Lawton understands. "Us Lumbee are like that, too."
>
> "So maybe it isn't color or anything like that that makes good cornbread.
> Maybe it's knowing how to make the best of a bad situation, or getting a dol-
> lar out of fifteen cents." Manna pauses, looking into a world that Bill Lawton
> cannot see. "You know what? Southern food is all 'soul food.' You cook it, your
> soul knowing that no matter what color you are, if you live long enough, life
> will break your heart." (125)

Sure enough, Manna's heart is broken, too, when the baby she loves is taken
back by her young mother, who reappears at a church revival. Significantly, a
Diné man who is part of the revival takes pity on her and, without a word of
pretext or request, inexplicably gives her cash to "get as close to home as you
can." Speechless, she thanks him with her tears, which he rubs into his brown
skin; smiling, he jokes, "Paid in full" (115). Her tears, which patently conjure
the Trail of Tears, constitute a receipt, like the cornbread—a record of payment for a loss surrendered. They are also what bind the southeastern Indian
to the southwestern one, and his insistence that she go "home" is a reminder
that her persistence there is a vital form of resistance; it is, clearly, another
form of revenge and the "economics of eating" that Silas recommends and
that the Navajo man's exchange metaphor highlights: he provides her with
the capital to get there, and her journey back to the site of loss and sorrow
and resistance is the payoff that he shares by literally absorbing it into his
skin. Manna's return means something for all of them if she, the displaced
southerner, can get home again — or "as close to" it as she can. Silas seems to
know this, too. When she does leave, thanking him for essentially purchasing her soul (he had initially gained her friendship by purchasing her a ticket
into the powwow where they met) and caring for it, he shrugs off the debt:
"Reverse the charges," he quips (118). With both Silas and the Diné man fi-
nancing her journey, Manna effectively performs a service that is invaluable
to Indians everywhere.

But the ending to the novel reminds us that the economics of eating is, for both African and Native Americans in the South, a vital but perennially compromised form of survival. The solidarity that Manna initially experienced with the black Mississippi woman (who disappears from the novel after she leaves Silas's dinner table) and with the Lumbee Bill Lawton evaporates quickly. Bill does travel back to Cherokee with Manna, and while they live together as man and wife there is no passion in their relationship; as Bill soon discovers, Manna is still desperately pining for her first love, an alluring man named Thomas Crow, whom her mother had distrusted and turned into a tree (one of the few magical-realist moments in the entire narrative). This was the act of betrayal that had sent Manna on the road and away from home and family to begin with; in returning home, she attempts also to redeem her lost lover's life. She begins sleeping each night under the tree that houses his memory. In an act of true devotion, Bill takes the tree and uses his superior carving skills to shape the timber into the man he once was.

Thomas Crow thus returns to life, and he and Manna become a local sensation—and Bill, like another true selfless carpenter in religious history, seems to relinquish his own unspent desires in the process. A final section called "Jubilee" reports:

> Manna and Thomas go on TV. . . . A man calls from Toronto, wanting to make a feature film. . . . Strangers mail them gifts. A car salesman from Ohio gives them a Volvo. A lady from Forrest City, Arkansas, sends them a cashier's check for $500,000. Manna uses the money to open up a café, right in the center of downtown Cherokee. "Bread of Life," they call it. People come from all over the world for Manna's cornbread. . . . Of course, Manna doesn't do the actual baking. Famous people, like athletes and television personalities, send for special orders. (134)

The catalog of their good fortune continues; Manna even reconciles with her mother and becomes pregnant with a son—surely a sign that the cycle is broken—and the narrative ends with the conviction that all in their circle are "blessed." In an extravagant way, it seems, they have accomplished the supreme form of the "economics of eating" that Silas promotes; and their success stands as an exemplar of redemption for what all Indians have been deprived of for so long: "In this mean old world, it's not every day somebody's life turns out like it should" (136).

And yet, is this really how it *should* turn out for Manna? Should she exchange her love story for a feature film, or for a check that allows her to peddle her soul (food)? It seems no accident that she becomes a Cherokee Paula Deen, a trademark in her own right, a signifier of the blessed and yet merely a cardboard cutout of the real thing; her "bread of life," which she doesn't even bake herself anymore, becomes symbol rather than sustenance. While "Jubilee" is supposed to connote a time of celebration and the eradication of debt, it seems here to signify the illusion of freedom from the ownership of souls, the exchange of birthrights and traditions for a mess of pottage. Given the careful connections to African American kinship earlier in the novel, the reference to "Jubilee" here is clearly meant to evoke Margaret Walker's 1966 novel of the same name, a searing story of an ex-slave's struggle to survive in the South after the Civil War while battling vicious racism and inequity. What looks like celebration and freedom, these African Americans know, is largely a promise deferred in an environment inhospitable to such change. Simple survival becomes a hard-won commodity, a much more meager reward than the fantastical life that turns out "like it should." Likewise, in downtown Cherokee, where actors in antique dress peddle legend and tradition to tourists for a profit, their gift shops looking much like Manna's "Bread of Life" simulacrum, the trade is a deeply compromised one. Such recognitions tell us that Pettigrew's ending must be ironic; otherwise, its jubilant tone is too abrupt and incongruous to be sincere. Life doesn't end up "like it should," and that is precisely the point; allowing it to seem that way, even in playful or subversive fashion, is a costly simulation.

The difficult thing is that we live in a cultural moment that celebrates our collective transcendence of racist ideologies and social formations, and presumes that intellectual and tribal sovereignty — simply because it redeems colonial injustice and shelters beleaguered groups — is immune from the residues of these tainted histories and systems. As the following chapter will attest, we also tend to assume that "freedom" and "success" are quotients measurable by economic standards. But as this chapter has begun to demonstrate, those very principles and measures of success are the same ones that persistently and irrevocably drive human communities apart from one another. For African and Native Americans in the South, the spectacles and illusions of opportunity and emancipation have never yielded healthy communities and the maintenance of culture; instead, they demand a heavy payment and ensure constant competition, rupturing even those groups who have the most cause to find common ground. As these writers remind us again and again, the past is never past, and Jubilee is a glitzy chimera. Perhaps in the end, the tribes that remain in the South have the most to teach us about both the hope of solidarity and the peril of compromise — and above all, about the haunted, insular, and frail foundations of contemporary tribal nationalisms and sovereignty.

CHAPTER THREE

RECKONING THE FUTURE

Capitalism, Culture, and the Production of Community

The agrarian South is bound to go when the first page is turned and the first mark crosses the ledger.
—Andrew Nelson Lytle, "The Hind Tit"

There were never any family birth certificates for us, no paper marriages, no ownership of property . . . only story-names and family histories given to us by our relatives . . . and copied from the dusty ledgers of local libraries and government offices. Our personal accounting statement of forced assimilation. Our cultural debit column of war. . . . It was the perfect paper genocide.
—Kathryn Lucci-Cooper (Cherokee), "Finding Carrie"

Lurking at the occluded heart of the South's mightiest triumphs and tragedies is a torturous relationship to the almighty dollar. From the Removal of the Five Civilized Tribes to the erection of plantation dynasties, from the indignities of Reconstruction to the savage inequities of Jim Crow and the eventual rise of the Sun Belt industry, the region's heights of prosperity and depths of privation have been yoked inextricably and variously to competitive antagonisms, exploitations, and denials. In ways both practical and profound, the vectors of capitalism have proven the primary terms of southern existence, of Native experience, and of the multiple collisions between and among them: first, in the supplanting of indigenous lands and histories by spectacles of wealth and slavery; in the subsequent evolution of a rigidly biracial order that both obscured Indians and provoked their own defiant redefinition and essentialism; and finally, in the contemporary marketplace that both excludes and then tantalizes with unparalleled opportunities for growth and sovereignty. Both Native and non-Native southerners frequently reject capitalism's opportunities in favor of the brighter hopes of humanism, anticapitalism, and tradition; nonetheless, they also find their survival and identity thoroughly enmeshed in the principles and privileges of that same system. Put another way: the very economic system responsible for the destruction of both the South and its Indians becomes the paradoxical means to their common salvation and survival.

Paths to Prosperity: Capitalism and Compromise in the Contemporary Native South

In Kathryn Lucci-Cooper's essay "To Carry the Fire Home," she attempts to make sense of her "mixed heritage" as both a southerner and an Indian.[1] With aunties and grandmothers who managed to be both "devout" Christians and Cherokee traditionalists, Lucci-Cooper experienced what she deems "a reasonable coalescing of Christian principle woven within the warp and weft of Cherokee storytelling and handed down as a basket of mountain tradition. We never knew anything was different about us. We thought all people were pretty much the same, just a mixture of cultural identities" (4). What she refers to as "different" would seem at first her Cherokee heritage within the rural, Appalachian South; certainly this is part of her dawning sense of distinctiveness, but more than that, it is the family's economic status and their staunchly rural, antimaterial values that define them. Her mother's primary shame had long been "being thought of as poor in a working-class community," and only secondarily the fact of being Indian among immigrant whites who appropriated for themselves the mantle of nativism (6). The family's main concern is simply surviving in "southern Appalachia's coalfields" with its "apple trees and cornstalks," home terrain that they are determined to protect and maintain at all costs (6). For Lucci-Cooper, subsistence and simplicity are cultural mainstays and defining traits; Cherokee culture exists simply as a fact of her existence, a notation in the family Bible, secondary and incidental—not as something highlighted to mark and separate in the way that class does. Not until she leaves the relative comfort of home, that is, and enters an arena where the rude lessons of poverty activate her anticapitalist — and deeply, devoutly indigenous — sense of denial and resistance.

"In 1972," Lucci-Cooper recalls, "I boarded a bus bound for the university and became an urban Indian. Like so many others, I would never again be laced to the cradleboard of traditional innocence or wrapped in the green quilt claiming of those hollows." While Lucci-Cooper clearly retraces the vestiges of Removal here, she does so to place the experience within a manifestly contemporary context of ongoing dispossession and alienation from home and tradition. Either way, the fate is disastrous: not unlike the experience of her Cherokee ancestors uprooted, displaced, and made to feel forever unsettled, fractured, and "different," this Appalachian Indian finds herself unhomed and alienated in the modern city, close to her roots geographically and yet worlds apart in values. The place she leaves behind both willingly and reluctantly is not just an indigenous one — it is the mountain idyll whose inclusive heterogeneity and anticommercial values had "wrapped" her in a sense of homely belonging. In the city, by contrast, she finds herself "competing in a world of people who could not understand the language of my thoughts. A people controlled by material wealth and enslaved by issues of time. I was compelled to conform or fail. It was my first real failure" (4). Shuttled rudely into an arena dominated by capitalist priorities and time clocks, Lucci-Cooper defiantly clings to the refuge of Cherokee tradition as her compass of true value and freedom from the "enslavement" of capitalism. In the process, she implicitly emphasizes her Cherokee self above her Appalachian one, finding in the former a "language" and a tradition antithetical to modernity. Noticeably, the rhetoric of "enslavement" quietly places such competitive and material obsessions squarely in the realm of southern history and culture, and thus, she ineluctably erects a new boundary between her indigenous and her "southern" selves.

And yet, despite her desire to perform a splendid "failure" by refusing to conform to the dictates of modernity, she eventually finds herself powerless against the alien values and codes of this modern, academic world. Its effects, Lucci-Cooper recalls, are devastating and obliterating. Vainly resisting the coercions of the urban southern marketplace, her prior sense of self threatens to disappear in a strikingly physical way: in this new environment, it comes as a true shock to discover that, at five-feet-two inches in height, she "was not tall." She had always been told otherwise by her family, whose women all hovered under the five-foot mark; it is not until she arrives on campus among a sea of leggy coeds that she finds herself "aware of my less than impressive size. . . . I was not tall!"[2] The lesson is twofold: first, we witness the power of this Cherokee family, and particularly its women (in keeping with matrilineal tradition), to create and sustain a reality that is supremely self-enclosed and relative, refusing the "standards" of the outside world where women regularly exceed five feet in height and material markers determine one's worth. With the loss of these internal, familial standards, Lucci-Cooper suffers a coterminous "diminishment" of not just her physical stature but her very identity. Importantly, just after relating the blow to her perceived size, she recalls a "second recission": a Lakota/Greek Orthodox priest, introduced to her by a well-meaning professor, dismisses her haughtily with the remark, "I mean, really, is everyone around here a Cherokee?"[3] In a landscape where claiming to be Cherokee has grown both as common and as apocryphal as playing cowboys and Indians, as we have seen demonstrated persistently in the previous chapters, Lucci-Cooper understands for the first time the gravity of being not just small but utterly invisible in southern social space. More than that, the priest does not simply deny her indigeneity: he flatly lumps her into the surrounding populace, rendering her white or black along with "everyone" else who simply plays Indian. As a fellow Native especially, the priest lays bare a cultural truth that robs her of a past and a knowledge as comfortable as sleep, a fact of her existence that she had never had cause to question, like her grand stature or her easy heterogeneity.

What this example makes painfully clear is the power of intrusive economies and standards — in the form of capitalist priorities and "real" Plains Indians — to transform southern social space and marginalize its occupants in the process. Native and non-Native southerners share a profound sense of material dispossession in the historically parallel (if not morally synchronous) conditions of Removal and Reconstruction. In both instances, a colonial process imposed a new, alien, unsettling economic order upon societies that had long defined themselves along alternative lines and values. Whether such suppositions are accurate is a matter of much debate, as I have argued elsewhere, particularly in regard to the South's professed loss of the "humane," genteel order of slavery.[4] But what is undeniable is the power of capitalist forces, principles, and effects to utterly suffuse the communities it encounters, and to activate reactionary, antimaterial fetishes as well as deep material hungers and lusts always already encoded even in presumably anticapitalist environments. Crippled and codified by forces from without, both the Native and non-Native souths thus share their conscription as "backward," dependent communities within a quasicolonial economic structure. For both entities, the often traumatic conversion to inimical economies transformed their formerly closed, traditional societies into seemingly alien, capitalist orders. Indeed, the prevailing model of American capitalist growth relies on the suppression of certain such vulnerable sectors, overcome by military aggression and subdued by ensuing colonial policies. What noted economist Andre Gunder Frank termed the "development of underdevelopment" ensures that the system as a whole can flourish only when peripheral regions and communities remain backward and impoverished.[5] Dependency theory emerged primarily through scrutiny of capitalist development in Latin America following multiple colonial revolutions; since then, scholars have applied similar logic to explain the disastrous effects of post–Civil War Reconstruction policies on the U.S. South's sluggish economy and culture. Likewise, theorists such as Joseph Jorgensen and Richard White have blamed Indian Country's pervasive poverty and underdevelopment on the "history of super-exploitation" cultivated carefully by U.S. colonial economic practice.[6]

Accompanying the extreme effects of material privation is, naturally, the perceived loss of cultural integrity and identity as well. For white southerners, the introduction of ledgered mechanisms into the pastoral humanism of agrarian space heralded the complete annihilation of quasi-aristocratic refinement, manners, and tradition. Likewise for Natives, the "paper genocide" of Removal, followed by the ascension of a biracial order and a cutthroat economy, ensured that those left standing in the South would rarely be seen, counted, or given the chance to subsist and thrive by their own cultural mechanisms. Both groups have since decried the corrosive effects of compulsory participation in a strange, dehumanizing, deracinated capitalist marketplace — one that converts its very citizens into ledgered columns and debits, stripped of value and integrity. In the calculus of Removal and the suppression of its resisters, as Lucci-Cooper describes it, white southerners invented "generic paper definitions of who is and who is not, *the whole, the tribe . . .* arranged, numbered, and cataloged on the pages of governmental documents . . . [and] large ledgers . . . [that] traced their movements and kept an accounting of their material losses." In the marshalling of numbers, figures, and accounting, whites accomplished the "paper genocide" of her people;[7] yet they also ensured that the people would live on as statistics in ledger books and commodities in a human economy of devaluation. The terms of exclusion for Native southerners bind her ancestors uncomfortably to a rhetoric of illegitimacy and dispossession that similarly plagues white, post-Reconstruction southerners —those unreconstructed elite who condemn the ledgerbooks that came to rule and devalue their culture after the demolition of plantation slavery (as Andrew Nelson Lytle puts it sharply in the epigraph here, taken from his essay for the 1930 Agrarian manifesto, *I'll Take My Stand*).[8] At the moment of Removal, Cherokee Indians were given a choice between "ownership and life"; by resisting Removal, her grandparents "chose life," or thought they did.[9] What Lucci-Cooper discovers generations later is that ownership and life are mutually constitutive conceits in American society.

The production of community—indeed, the *re*production of community—arises in response to these commercial threats from without; however, it is also intimately affected and conditioned by those very forces. Put another way, in the effort to regain worlds and values lost, both Native and non-Native Souths often find themselves ineluctably entangled in the very economies they mean to resist, and they in fact reconstitute communities along distinctly material lines. Paradoxically, such efforts differentiate the Native even further as a culture apart and distinct from the rest of the biracial South, as the economy that has such terrific power to erase also offers the unparalleled opportunity to be visible—such as those that elevate the Mississippi Choctaw industrial complex or the Eastern Band of Cherokees' indigenous theme park. Such developments constitute important and pragmatic decolonizing maneuvers in a space where simple assertions of identity have long been denied remnant Indians; the problem arises when its participants repress or deny their marked transformation by economic forces and priorities. Lucci-Cooper's awakening into the full force and meaning of her Cherokee heritage, for example, happens only in the discomposing arena of capitalist logic that threatens to obliterate it. In the effort to assert and retain the indigeneity that has been callously denied her—apparently all along, and without her knowledge—Lucci-Cooper clings even more fervently to family and tradition. Yet even as she proclaims and nurtures an idyll of authenticity, she simultaneously uncovers an irrepressible language of financial concerns, transactional erasures, and terrible material compromise. In short, she reveals how vitally the reality of economic anxiety and pressures have always already undermined her choices and her very identity. As Rosalind Krauss argues, following similar ideas proposed by Fredric Jameson, this might typify the very character of art in the age of late capitalism: "In its very resistance to a particular manifestation of capital . . . the artist produces another version of that phenomenon which can also be read as a function of it, another version, although possibly more ideated or rarefied, of the very thing against which he or she was reacting."[10] What is most difficult to admit here is that the corrupt "alternative" or "reaction" offered by Lucci-Cooper and so many Native writers is indigenous culture itself.

Initially, she laments that her mother before her had crumpled under the weight of prejudice and biracial pressures and, in the end, had chosen to embrace her husband's (Lucci-Cooper's father's) Sicilian culture rather than her Cherokee birthright. Lucci-Cooper steels herself against "negotiating a similar trade within my own life" and determines to follow her grandmothers' teachings; so she leaves college early, gets married, and becomes a "full-time mom" (6). While her defiance is remarkable, it is nonetheless difficult to ignore her salient metaphors of commerce and industry — insistent turns of rhetoric that render her cultural identity a trade negotiation and her maternity a job. One might argue that these are fairly ordinary, casual figures of speech; but such nonchalance makes them more rather than less worrying, as they indicate a kind of conceptual shorthand so fully entrenched as to be unremarkable. Lucci-Cooper reveals explicitly the ways that she has had to acquiesce to the "realities of today's economics" — first and foremost when she laments that financial demands have kept her locked in that urban environment and far away from the mountains, a pragmatic "compromise [that] allows my husband and me to provide for our four sons" (11). Put simply, she is trapped in a world of enumeration and diminishment, where she has to manufacture identity and authenticity at grave cost, and she cannot "go home again," as fellow Appalachian writer Thomas Wolfe put it, to the geographic and spiritual place of comfort that she knew as a child; still, that very compromise is what allows her family to flourish, and for her husband to "provide" for their continued nourishment and health. We would expect Lucci-Cooper to be attuned to these insidious patterns of capitalist rhetoric and capitulation: after all, she recalls being a fierce devotee of antiestablishment causes, a member of the "Socialists of my college campus, then among the Communists, and finally among the anarcho-syndicalists. My prayer offerings became picket signs; political chants and slogans were my prayer songs."[11] With an ease that goes unquestioned, she elides anticapitalist ideology with indigenous tradition, a place where battling the economic system is tantamount to prayer, and where antiestablishment activism restores her faith in a community long steeped in alternative values. In short, she unquestioningly maintains the divide between "tradition" and "modernity," between indigeneity and capitalism, that has long relegated Native Americans to roles as prehistorical, preindustrial relics. Under such a binary, to embrace capitalist development and prosperity is to both ensure and destroy one's survival *as* an Indian.

Such a binary is pragmatically insupportable, though, in a world where survival is contingent on participation and competition in a capitalist marketplace. The same has proven true for Indian nations across the U.S. that have lifted and invigorated their communities through industrial enterprise and gaming operations. Indeed, for many tribes, the entry into a broader consumer marketplace with the help of casino revenue and numerous other business ventures is precisely what has afforded them the opportunity to pursue and strengthen political viability and sovereignty. In the South, as elsewhere in the nation, the Indian tribes that have achieved the most visibility are, quite simply, the ones that have acquired the most wealth: the Mississippi Choctaws, the Eastern Band of Cherokees, and the Florida Seminoles. Not coincidentally, these nations have also enjoyed the most success in reestablishing sovereignty and self-determination. Former chief Phillip Martin, the figure largely responsible for transforming the Mississippi Choctaw economy, ardently celebrates the mutually constitutive process of fiscal growth and tribal health even as he acknowledges the occasional hesitancy of his community: "Sometimes, your own people will fight progress if it means giving up the security of the known, regardless of how miserable the circumstances of that known world may be either for themselves or other tribal members." For Martin, negotiating a capitalist economy need not categorically signal the death of traditionalism, either: "One can often change a bad situation with perseverance without sacrificing tribal culture and language in the process," he maintains.[12] In *High Stakes*, her remarkable analysis of the Florida Seminoles' economic rise via the nation's first tribal gaming enterprise, Jessica Cattelino insists that the "fungibility" of revenue allows it to be converted into wholly beneficial, nutritive cultural projects and growth.[13] Similarly, a recent collection of essays edited by Brian Hosmer and Colleen O'Neill demonstrates the fine balance accomplished by those Native groups pursuing alternative pathways to economic health in ways that explicitly nurture rather than extinguish tribal principles. My aim here is not to dispute this compromise, nor is it to resuscitate an unproductive dichotomy between indigenous identity and modern capitalism. Instead, it is to expose how deeply such debates and processes have been fundamentally yoked to the notion of culture from the start, making conceptions of indigenous community always fragile constructions tethered, for better or worse, to material concerns.

Tribes in the South have had little choice but to secure both the financial and political futures of their communities through savvy economic development; but to both insiders and outsiders, that shift has raised questions about the nature and adaptability of Indian culture. Casinos have engendered the most divisive debates about the seeming incommensurability between fiscal entanglements and Native values, to be sure; but these concerns are not limited to the flashier gaming enterprises. In ways less visible and controversial, Indian tribes have engaged in myriad business endeavors that strengthen the economic health of the community even as they seem to imperil traditional notions of indigeneity. On May 20, 2009, the *Sylva Herald and Ruralite* newspaper in Jackson County, North Carolina—home of the Eastern Band of Cherokee Indians—reported on the unlikely union of strange bedfellows: "Tribal Council approves Wal-Mart Lease." Perhaps more surprising than the idea of an anachronistic Indian shopping for cheap toilet paper is that of an Indian doing so at *Walmart*—arguably one of the most visible emblems of southern culture, economic savoir-faire, and purported family values. But Eastern Cherokee leaders seem hopeful about effecting in their own depressed Appalachian community precisely what Sam Walton accomplished for the rural Arkansas economy where he birthed his megabox superindustry. According to Principal Chief Michell Hicks, a local Walmart presence "will help our tax base, it will help us create more jobs, mostly construction at first and then jobs once the store opens. It will also help us recruit other real estate opportunities in Cherokee, which is something we've been trying to do."[14]

What seems at first an anomalous collision of quintessentially Native and contemporary southern consumer cultures becomes, in their common effort to reconstruct devastated economies and landscapes, an unexpectedly kindred partnership, and the kind we see more and more of throughout Indian country. Native Americans nationwide are striving to support a holistic, essential, vibrant identity both apart from and complicit with contemporary civilization. More often than not, though, the "apart" quotient of Native identity resurfaces with urgency as a way to emphasize (if not exaggerate) Indians' inherent distance from the dominant society's rampant materialism. What is most troubling about these laments is the degree to which they perpetuate the "modern"/"traditional" dichotomy long used by colonial societies to enforce a sense of immutable hierarchy and subaltern inferiority between national and racial groups.[15] In both the Native and southern cases, the effort to recast the past as a precapitalist space plays directly into such notions, as both groups attempt to portray themselves as anticapitalist societies with values and practices antithetical to market principles and corruptions. But when an inequitable, competitive, and exclusionary marketplace becomes the very arena for such pageants, it threatens to poison the very basis of cultural identity itself.

Indeed, the economics of survival have given way to a variety of formulations and performances of cultural authenticity and difference, many executed under the rubric and with the support of capitalist institutions and occupations. Throughout the South, tourism has long been an essential feature of an economy accustomed to peddling its environmental, historical, and cultural distinctiveness. As historian Richard D. Starnes carefully points out, though, such enterprises do not merely reflect culture; they create it. As a persistently "causal force in southern history," tourism broadly has transformed communities, landscapes, social perceptions, and race relations, and not always in prosperous or progressive ways.[16] The industry tends to drive an even greater wedge between classes of leisure and labor, for instance, and cultivates resentment among the working-class and racial minorities who generally figure as employees or outsiders rather than beneficiaries. More difficult to apprehend, and yet equally disastrous in its effect, is the way the "selling" of southern cultures has vitally influenced the construction and performance of particular stereotypes (one need only think of Paula Deen's down-home branding or the infectious appeal of Larry the Cable Guy's exaggerated and apparently artificial redneck pageantry). In the effort to assert the survival of tradition, culture in fact becomes something of a fetish, an anxious effort to resurrect and repossess a world that cannot be redeemed. The idea that culture could not survive these entanglements is a notion we cling to as a matter of integrity and survival. As Terry Eagleton has argued, "The more pragmatic and materialistic civilization becomes, the more culture is summoned to fulfill the emotional and psychological needs that it cannot handle — and the more, therefore, the two fall into mutual antagonism. . . . Culture is the repressed that returns with a vengeance."[17]

Scholars like Alexis Celeste Bunten argue earnestly for a distinction between indigenous and nonindigenous tourism, though, suggesting that Native tourism might transcend these vexed politics and performances. She encourages instead the possibility of "'Indigenous capitalism' as a distinct strategy to achieve ethical, culturally appropriate, and successful Indigenous participation within the global economy."[18] Yet if we consider the possibility that "culturally appropriate" formations are themselves the product of commercial interests and projections — what John L. and Jean Comaroff call "ethno-commodification" in their wide-ranging study *Ethnicity, Inc.* (2009) — then such sanguine interpretations of the new market for "genuine" Indian experience must relinquish some of their potency. Defenders of Native "authenticity" and "indigenous capitalism" are not necessarily wrong; they are simply, for all the best, most hopeful reasons, downplaying the essential "triangulation of culture, identity, and the market."[19] Far from erasing culture, the Comaroffs argue, mass circulation, in fact, "reaffirms ethnicity — in general and in all its particularity — and, with it, the status of the embodied ethnic subject as a source and means of identity. . . . The implication? That aura may reside as much in the duplication of objects as in their uniqueness (Steiner 1999), in their becoming what Bruner (1999) calls 'authentic reproductions.'"[20] In other words, the fetish of culture, often produced in well-intentioned, earnest efforts to both redeem and preserve tribal identity, *becomes* the reigning version of cultural legitimacy.

A salient example of this phenomenon can be seen in Cherokee, North Carolina, where Indians cater to the local tourist industry by advertising excursions in the Qualla Boundary, a reservation community tucked away from the interstate and a veritable step back in the past and into national legend. Like any theme park, the Eastern Band of Cherokees' business is highly self-conscious and calculated, just another prong in the larger financial empire that includes the local Harrah's Cherokee hotel and casino complex (and, of course, the potential Walmart lease, which has languished since the recent economic downturn).[21] By emphasizing historical epochs and performances, the Cherokees actually diminish the lesser-known fact that prior to Removal, the Cherokees were "probably the most thoroughly acculturated Indians in nineteenth-century America."[22] They had a highly functioning community, government, constitution, written language, and newspaper — all modeled on white precedents but retaining significant elements of Cherokee culture. When the Eastern Cherokees open their doors to outsiders now, they don costumes and put on plays, acting out elaborate reconstructions of traditional dances "in period garb and makeup."[23] Begun in 1950, the long-running historical reenactment "Unto These Hills" replays the drama of the Trail of Tears to huge audiences and sizeable profits. Nearby, Oconaluftee Indian Village allows visitors to experience everyday life in an eighteenth-century Cherokee town.

Visitors must know, on some level, that these are real contemporary Indians only acting the part of their traditional ancestors; or do they? And what about the Cherokees themselves? One visiting journalist, present during the filming of a historical reenactment, reflects:

> Native Americans have spent a great deal of time and money fighting the stereotype of the savage Indian, especially the half-naked, weapon-bearing mascot-type. Yet to attract tourists, the Eastern Band had decided to pay a production team to film Native Americans running around the woods half-naked, carrying weapons, delivering punch lines — essentially becoming caricatures of themselves.[24]

The most distressing part of the journalist's account is the observation that "Nobody on the set that day seemed to find this [charade] odd or unsettling or even ironic — not the director, not the camera assistant, and not the makeup artist; none of the creatives from the agency that came up with the ads; and none of the talent, all of them registered Cherokees, authentic as can be."[25] Yet it would be wrong to assume that these Indians don't harbor a clear sense of the compromises they make in order to survive; it's just that such acquiescence to an inimical economy has become so regular and ingrained as to be not just justifiable but supremely necessary and routine. As Joe Feather, one of the tribe's most popular performers, muses, "The people who come to see me know nothing about me. They want me to feed this monster they've got inside them, and it makes them feel better if they come here and give me a dollar. But we're in America, man, and we have to *survive*. And I will do anything to help my family survive."[26] In a depressed Appalachian countryside where travel and tourism have replaced logging and hunting as primary forms of subsistence, the Cherokees adapt to the changes and play the role that will most help them "survive." Significantly, that often means consciously skewing even the facts of their own culture and history. As Henry Lambert reports, these "Cherokee 'chiefs' soon realized that their income was tied to their exotic appearance," which non-Natives associated with Plains Indian stereotypes such as elaborate feathered headdresses rather than more modest yet accurate Cherokee customs like buckskins. "If you are going into show business," one performer noted simply, you have to "dress for it."[27] Despite their best efforts to give the public the cultural experience of their wildest and most stereotypical imagination, and even despite the help of the tribal casino operation, most members of the Eastern Band of Cherokee remain at or just above the national poverty level.[28] This condition is in keeping with broader trends: according to a ten-year (1990–2000) study by Taylor and Kalt, "The family poverty rate for all Indian areas that were specifically involved with gaming was 36 percent," a rate more than double the national average.[29]

While the economic "survival" afforded by tourism is meager at best, equally worrying is the increasing recession of the tribe's actual history in the wake of its performative fabrications. At best, the split between the pageant and the reality is one maintained consciously and carefully by the community's entrepreneurs. At worst, as Starnes reports, many Cherokees now "embrace a counterfactual version of their own history and culture," effecting what sociologist Larry French has described as "nothing less than 'cultural genocide.'"[30] Today, the tribe maintains two distinct websites: one, an internal communication source to report on tribal news and community happenings;[31] the other, a patently market-driven advertising threshold to promote travel and tourism in Cherokee country.[32] On this latter site, we see a revolving series of four different images: all feature a warrior in traditional dress and war paint displaying various poses and gazes of intense reflection or challenge. Each highly stylized photo bears a slogan: first, a painted aborigine heralds the caption: "Most people don't realize that Asheville borders another country." There is savvy truth to this statement, which might read "most people don't realize that Cherokee Indians live right next door to 'real' North Carolinians." However, that's neither what the ad claims nor what American tourists would want to acknowledge; instead, the assertion of "another country" transports us back to a precolonial era. Accordingly, the next image in the series features a close-up of a masked warrior staring intently at the viewer, an arresting image promising "Not just stories around the campfire. Legends." Rather than delving more deeply into the *reality* of tribal survival and cultural continuity, we shuttle backward and further away from both contemporaneity and realism. A dose of adrenaline, like the kind that fevers a good John Wayne film, appears next: "Travel on the Blue Ridge Parkway without a Cherokee Guide is ill advised"; with this warning, a contemplative, befeathered Indian stands solemnly in wait, ready to shepherd the plucky traveler through a mysterious landscape of dark adventure. Once in this fantastical territory, the website promises a full panoply of bona fide indigenous images and experiences: "Captivating dances, tomahawks, blowguns, drumming, peace pipes, ancient clan masks, stirring legends, bows and arrows . . . are we there yet?" The fusion of clichéd consumerism and cultural preservation seems both deliberate and savvy; and while such efforts may attract caravans of suburbanite station wagons with cranky children in the backseat, hungry for a spiritually redemptive and authentic tour of indigenous fantasy, they do more damage than good to fragile notions of cultural survival and purity.

Still, the very emphasis on "authenticity" is itself problematic, a refraction of political needs, racial bifurcations, and market expectations. In ways both explicit and subtle, the imperfect reproduction of nation and sovereignty through these economic mechanisms actually intensifies rather than diminishes racial antagonism and competition. As the writers in this chapter evince with startling frequency, the particular trauma of economic dispossession and recuperation in the South has long conditioned the often violent, divisive contours of race and culture: to compete and survive economically in an embattled colony is never a project pursued in isolation, but over and against neighboring groups and cultures, often in overtly antagonistic ways. In the same way that the economics of slavery spawned a monstrous racism that would otherwise (arguably) not have developed as radically, the competitive economies of the reconstructed South engender new and divisive contours of racial and ethnic separatism. As we saw in Barry Hannah's fiction (chapter 1), the most successful and visible tribes are increasingly likely to suffer the disdain and suspicion of their non-Native neighbors, many of whom resent what seems like "unnatural, even scandalous special treatment from the federal government."[33] Economically viable tribes are deemed unworthy of continued recognition as Indians, as Alexandra Harmon argues in *Rich Indians* (2010): "In the reactions to Indians' new and growing wealth, moral judgments of economic behavior merged with ideas about Indians. Whether the ostensible subject was revenue sharing or the moral acceptability of a revenue source, conceptions of Indianness underlay the positions people took. Normative generalizations about Indian propensities — often paired with contrasting characterizations of non-Indians — were common. Some Indians detected and resented a widespread assumption that making money was inconsistent with Indian traits."[34]

This animosity could and often did grow combative. During the astounding transformation of his tribe from a poor community of sharecroppers to a lucrative business and gaming complex in the latter half of the twentieth century, Mississippi Choctaw chief Phillip Martin continued to battle regional conservatism and public misperception. As Martin recounts delicately in his autobiography, the agency doctor took to carrying a .45-caliber revolver for protection against those who "had a way of trying to keep the social structure intact and were often slow to accept change."[35] Unwaveringly, though, Martin remained unapologetic about the means by which he secured the phenomenal growth of his people: "I am a capitalist," he states. "For me, capitalism is the opportunity to make a living through your own abilities."[36] Of primary importance is the issue of autonomy and control, and Chief Martin consistently defends the integrity and honor with which he executed the tribe's business and growth. Indeed, what is at stake often is not just economic solvency but the less material benefits that come along with it: namely, the right to exercise your "own abilities," to maintain and manage both the present and the past — basic rights stolen from the Native southerner in ways that are made visible on a daily basis.

In multiple ways, these privileges have been repossessed — imaginatively and narratively, as we have seen in previous chapters, as well as materially, in the collection and memorializing of Native "artifacts" that condemn the Indian to a past anterior and obsolete. But does purchasing back those relics — both literally and metaphorically — necessarily liberate them from the economy of value and violence in which they are so thoroughly saturated? Can a repossession and performance of those usurped elements of culture be empowering simply on their own terms? Perhaps — but not without complications or consequences. Lucci-Cooper recalls an episode her father experienced while trying to buy a used car in rural Handley, West Virginia. He had gone to meet with the seller, a white man who "proudly took him on a tour of the many ancestral bones he had collected and paid for over the years from various sources throughout the Southeast." The most grotesque sample, which the man unveils gleefully, is "the head of what looks like a young child, and it still has the stone arrowhead lodged in the bones that form its skull."[37] As Lucci later relates this story to his daughter (Lucci-Cooper), the notion of a white man purchasing and claiming to be the *"owner"* of "authentic" sacred objects that include human bones fills her with disgust. She is "not surprised" when her infant son later "spit[s] up the whole of his meal" breastfed to him during the telling of this awful anecdote, one unfolding, not incidentally, against the backdrop of a routine commercial transaction — an attempt to buy a used vehicle.[38] Lucci-Cooper's infant son rejects bodily what contemporary southern Indians have internalized in the centuries since their colonization and eviction: Native extinction, verified in spectacles of obsolescence and yoked irremediably to the objects of consumption that supplanted them, becomes a commodity of inestimable worth in the development of an American nation and U.S. southern ascension. This recognition is a chilling one, particularly in an environment where human bodies continued to be considered property even after the nuisance of Indian life was supposedly exorcised. And yet, although the baby refuses the story along with the meal, he does not get his food back. Like Lucci-Cooper and the rest of her people, a profound emptiness and loss seem the most palpable consequences to the sale and seizure of their own images and bodies.

This incident — made more disturbing because it is all too real — is a striking metaphor for the narratives we will explore further in this chapter, which taken together constitute a troubling narrative about economic development in the Native South. While much of the existing scholarship on indigenous economics is concerned with whether culture can survive and thrive in confluence with modern capitalism, Native southern writers seem concerned with the quality and character of that endurance, the possibility of recovery after the revulsion and regurgitation, so to speak. The prognosis—not just for Indians, but for all Americans—is difficult. As their narratives attest, economic processes and conditions wreak havoc on Native culture and communities in increasingly extreme and undeniably physical ways, much as Lucci-Cooper's infant son reacts violently and viscerally to the knowledge of his people's commodification and dehumanization. In ways that yoke their cultural violation firmly to these economic rubrics and rights, Native writers in the South figure their simultaneous invisibility and cultural impoverishment as a cruel assault on physical bodies, families, and communities, a sense of despair and annihilation so severe that it manifests like Lucci-Cooper's haunting "recissions"—as violent, wounding, corporeal sunderings of self, community, and integrity, all provoked explicitly by the obliterating instruments of economic logic.

Consequently, the effort to reclaim cultural sovereignty among southeastern Indians takes both the path and the character of financial recompense in a calculated effort to redeem what has been stolen. What we find in these collisions of fiscal pragmatism and cultural reclamation are sober reminders that these are mutually inextricable categories, and most important, that such a confluence haunts southern Natives and non-Natives alike in uncannily analogous ways. Like the arrowhead lodged in the skull of the Indian child in the white man's mausoleum, Native southern writers regularly feature narratives about children not just taken away but in fact sacrificed by their own families, a textual preoccupation that discloses an anxiety about the foreclosed futures lost in these new, fetishized acts of economic volition. Indeed, we must attend not just to the hope encoded in capitalist development but to the terror.

Savage Economies: Reconstructions and Deconstructions of Community

In a recent collection of essays exploring the notion of the "economic sublime," Jack Amariglio, Joseph W. Childers, and Stephen E. Cullenberg seek to uncover the pervasive "horror [of] the all-encompassing features of a globalized economy" that has infiltrated every aspect of our lives yet evades precise representation or control.[39] Similarly, Slavoj Žižek has recently suggested that the manifestation of violence is simply the most visible of a "triumvirate" of brutality: its companions are "symbolic" violence, "embodied in language and its forms," and "systemic" violence, regulated and normalized by social institutions.[40] Because subjective acts of violence are consistently figured as aberrant — flagrant disruptions of a peaceful, orderly society — systemic violence is thus rendered invisible, its effects wrought by hidden hands. As Antonio Hardt and Michael Negri further suggest, the diffusion of late capitalism has blinded us to its quotidian assaults conducted "impersonally" and routinely.[41] As the reach of capitalism has expanded, so too has its immanence; the borders of cultures and nation-states tend to dissolve in the wake of a higher sovereignty — that of capital and its encompassing authority.[42] The literature of the Native South in many ways offers a dramatic reification of this economic terror, one that threatens to annihilate the remaining reservoirs of tradition and culture perceived to be integral to indigenous societies, even as it tantalizes with unparalleled opportunities for survival and nourishment.

In chapter 1, we saw characters in works by Stephen Graham Jones, Louis Owens, and LeAnne Howe acting out violently against the losses and erasures that conscripted them; for all of them, both cultural thefts and economic privation lie at the heart of their characters' actions, and invariably, violent vengeance fails to yield any palpable relief or sustenance over those circumstances. An even more distinctly material genealogy of this crisis emerges in Cherokee writer Geary Hobson's spectacular short novella *The Last of the Ofos* (2000), which we discussed briefly in chapter 2. Hobson's protagonist is a man named Thomas Darko, the last surviving member of the "Ofo" — or Mosopelea — tribe of Louisiana. Darko is not just the Last Mohican for the Deep South; rather than a quietly vanishing remnant of a once-populous tribe, Hobson figures Darko as a member of an indigenous community that has always been fragmented, mixed, scattered, and occluded. Clustered among pockets of remaining Tunica and Biloxi families, the Ofo have their own small "postage stamp" of soil, Hobson tells us — clearly conjuring the metaphor Faulkner used to describe his own famous literary empire, and in doing so, asserting both territorial and cultural rights not just to American land but on southern soil in particular (7). Allusively, Hobson also exercises his authorial right — like Faulkner — as "sole owner and proprietor" of a fictional community, a notion at once liberating and meager.

This fragile, mixed Indian community suffers deeply not just from their social isolation but from severe poverty; Hobson makes clear that long after literal Removal, economic forces are finally the ones to decimate the Ofos when "that damn old railroad track" comes along and quickly gathers a reputation for "being a real people-killer" (19):

> The number of our people that has died on that damn thing would make a whole cemetery by itself. Long time ago, a chief's brother and as stout a warrior as you would ever see, so I heared tell, was found dead on the tracks all cut up in a lot of parts. And not long after that, that man's sister, a medicine woman name Arsene, got hit by a train and killed, too. The Texas and Pacific Railway Company, it was called, but the Runover and Kill Company it was called, too. And then, they was my own family and how they all git wiped out by a train—but I'm getting ahead of my story. Only Sun Father knows the honest real count of how many of us Ofos and Tunicas and Biloxis got sacrificed on them tracks—and a whole bunch of mules and cows and horses and dogs, too. I spect—no, I *know*—they all had they lives and they cared about them. (19)

The advent of the railroad kills not just anyone but the brother of a chief and formidable warrior, and later his medicine woman sister. The culture for which they stand as obvious, powerful metonyms is torn apart violently—"all cut up into a lot of parts"—by the engine of progress and its powerful ability to steamroll human lives and demolish tribal integrity. When Darko later loses the remaining members of his own family, it happens in one cataclysmic crash: not surprisingly, "they all git wiped out by a train." In the "story" of his people's "sacrifice," Darko forcefully assumes the right to narrate and to name, to "call" the railroad company by a name better suited to its business; and while he defers to a greater power for a true assessment of how dearly such progress has cost them (something "only Sun Father knows"), he won't relinquish the one thing he emphatically *knows* for sure: "they all had they lives and they cared about them."

If there is a moral to Darko's narrative, it seems to be this repeated accent on the significance of every small life in the face of all-consuming incursions. It is a mantra he intones at key moments in the text, and always in instances when a life has been curtailed recklessly and selfishly by industrial or material forces. In one such example, Darko and his gang have a run-in with *the* Bonnie and Clyde, who are revealed to be the basest and soulless of criminals: they shoot a dog to bits for plain mean fun, leaving Darko to tend the corpse in horror. After they disappear and he "begin[s] collecting the body parts," he addresses the mutilated animal sorrowfully: "You had a life and you cared about it, too" (55). Like the men and animals "cut up in a lot of parts" by the train, the dog falls prey to Bonnie and Clyde's vicious, greedy steamroller. What these examples imply is that the lesser creatures will be sacrificed in cold blood so that the elite may survive, and that such hierarchy is not a natural aristocratic or Darwinian fate but a criminal enterprise. In the particularly vexed and competitive economy of the struggling South—whether during Reconstruction, the Depression, or subsequent periods of recovery—capitalist development proves to have cruel consequences for the Natives laboring to maintain a competitive breath and to forestall their own erasure.

As we saw in the previous chapter, Bonnie repeatedly calls Darko a "nigger," effectively nullifying his already frail claim to his rapidly diminishing community. After he corrects her, she simply sneers: "Oh, git out of here, nigger boy. They ain't no more Indians around anymore. Everyone knows that" (51). It seems significant that the mouthpiece for this broad cultural assumption comes from a member of the criminal upper class, one who mutilates lesser creatures just as the passing train eliminates the Indians who stand in its path. Her dismissal of Darko's indigeneity is inextricably entangled in the dark web of an eviscerating and indelibly biracial economy; and for the remainder of the novella, we see Darko's status as the "last of the Ofos" as a simultaneously genealogical and material crisis: "I was a poor man, but not jist cause I had no property. No, I was poor cause I no longer had a family. This is real poorness. It can't never get no worse than that" (64). Darko's admission does not simply recalibrate for us a sense of where true value lies; instead, it reminds us of how deeply entwined are the modes of economic subsistence and the survival of the indigenous southern family and tribe itself.

Throughout Native southern literature, there are abundant instances in which social invisibility is similarly figured as a radical dismemberment accomplished by cruel economic forces and proxies. Such frequency unveils a deep sense of ambient violence woven into the Native southern experience from its earliest moments. In Louis Owens's short story "Yazoo Dusk,"[43] he returns to the swamp world of Luther Cole in order "to reconstruct, or construct for the first time, the Mississippi my father's Choctaw-Irish-French family knew."[44] Luther Cole appears here as a much younger man in love with Onatima Blue Wood, the mixedblood daughter of a wealthy Choctaw planter and his white wife. A heartsick Luther lays watching for the girl outside of her grand plantation home: "Fourteen years old and he knew he'd already been in love all his whole life and more, with the Yazoo just a hundred yards down the hill telling him violence would indeed lay hold of every goddamned thing the moment he moved. Hadn't it already taken hold of everybody he came from all the way back to Red Shirt and more?" (221). It becomes immediately clear that the "violence" Luther intuits is no mere hyperbole for his unrequited love but something that saturates the very place of his birth — the Yazoo River — and binds him indissolubly to "everybody he came from," like the storied Choctaw warrior Red Shirt. The love that he has for Onatima paradoxically but undeniably connects him to a kind of violence his people have been enduring for centuries: "all his whole life and more" he has possessed not just this love, which is plausible only in sentimental terms, but more potently, the knowledge that any act of desire and volition on his part will be met by immense pain and grief.

The heartache that Luther feels has a genealogical anchor because of what his particular beloved represents: not just the mixing of blood, which is also Luther's condition, but the entry into an elite world purchased by that white strain. When Onatima narrates a subsequent section of the story, she makes clear that the family's financial fortune has in no way alleviated the difficulty of being Indian in Mississippi: "If you think it's easy being an Indian girl, you're crazy. People think because my father's rich, or richer than most in these parts anyway, that it's all easy" (224). Onatima becomes well educated and proper, wears white nightgowns and fancies herself a "princess" (225); but she also battles the diminished expectations of the genteel white society around her, where the teachers "acted like a prize mule had sat up and recited the Lord's Prayer" whenever the girl exhibits a shred of intelligence (224). As much as her breeding and learning fail to earn her a foothold in white society, she also struggles to assume her Choctaw heritage. While Onatima's Indian grandmother teaches her Chahta ways and words — "alikchi medicine," "the real stories. . . . Deep woods stories, olden time true stories" (224) — she cannot share any of this with her "modern" father. Her liminal crisis deepens when her father plans to marry her off to a white planter, a man named Granger; torn between two potential lovers, Granger and Luther, she suffers the pain of being caught between worlds: "[Luther] would take me away, across the river to that life his kind of Chahta lived, not understanding at all the way these two worlds had steel hooks pulling from both sides until

I thought I would be left just bloody muscle and broken bone" (225). The "hook" that pulls Onatima away from Luther and into the world of the white elite is figured curiously here as an alluring force, the one thing—however painful—keeping her from retreating with Luther into the swamp. And yet the tug from Luther's side of the river proves no less injurious.

Whatever side she chooses, it seems, Onatima's fate will be one of "bloody muscle and broken bone" simply because she has to choose at all in a world that parses identity along racial and economic fault lines. As Luther already knows, to be Choctaw is to exist "like a piece of flesh caught on a briar and just ripped from the body, except this time it was the body itself ripped away, leaving that bloody piece behind" (228). The metaphor, which appears at the end of the story, comes from an unnamed "Teller" who imagines Mississippi's remaining Choctaw as bits of bloody flesh left to bleed in the Yazoo swamp. The ones who "turned back from that awful walk, straggling home," arrive with nightmarish stories of "dying children and old folks" and "White farmers charging ten times the price for any kind of food" (228). Smoothly, he elides the devastation of Removal with the economic exploitation that instigated, accompanied, and followed it: defiant Choctaw would return home with the knowledge that their barest survival would cost exponentially more than it should, draining further the already shredded tribal body. Like many actual Choctaw progressives, Onatima's father chooses to become a "white farmer" in his own right, and a slaveholder as well, not necessarily to get rich but simply to survive. Predictably, Luther deigns him an "apple": "an Indian who was not just red but red-brown on the outside and white like all rich people on the inside" (225).

In the post-Removal world of the Choctaw, "white" becomes a signifier for money and its power to belittle and demean those perceived to be less, like the "poor Indians," which often entailed radical self-effacement as well (226). Being white does not simply mean being "rich"; it means achieving such security at the expense of others and the erasure of Indian values and tradition. "Rich white folks were like that," Luther knows, "living *big* and wide across everybody's lives, like they owned the full moon and the whole sky of stars and everyone who walked or ran way down below moon and sky" (226). While the Teller mourns the ensuing war "when so many Indian people got cut to pieces for something that didn't mean a thing to them" (228), what he is really suggesting is that the Confederate cause and its perverse economy of human labor should not "mean a thing" to the Indians — a fact betrayed by men like Onatima's father, who sacrifices his indigeneity and his integrity for material gain. The "rich white" man who wants to marry Onatima thus threatens to possess and diminish her vibrant presence; worse, her own father is keen to trade her into that fate simply to secure his own tenuous position in the social hierarchy. What is palpable for Luther is that his love for Onatima, for all that she represents of his tribes' losses and their continued sacrifices, threatens to cut him to pieces, too — in a way that his people have been experiencing for as long as his collective memory can recall.

These violent recissions of intrusive colonial and economic forces emerge again and again throughout contemporary southeastern Indian literature. What is being imagined, it seems, is a new world order in which the body politic of the tribe has been brutally sundered, and in which even interpersonal relationships become charged harbingers of doom and betrayal. Much of Luther's angst surrounds the presumption that Indian survival and "white" capitalism are mutually exclusive entities, embodied textually in his and Onatima's very real sense that giving in to such forces entails utter annihilation of one's indigeneity; his ultimate decision to shun both the white man's world and that of this tribe signifies how deeply antagonistic the two worlds have become. Luther elects the shadowy swamp world over both, and we know from later works by Owens (*The Sharpest Sight* and *Bone Game*) that Onatima eventually joins him, but only after a series of disastrous events culminating in her apparent murder of her own husband, a man she was forced to marry as punishment for betraying her father and seeking a dark-skinned Indian lover.[45] A chasm of violence both actual and metaphorical consistently opens between indigenous culture and the imposition of alien, unwelcome desires that turn families against one another viciously.

The history of economic relationships between the white elite and a dark underclass in the South has long cultivated a supposition of natural hierarchy and absolute incompatibility between races and orders, engendered by a very real project to dispossess and unhome the region's indigenous and to settle the land with the labor of African slaves. Colonial processes were fueled by such assumptions, but they also helped manufacture and sustain them in the social formations that followed. In 1830 the fourteenth article of the Treaty of Dancing Rabbit Creek offered Choctaws the choice of removing to Indian Territory or remaining and becoming landowners in Mississippi: agreeing to become citizens of the state meant they would sacrifice membership in the Choctaw Nation, its headquarters removed to Indian Territory and severed from the remnant tribe in Mississippi, in exchange for "a reservation of one section of six hundred and forty acres of land, to be bounded by sectional lines of survey . . . but if they ever remove [they] are not to be entitled to any portion of the Choctaw annuity."[46] The treaty was negotiated by several Choctaw leaders, most notably Greenwood LeFlore, who was already a wealthy plantation owner and clearly a historical model for Onatima's father. After Removal, he was elected state senator, advocated assimilationist policies for Indians, and later fought for the Union in the Civil War, the conflict that "cut to pieces" Indians who never should have abdicated their honor. Historically, these resignations of tribal sovereignty were agreed upon by just such well-placed, often mixedblood men who harbored material motivations and rewards; and the cost to their communities was grave: the loss of holism, sovereignty, and scores of actual lives.[47]

Becoming American, with all the trappings of civilization that condition demanded, meant divorce from the tribal nation and purchase into a competitive biracial economy, or relative invisibility and erasure. While an African American can achieve financial success without necessarily abdicating racial authenticity, the choice for Indians is a doggedly binary one: Natives who succumb to the temptations of materialism are quickly perceived as "sellouts." The political incentive for maintaining such a division has motivated numerous tribal activists and scholars at various periods and crises in American history; what is more, the rhetoric of indigenous moderation, sustainability, and equal distribution has been taken up by no shortage of non-Natives eager to locate anticapitalist alternatives. However, new scholarship is also uncovering the extent to which capitalist energies have always energized Native societies struggling to survive colonial incursions. In *Rich Indians* (2010), Harmon insists that Natives have long been embroiled in economies of accumulation and prosperity, despite terrific controversy within their own communities and surrounding white society. She documents seven discrete instances of historical Indians who achieved great wealth — several of whom did so on southern stages, including the Powhatan of colonial Virginia and the wealthy planters of the antebellum Southeast. Not surprisingly, her later examples involve the profusion of casino tribes since the 1990s. What is at stake, though, in recognizing these capitalist conversion narratives as pervasive, tyrannical, and fatal to both the Indian and the white idylls of the Southeast? The issue is not so much whether "culture" can remain intact in the face of economic interests; rather, it is that in the process of attempting to reassert community on an anticapitalist foundation, something new is imagined altogether. Through the intervention of narrative—stories about the past and possibilities for a redemptive future—both the apocryphal South and the Native Southeast manage to spin new tales about their own communities that do not just justify but repress altogether the ways in which economic interests underlie and determine the very basis of community.

In Hobson's *Last of the Ofos*, for instance, Thomas Darko's entire existence oscillates anxiously around the need for both economic and cultural survival while repeatedly conjuring the grave incompatibility of the two endeavors; hence, his various occupations seesaw alternately between the twin poles of crime (figured or induced by capitalism) and performance (the hyperbolic maintenance of tradition in the face of such criminal threats). He is continually haunted by his run-in with Bonnie and Clyde and all that their outlaw behavior represents and demolishes; importantly, we are reminded that he met them in the first place while entangled in the same criminal underworld. Put another way, he could just as easily be implicated in the cutting to pieces of the helpless dog and, by textual extension, the demolition of his own tribe and family by the railroad, or (as in Owens's story) giving his own progeny over to the steel hooks of a white slaveholder. All that saves him is his lack of both agency and offspring. Floored by the potentiality of his self-defeating behavior, though, Darko attempts to align his own work with that of a more sympathetic criminal, Pretty Boy Floyd, who significantly is rumored to be "part Indian." Like Darko, his illegal activities are motivated by necessity—but they also have a distinctly antiacquisitive, commonwealth aspect to them: "He was different from them two grubworms [Bonnie and Clyde]. Ruther he was one who always stuck up for his own kind—the poor folks all around the country. . . . He was straight-up with his own people. It was them blood-sucking banks he was hell on" (57). Darko thus enacts his own Pretty Boy Floyd–inspired turn of generosity by helping a man and his family stranded on the side of the road, giving them cash and a new tire and refusing recompense. While the mode of his goodwill is obviously inspired by indigenous values and communal goodwill, it is significant that Darko's "own kind" also includes poor whites. The man he helps is a "poor-looking, skinny white feller in overalls"; moreover, he remembers that "it was cold that day—a strong, wet, rainy wind out of the north—coldern a banker's heart" (58). The metaphor doesn't seem accidental, nor does the direction of that cold wind from the north. In such moments, the community that Darko identifies with most acutely is a poor southern one undone by the battering winds of aggression and interference "out of the north." While Indian values surge forward here as a ballast, they do so in service of a community where class affinity ultimately matters more than race. The "blood-sucking banks" rob one's life and soul, but they also clearly drain one's blood and heritage: the only relationship left that matters and binds these men is one of class, making their racial difference a social fiction more than anything.

Nevertheless, such blood-sucking forces have the effect not of lasting intercultural solidarity but rather resurgent conceptions of tribal distinctiveness and preservation. Darko repeatedly laments his status as the "last" of his tribe and feels the awful responsibility of continuing that line; yet he also knows that material circumstances have curtailed his possibilities and compelled him to be at various times a physical laborer, a criminal, and a cultural sellout:

> I run whiskey; I worked the wheat fields some all through the Great Plains; I butchered livestock in Fort Worth. I roustabouted and drilled in near-bout ever oil field in Louisiana. Shoot, for a while I even farted around as a rodeo clown out in New Mexico and Texas. Was a time, too, I dug taters in Colorado and Nebraska, and part of another year I like to froze my tail off working construction on the Alcan Highway up in Yukon country. . . . I walked some real-mean streets in big cities . . . always carrying with me a loaded .38 pistol or a straight-razor. Most times I carried both. I even went out to Hollywood one time to be in a picture-show about feather-bonnet Indians, and I even pretended to be one, jist so I could git the job, and I got it, too, and some other ones besides. Another time, jist cause I got a Louisiana accent, they had me play a Cajun in a show about jazz music. You got to have lived through the 1930s and 1940s to know what I mean. And you got to be Indian, jist like I am, to know how much that galls—that having to act like something else other than what you be. (4–5)

What is so striking about this passage is Darko's awareness of his dual heritage as both a working-class man *and* a member of an elided and stereotyped race; a poor southerner *and* an Indian; a "clown" *and* an essential, unspoiled self that he must shroud but believes in nonetheless. Moreover, he knows that the blurring of these borders — and the presence of the borders in the first place — happens as a result of economic necessity: you "got to have lived through the 1930s and 1940s" to understand exactly how one comes to such sober, self-effacing choices. Laboring in the decades of the Depression *and* being Indian are compatible experiences, as both require one to sacrifice safety, integrity, and authenticity — to "be something else" in order to survive financially. Playing a Cajun galls Darko as much as mimicking a rodeo clown or an Indian, apparently — none approximates his own mixed cultural inheritance in an unseen deep southern existence that features neither war bonnets nor trumpet solos. Yet the necessity of economic endurance makes the pageantry of cultural stereotype — and deepening division between those roles — ever more potent and inescapable.

Hobson's novella envisions the inevitability of that fate with brilliant subtlety. Inevitably, Thomas Darko's exploits as a whiskey runner land him in jail, a harsh reminder that even his most desperate and sympathetic acts will eventually be curtailed by a judicial system engineered against Native prosperity. His incarceration functions as metaphor, too, for his social isolation and invisibility, and the impossibility of exercising even his rights to racial performance. While locked up, he realizes fully the limitations to his agency and the very anomaly of his existence in the South: "It was like the State of Louisiana had no clear idea of what kind of a person I was. Sometime I was put with niggers and sometime with white men, but most of the time I was kep in a place off by myownself" (56). The jail thus represents a microcosm of his life as a southeastern Indian — a fate of anomalous solitude in a space of surveillance and control. Fittingly, it is while serving time there that he receives the news of the wreck that kills his entire family; the tragedy simply magnifies the terrible loneliness he already experiences and elides for the reader how intimately his isolation and futility are tied to the industrial-capitalist forces that obliterate his entire tribe.

Being in prison thus means continuing to toil, and now he does so blindly and automatically in an effort to dull his immense emotional pain. As Mark Fisher avers, under capitalism, "Work and life become inseparable. Capital follows you when you dream."[48] For Darko, his life is circumscribed by labor:

he stops keeping track of the days, no longer able to see himself in time, and does nothing but "work—plow, hoe, saw, tote, fetch, and run" (62). He stops talking to people altogether, and becomes painfully aware that "I might never git to speak the [Ofo] language again since everybody but me was gone" (62). The misery of remaining alive and silent — "like a lone cypress in a cleared-off bayou bottom" — is little different than being cut to pieces by a passing train or a cold-blooded, money-rabid gangster. The fact that all he can do after such a crisis is "work" reminds us none too subtly that such activities have long marked his less-than-vibrant state, that they are a harbinger of social death rather than a stay against it. The conviction that, beneath all this, he has a life of his own and that it *matters*, is a quiet truth he can communicate to no one.

Even after Darko is released from jail—and subsequently discovered by the Smithsonian team who studies him and preserves his soon-to-be "dead" language—he never elects to ward off the end of his tribe simply by pro-creating. He certainly has opportunity: briefly married to a fellow Native woman from a nearby tribe (who abandons him while he is serving his sentence), he also has subsequent affairs, including the one with the black maid Melba in Washington, D.C. (discussed in chapter 2). But Hobson apparently decides, in part, not to reconstruct history. Darko is based on the real-life "last of the Ofos," a woman named Rosa Pierrette of Marksville, Louisiana, and Hobson remains true to this somber source.[49] To render Darko's fate differently would defy the historical record and deny the gravity of indigenous loss in the South, a place where the actual extinction of tribe and community has been an all-too-real fact. Yet Hobson's meticulously crafted novella tells us also that often such extinction is more metaphor than reality, that physical procreation might actually be irrelevant when life under capitalism has been deadly and infertile. To choose to extend the family line by reproducing would further the Ofo genealogy but would constitute a false choice, given the poverty of opportunity and visibility in Darko's world. Instead, Darko's lonely life is marked by criminal enterprise, desperation, selling-out, and ultimate isolation. Likewise, numerous other southern Native authors signify the metaphorical—if not yet literal—death of community and family in a profusion of narratives that feature young people being sold, traded, pawned, or otherwise sacrificed to an economy that has already all but consumed their futures.

What You Pawn I Will (Not) Redeem

Central to economic thought from Karl Marx to Justus Möser, Edmund Burke, and Jürgen Habermas has been the anxiety over capitalism's "spill-over" properties — that is, how market principles are likely to contaminate and erode essential human relationships.[50] Most cataclysmic is the prospect that capitalism's tendencies toward abuse and control would deteriorate and eventually destroy the family itself.[51] Whether or not the advanced state of breakdown in the family unit nationally can be attributed to the incursions of capitalism, it is indubitable that the fear of crumbling kinship ties seems to have come to fruition, and the crisis is more often than not marked by conflicts over money, addiction, betrayal, and hungers with deep material roots. At its worst, such dissolution signifies what Fredric Jameson would identify as a profound failure of future possibilities, the mood characteristic of late capitalism; in *Capitalist Realism*, Mark Fisher builds on this supposition by identifying in our present moment a rampant atmosphere of "sterility," a culture unable of producing anything new, and ensuing generations of young people "no longer capable of producing surprises."[52] In a seemingly benign way, Fisher demonstrates, television shows like the popular *Supernanny* — in which a child-rearing expert swoops in to troubleshoot families in crisis — actually help us to diagnose the myriad ways in which children are not misbehaving quite as much as the parents are: "It is the *parents'* following of the trajectory of the pleasure principle, the path of least resistance, that causes most of the misery in the families."[53] In a strikingly similar way, Native southern writers are beginning to indict not the pathless new assimilated youth but rather the terrible agency wielded by the elder generation. As failed custodians of tribal holism and continuity, these textual parents have been materially and emotionally impoverished to the point that the future itself — and the children who embody it — are seen merely as disposable entities, inevitable casualties on the road to momentary profit or satisfaction.

It is difficult otherwise to explain the alarming profusion of Native southern narratives that feature children sold, traded, or otherwise sacrificed for material gain, much as Onatima's father uses his own daughter as a bargaining chip to purchase his class ambitions. In Florida Creek author Chip Livingston's short story "Pond," for instance, a young Miccosukee man named Pond leaves his Florida home to go searching for relatives and tribal connection out west; as an adopted child in the South, he has grown up feeling bereft of both. By the end of the story, he discovers the true story of his origins from a cruel cousin: his name is *"Pawned, not Pond,"* she tells him, because his real mother was *"a nasty alcoholic who took you to a pawnshop to get rid of you. . . . She was trying to get some money so she could buy another bottle of whiskey. . . . [My uncle] felt sorry for you, I guess, or for your mother, and gave the woman the ten dollars he had gotten for his own mother's beads."*[54] Up until this point, Pond has been making up stories of his birth and his family in order to cover the aporia in his origins; he simply doesn't know where he came from, and even his name turns out to be a fiction. As Owens has said, drawing on his own personal experience of familial loss and betrayal, "I know that we invent what we need to be true, imagining and rewriting until there is some kind of text that gives us back a self."[55] Pond's story of his own life is clearly the version that he needs to be true even before he learns the real narrative in which he is both sold and purchased in one swift breath.

In a story called "Jukebox," Pamela Masotti (Cherokee with roots in Florida and Texas) shows us yet another drunken parent — this time a father — who is purported to be so drunk and "scheming" that "he will soon be trying to trade his only daughter."[56] Like Livingston's, Masotti's story also suggests that alcohol pushes a parent to unimaginable exchanges, thus tempting us to read these narratives as grave critiques or parables of the desperate addictions plaguing many contemporary Indian families. Yet there is something markedly more peculiar and urgent about these exchanges in both detail and frequency — something that points toward a deep, self-interested hunger and a reckless disregard not just for family but for its most vulnerable members. Neither story ends well: Pond heads back to Florida, rejected and humiliated by his cousin, back to the father who procures him for the price of his own mother's beads; and in Masotti's story, the mother murders her drunken husband, transforming herself into the "protector" who makes the world "safe" and "takes care of the evil" for her children.[57] In both cases, the ironic solution to the problem of "evil" and addiction involves more evil, a relentless participation in the economy of abuse and narcissism that leaves these children vacant, isolated wanderers searching for true safety and protection.

A more extensive and thorny version of this tale emerges in Dawn Karima Pettigrew's debut novel *The Way We Make Sense* (2002), discussed briefly in chapter 2, which begins with a young girl being sold by her father to pay a rodeo entry fee. When Jack StandsStraight's pockets turn up short, he enumerates the assets in his life that might serve as payment. His daughters Carolina, Georgia, and Tennessee Jane are too valuable to spare. But a fourth—Indiana—proves expendable; she is, in effect, sold. When Jack's wife, Oklahoma, learns what her husband has done, she wakes Indiana and sneaks her onto a bus headed south in the middle of the night, bound for North Carolina's Qualla reservation where Oklahoma's people remain. Saved from being sold away to a fellow rodeo rider, Indiana is nevertheless torn from her family; the metaphorical circumstances surrounding the transaction unmistakably connote not Removal but slavery, as she is effectively sold down the river. The trail takes her back to her North Carolina ancestors in a homecoming that proves more ominous than joyous.

As in Howe's *Shell Shaker*, Pettigrew is also at pains to show how the southern origins of this Cherokee family haunt and steer them in the Oklahoma diaspora. The character Oklahoma—like so many of the state's people—is originally from North Carolina, a land she describes to her daughters as a "heavenly" place: "lovely and full of green and rain and mountains." They live in Oklahoma now, though, because "Daddy is happy here, where he can be a cowboy" (15). What tantalizes about the west and Jack are unmistakably white, Euramerican values: Jack is "handsome as a fifty-dollar bill" with "skin the color of a new penny," a chin "like a movie star," and teeth "incredibly white, like flakes of Ivory Snow detergent."[58] Unlike many Native families, Jack never acknowledges being from anywhere else but Oklahoma; he is a "cowboy" American seemingly without a past or a conscience. When he once ended up briefly in the South for a Baptist meeting, he is taken by Oklahoma's "copper beauty" (16); the choice of descriptors clearly evokes, like Jack's "new penny" sheen and Ivory soap purity, the transmutation of the Indian into a commercial culture that overwhelms and rewrites him, replacing "real" individuals with Hollywood doubles and "incredible" smiles. It is impossible not to read Oklahoma's exchange—the sacrifice of "heaven" and home in return for a specimen of dazzling, surreal, "white" wealth and beauty—as a parable for the Cherokee's bitter exchange in their reluctant treaties and promises of ownership and prosperity in the new land of Oklahoma. What she gets is as paltry as the dusty land greeting her ancestors at the end of their horrific migration: for all his glint, Jack StandsStraight is unremittingly poor. The very first lines of the narrative promise that this will never change: "No matter how he ties his life together, the knot at the end of Jack StandsStraight's rope is poverty" (9). To be at the "end of one's rope" is to be completely desperate, unable to hang on any longer—in that space, at the end of all his efforts, Jack invariably confronts the unrelenting poverty that rules his existence and determines his choices.

Presumably, Oklahoma's southern parents chose her name in order to honor the ancestors who had not been able to resist their removal. From the start, then, she is marked as a signifier for a loss—a Native South and a remnant tribe evacuated, the tribal body continuing elsewhere in a place called Oklahoma. It seems inevitable that she, too, will be drawn away by the allure of something better; but once made, the decision plagues her. The pattern of reproducing and reifying loss continues in the naming of her own daughters, all spectacularly beautiful and sweet, who allegorically represent both the lost South and a prior, more enriching sense of value uncorrupted by materiality and desperation. Three of the four StandsStraight girls are named explicitly for southern states: Carolina, Georgia, and Tennessee Jane. Carolina, not surprisingly given Oklahoma's origins, is the family favorite, a sturdy and fearless horsebreaker who "can make real StandsStraight men someday." Her promise of making "real" what has yet to materialize seems destined, by implication, to remain an unfulfilled promise. Georgia is Oklahoma's best company because she "looks like her own Mama, way over in North Carolina," a comfort that "helps Oklahoma to bear the flat places and the wind out West, and to stay with [Jack]"; put simply, she is a reminder of home that helps Oklahoma to "bear" the land bearing her own name, the flat and empty space that embodies her vacant self. "I know better than to think that Mama can survive without Georgia," another daughter tells us knowingly (20). Finally, Tennessee Jane is "useless" but the kind of pretty that "makes bankers, doctors, and even Hollywood come calling"; her "dark gray eyes and smile on fire from Heaven are better than an old-age retirement policy" (10). Like the others, this Heaven-ly girl is clearly meant to evoke the "heavenly" homeland for Oklahoma herself, and presumably for all of Oklahoma's displaced Indians, for whom life "without Georgia" is hardly endurable; but her rare beauty and Hollywood looks are her inheritance. Because of what they represent, the daughters' collective splendor is worth more than mere currency; like the southern states and the lost past they represent, the girls are priceless, precious, and "rare as good gold" (11). Yet, of course, they are not. The daughters are inevitably weighed, measured, and priced; they are appraised for their glittery potential or likely loss: a "someday" promise, an "insurance policy," a ghostly comfort, a "useless" beauty.

The fourth daughter — significantly, the one who is sold and scurried south to North Carolina before the final transaction can occur — is named, not after a southern state, but Indiana. Known prior to statehood as "Indian Land,"[59] Indiana's namesake makes her a veritable proxy for all removed Indians; however, despite close geographic and filial ties to the South, Indiana was also the first western state to mobilize for the Civil War on behalf of the Union, a history that pits Indiana herself as a metonym against the Natives who remained and defended the South. Strikingly, Pettigrew chooses this particular daughter to send as an envoy back to her mother's people in North Carolina. This is the sequence of events in *The Way We Make Sense;* but in her later novel, *The Marriage of Saints* (2006), Pettigrew returns to the same characters and plotline in order to rewrite it: in this later version, Indiana never makes it to Qualla at all, but "fell down a well," the day before she was to be claimed as collateral.[60] The revision is disturbing, as it throws into doubt the reality of the events — or at least their importance and efficacy — following Indiana's escape to Qualla, which constitute the remainder and majority of the initial novel. In the slippage between outcomes, Pettigrew suggests that returning South, and concomitantly escaping a heartless economy of sacrifice and waste, is but a fantasy. More importantly, as the bulk of *The Way We Make Sense* follows not just Indiana but her daughter Manna, we are forced to doubt the very possibility of fertility and continuance, particularly back in the region remembered as a blessed, sacred place uncorrupted by the cowboy economy that ruins the StandsStraight family.

Pettigrew's later revision simply exacerbates what is already a potent issue and worry throughout the first novel: whether an escape from these fatal economies and desires is possible, and whether the South can credibly function as the site of anticapitalist fantasy. To begin with, the entire account of Indiana's hurried bus ride and journey back to Qualla, her reunion with her grandparents, and her upbringing there (events that span several years, at least) are skimmed over briskly in the narrative and conveyed not in prose but a series of spare, episodic verses. It is as if the story cannot be told at all in the conventional way, just as Thomas Darko "was never known to have uttered a single Ofo word publicly" (114). Perhaps such sacred cultural knowledge is not intended to be shared, or it must be protected; more cynically, she suggests that there exists no plausible story to tell here at all, that Indiana does die — in a well, or in heartache — at the moment her father deems her worth little more than a ticket fee. What the poems do disclose is a refusal to succumb to any sense of false hope or easy redemption from such a cruel fate. Each piece in this poetic interlude begins with a title and a caption indicating the speaker and the occasion, giving us snapshots of Indiana's departure and her new life in Qualla. The first poem is titled, fittingly, "Trail of Tears," and it is narrated by Oklahoma "grieving" for her lost daughter:

> If I wake again in Eden, I'll say no,
> whisper winter instead of yes,
> save my hope this drought,
> spare my faith this famine.
> If I wake again in Eden,
> I'll not be fooled.
> My eyes are open.
> Snakes know nothing of grace. (2)

On the one hand, Oklahoma acknowledges tacitly here that she has been blinded by her love for Jack, and she vows not to be "fooled" again. At the same time, though, it is her Edenic fantasy — recalling her perception of "Heaven" back in North Carolina — that she is determined not to be "fooled" by again. Uttered in the narrative moment immediately after Indiana's departure, and indeed, taking the place of any narration of the trip or the transition, the poem offers a dismal foreboding of her child's fate, as she simply vanishes from Oklahoma's life and the text, to a place apparently as feckless and untrustworthy as Jack.

The next two poems confirm Oklahoma's sense that a combination of vanity and dollar bills have paved this expressway of ruin: "The Alchemy of Shame" features Jack StandsStraight as he "holds down the fort at the End of the Trail Gift Shop and Trading Post" lamenting his role as "businessman, / bonedigger, / graverobber, / ghoul" (25). Literally, he is selling Indian artifacts to tourists; tacitly, he admits regret for trading his own daughter like a plastic papoose. But why a "bonedigger" and a "graverobber" rather than a killer? In effect, his "business" transaction amounts not to an original sin but a kind of cultural necromancy, as he raises the specter of a child representing the birth of removed and "extinct" Indians (as her namesake heralds), transformed into American national space, and returns her to another region supposedly evacuated of Native traces. It is no mistake that the trinket store is at the "End of the Trail": on the one hand, it signifies that Oklahoma marks both the geographic and cultural "end" of something; more incisively, it borrows the name of an infamous sculpture fashioned by the nineteenth-century artist James Earl Fraser and displayed at the National Cowboy and Western Heritage Museum in Oklahoma City. The piece features an exhausted Indian warrior on horseback, slumped over with his spear facing earthward, an obvious depiction of a once noble but now gloriously vanquished race. When it appeared at the entrance to the 1915 Panama-Pacific International Exposition in San Francisco, California, it was accompanied by a caption explaining that "The drooping, storm-beaten figure of the Indian on the spent pony symbolizes the end of the race which was once a mighty people."[61] The gift shop of mass-produced Indian trinkets is indeed the End of the Trail for Pettigrew's generation, and it is one where Jack StandsStraight himself runs the cash register.

What hope lies back at the beginning of the trail, then, in the Cherokee's ancestral home? The third poem, "Southern Comfort," confirms Oklahoma's despair yet again: it issues from a prayer meeting of women who plead for their men to "come home victorious, / not drunk" (27). Like alcohol or land or money—or any other forms of intoxicating, self-medicating compensation—the return to a place of authenticity and hope, the redemption of the South, will deliver no true "comfort," the title implies. It is merely a drug to feed an emptiness that cannot be quenched or healed. We gather from these bleak snippets of verse that Indiana's life in North Carolina follows much the same course that her mother's did. Like Oklahoma, Indiana falls in love with and marries a too-handsome man (Joe Turner) who ends up abandoning her. We never learn of their courtship directly: significantly, it is only *after* Joe Turner's departure that the narrative reverts back to regular prose (slipping occasionally back into poetry at times during the remainder of the novel); and again, we are left to assume that the details of their romance are in some way ineffable or perhaps entirely fantastical.

When the narrative does pick up, Indiana is left alone, abandoned and pregnant with a daughter whom she will name Manna. When this next girl in the clan grows, she threatens once more to repeat the cycle of loss.

Like the love that awakens Luther Cole to the histories of violence in his collective memory, the botched romances of these women stand for more encompassing and material thefts; and the implication of it all is that the possibilities for true connection, community, and solidarity have been demolished by the petty, self-interested motions of the new American order they inhabit. Indiana tries to instruct her daughter in the "School of Weights and Measures": when young Manna begins to be courted by a dashing Cherokee named Thomas Crow, Indiana worries that he is "too good-looking for his good or Manna's. I know what I'm saying. I had a husband and a daddy that were that kind of handsome, and I don't have to tell everything I know to say what they cost me." In one of the rare mystical turns in the novel, Indiana performs this salvation by actually changing Thomas Crow into a tree; to her daughter, she simply says, "That's what I'm doing, saving you your weight in heartbreak" (73). Like the mother in Masotti's story, Indiana performs an act of evil in order to "save" her daughter from an anguished fate; yet in the zero-sum world of this new accounting, whatever is pawned must be paid for in kind, and whatever weight is "saved" from heartbreak reverts back to the protector.

The lesson, we gather, is cumulative: regardless of place, these Cherokee women have lost the capacity for pure, uncontaminated love in a world that weighs and measures and abuses human bodies; where women are perennial victims in a game of vanity that threatens to intoxicate the tribe's men and displace the very weight and being of the women who love them. Oklahoma was betrayed by Jack's lust for fame and fortune. Indiana's husband, Joe Turner, was destroyed by the Vietnam War, unable to respond humanly to anything upon his return, and realizes too late that fighting for America constitutes the greatest form of irony and hypocrisy, that Indians were compelled to fight and kill "men, children really, who are us only they live in Vietnam and not Oklahoma or Georgia or Alabama or North Carolina. . . . There's no difference between me and the guys I'm killing except they got to keep their long hair" (41). Joe never recovers from what he views as fratricide and suicide, all in the name of American conquest and colonialism, and this precipitates the "vanishing act" that leaves Indiana alone and bereft. Thomas Crow, Manna's young lover, promises to "run right through" and "crush her up" in the same way, much like the Runover and Kill Company in Darko's world. But Manna is too precious for Indiana to let that happen:

she is a beautiful girl with hair "so black that the shock of finding silver in it is like starlight or finding a silver dollar you weren't expecting" (72). In other words, her beauty is pure and unadulterated, and she represents a value antithetical to a world of silver dollars or new pennies or Ivory soap flakes.

Still, it is not purity that Indiana aims to protect but precisely the opposite: she *wants* to find silver dollars and richness wreathing her daughter's body and life. What she rails against so fervently is not the currency of the American Dream itself but the fact that it continually forecloses or exploits the people deemed less worthy, the ones drawn in by the sheen and promise, only to leave their families and their women wanting. What Indiana learns finally from the betrayal of her father and the disappearance of her husband is not to eschew the mechanisms of power and accumulation, but rather to harness them for one's own survival. Otherwise, the "cost" is too great, and the body does suffer its weight in heartbreak and suffering, the devastation of being sold or sacrificed to pay the mounting bills of participation in American life: killing for the national cause, or simply winning a rodeo to "pay the note on the land" and secure the American Dream (15). If Manna is determined to find a man (not "love"), Indiana demurs, "at least get one that's got enough of the American Dream to take care of you. What are you going to be with Thomas Crow? Poor? Wore out? Left?" (73). Indiana's warning is an early version of the "economics of eating" that Manna herself will eventually learn: do what you must to eat and to survive, and worry about love and happiness and fulfillment later. "What you love you will lose" anyway, Indiana warns (75). Once again, the implication is that loneliness and isolation are, like Darko's, their ineluctable fate.

First, Manna must leave home and the South in order to find her own lessons and perspective, only to discover that she cannot outrun her past or her solitude despite the kinship she develops with various Indians along the way — other Cherokees, a Chickasaw, a Lumbee, and a Diné. But no matter how far she roams, the memory of home and the peril of being robbed of her love and spirit haunt her. Significantly, after hitchhiking her way to New Mexico, she ends up in a flophouse where she is brutally raped. As she crouches in the dirty bathroom bleeding onto a towel, the narrative intervenes with a poem called "Practical Wounding" that eerily recalls Oklahoma's "Trail of Tears" elegy:

I went fishing for hope in winter,
Slipped on the ice and fell headlong
Into fists, thunder, broken glass.

The scars on my heart are healing nicely,
    Thin trophies from love bingo.
    I should have stayed at home,
    Eaten hominy.

Shards of heart flavor all my kisses.
They taste of copper pennies spread with jam.
Press hard, find honey in all my bruises. (79)

Love is figured soberly as a game of bingo where winning entails only the slender rewards of slowly healing scars. As her mother warned, she is destined to lose; her splintered heart takes on the complexion of her grandmother Oklahoma before her (a "copper" beauty) and her grandfather Jack (the color of a "new penny"). The devastation of their desires has everything to do with their identity as Indians who "should have stayed at home," not gone in search of fortune or love or a mythical something better. The revelation is an absurd reversal of natural human desire, but it reveals how perversely entangled are the economies of material and emotional satisfaction, and how deprived this family has been of both rewards. Hearts are shattered like pennies, and any kisses she has to give now will taste like metallic coins — in the smallest denomination possible. Moreover, for what seems like the first time, she becomes explicitly aware of the irony of her name: the biblical term for the honeylike substance that God provided the Israelites for their journey in the desert, "manna" oozes from her bruises. An embodiment of both pain and consumption, Manna is defined by the identity that will cause her always to be food for others, liable to be raped and discarded, and never to be satisfied herself. Importantly, "heart," "copper pennies," and the "honey" of manna all serve the same function here: they are gifts, or kisses, for others that spring from Manna's own pain. "I should have stayed at home, / Eaten hominy," she laments; but given the pervasiveness and mobility of her despair, how would staying "home" and eating "hominy" — a particularly Native American form of the southern staple "grits" — have made her fortune any different?

The answer seems to lie in the homonym of "home" and "hominy" — a harmony of sustenance that promises to fulfill, at least in her fit of nostalgia and regret. But can it? When she finally emerges from the bathroom into the now-deserted house, Manna is alone and ravenous. She finds no food, but she does find a different kind of nourishment. Just as Indiana was left alone and pregnant with Manna, the honey for her mother's own wound of abandonment, Manna wakes the morning after her violation to find an abandoned baby, about two years old, standing in the vacant kitchen. "Somebody forgot this little girl, left her by herself in this empty house," Manna thinks. Clearly a stand-in for both Manna and Indiana, and a sign that the reproduction of forgetting will not end, the child "reaches up for Manna, who lifts her from the floor and understands." Manna finds herself paralyzed in a moment of narcissistic reflection, staring into the brown eyes of "a baby, but not exactly"; and the baby calls her "Mama," which is like "Manna" but not exactly (80). Appearing directly after her rape, the child represents the fruit of a horrible violation — again, a comfort and a reward *produced* by the evil itself. Manna's awareness of this supreme impoverishment does not set in until she opens her pocketbook and discovers it is "No use. Some stranger has discovered her money." In a fit of despair, she crashes her make-up compact against the kitchen sink, shattering the mirror and cutting her fingers. She sinks to the floor and "sobs for her heart, for Thomas Crow, and for her mother, whose fault this all is. Tears for the loss of her joy, her stolen stash of money, and the ache between her thighs stream from her eyes, over her cheeks." Breaking the mirror allows Manna the momentary chance to destroy her connection to the blank surrender and solitude she sees in the forsaken child, and yet it — like the theft, the rape, and the betrayal by her parent — is "no use." In the litany of losses she enumerates as she cries, she tacitly equates happiness and family and love with money; the flood of "tears" for it all conjures again the trail of tears, and the ache of losses that simply continue accumulating. "Manna's tears produce no miracles," we are told (82). She wipes her eyes, apologizes to the terrified baby, and sets about finding food to sustain them.

This doggedly practical response to her "Practical Wounding" (which suggests that she is almost wounded, but not quite) is her habit; like Thomas Darko, she simply forges on and works, intent on mere survival. Not surprisingly, the quest for food and nourishment turns explicitly cultural: as Manna and the baby together scrounge for provisions, they find a flyer that leads them to a local powwow where they hope to partake of the feast. All the way there, the baby chews on the paper advertisement; as she ingests bits of the flyer, we understand that she is swallowing a new and unfulfilling form of material consumption — the kind that has infiltrated Native ritual, converting it into performative ads on glossy paper, "the color of weary goldenrods," which will not satisfy the kind of hunger that plagues Manna and the child (83). Sure enough, Manna finds herself again a consumed object within this economy. Like her mother before her, sold away for a rodeo entry, Manna finds herself bought for the "price of a powwow ticket" (95) by a Vietnam veteran in a wheelchair (possibly a double for her own war-wrecked father) who sees her trying to gain entry and sends his nephew, one of the dancers, to pay her admission. Structurally, the event might signal a redemption for the specific trauma that marked her mother's life. But like the boy Pond in Livingston's story reckons, is it finally any better or less dehumanizing to be bought than to be sold? It is the idea of feeling wanted and valuable, perhaps, that makes the evanescent difference.

With seemingly no other options, Manna goes home with Silas Pipe and his nephew, a powwow grass dancer, where they grow comfortable living as an unconventional family, drinking processed drinks like Kool-Aid and watching the Lone Ranger and Tonto on television (as discussed in chapter 2). And sure enough, the baby is eventually taken from her, restored to her real mother, and soon Manna finds herself shuttling back to the reservation in North Carolina. What she takes back home with her is hominy: made into cornbread from a recipe her father had printed on the back of a hardware store receipt, the cornbread that made a black woman from Mississippi cry, and lured a fellow Lumbee, Bill Lawton, into her life and back home with her. The recipe promises to bring fulfillment and nourishment to her family and tribe, but as we already know, it portends only further loss. As a poem late in the book asserts,

> Multitudes of people, crying,
> Asking for manna and pleading for quail,
> Shouting, reaching, pushing, shoving,

> Salt and oil, flour and lard,
> Eating is everything, pass your basket . . . (133)

What Manna offers is greedily sought and devoured by the "multitudes of people" who push and shove their way to what she provides. After her lover Thomas Crow is resurrected and the pair becomes a pop-cultural sensation, an example of "authentic" Indian mysticism, they use their newfound fame and fortune to bring manna to the people in mass-consumer fashion: "Manna uses the money to open up a café, right in the center of downtown Cherokee. 'Bread of Life,' they call it. People come from all over the world for Manna's cornbread. . . . Of course, Manna doesn't do the actual baking. Famous people, like athletes and television personalities, send for special orders" (134).

Being deeply distanced from their heritage, from the very hominy that signifies home, tells us perhaps that one really can't go home again, even when all appearances—and magical resurrections—suggest the contrary. What seems to doom Manna and her "Bread of Life" is the fact that it was recorded by her vanished father on the back of a hardware store receipt; and in this world, what carpenters like Bill Lawton create are dazzling constructions, mystical acts of necromancy, and what bakers like Manna produce are gimmicks and brands. On the one hand, this represents Pettigrew's condemnation of the commodity fetishism that has suffused all our hope and life, where our lovers are ghosts and our nourishment is false. More potently, though, she decries that such trades have evacuated even (and especially) Cherokee, North Carolina, where actors perform historical pageants in full regalia that Eastern Cherokees never actually wore, much as Thomas Darko donned a war bonnet to play a Plains Indian simply because he needed the money. In such spaces, the illusion of genealogical continuity is simply a costly delusion: when Manna becomes pregnant with a son, what different or better fate will his birth herald? We are given no reason to believe that gender politics are finally the point here, and even if they were, a male child would hardly announce the liberation of a chain of bereft women. Instead, like so many Native southerners, Pettigrew quietly reveals what lies hidden under the glossy veneer of success, the dazzle of performance, and the hope of new life, love, and family: the "end of the trail" all over again.

"I Need It for Myself": Owning Self and Culture

The terrible trades suggested throughout all of these narratives remind us again and again of the fragility of culture and community under the debilitating codes and priorities of contemporary capitalist America. What looks like prosperity and propagation in the end can only feebly counteract the relentlessly vacant, isolating, and alienating conditions that have deeply wounded and altered those who must fight harder than ever to maintain communal visibility and sustenance in the removed spaces of the contemporary South. What we are left with, and what we need to be wary of accepting at face value, are the hopeful and forceful reconstructions of culture in spaces irrevocably ravaged by the multiple removals and sacrifices of colonial eviction, segregation, and advanced capitalist competition. It is just such a space — a lonely, insular, private, and narcissistic construction of tribal endurance — that haunts Alabama Cherokee writer Jerry Ellis's travelogue *Walking the Trail* (1991).[62] The book documents Ellis's efforts to retrace the Trail of Tears on foot, hoping to revive historical memory and decode the contemporary legacies of colonial loss and capitalist overdevelopment all at once. Ellis is not the first American Indian to undertake this symbolic voyage, and certainly he won't be the last.[63] What is unique about his trip is the direction of his route: an Alabama native, Ellis doesn't simply reenact the journey; he reverses it. "Rather than follow the original Trail from Alabama to Oklahoma," he decides, "I'll walk from Oklahoma to Alabama as if I were freed to return to my roots, a luxury taken from the Cherokee" (6). Along the way, Ellis reveals much more than he probably intends about the kind of "luxury" his contemporary freedom affords him: an ability to explore and own identity in ways that borrow more from the self-enclosed individualism of modern capitalist principles than the obscure teachings of his Cherokee ancestors.

Ellis makes clear that his journey represents a way to reconnect with his indigenous identity: "I long to know more about the man I am, where I came from, and where I am going" (6). Spoken by an Alabama resident journeying to the diaspora, this admission signals subtly that roots, home, and identity do not always cohere in obvious and sustaining ways for the Indians who clung to their native soil, but rather it is something he must leave the region to go in search of. This is also one of the first hints we get that this journey is for personal gain at least as much as it is a way to honor his ancestors; later, he admits that the quest is "not only for them" but also "I need it for myself. It'll give me a chance to do some soul-searching" (64). It's not long before we discover that in this twentieth-century landscape, such self-rewarding motivations—with acute emphasis on the mutable notion of "reward"—may in fact be far more primary and urgent than the latter.

At the start of Ellis's trip, he is guided by the assumption that the walk—and, by extension, the deliberate immersion in Cherokee history and spirituality—will release him from the unsavory aspects of contemporary capitalist coercion. Despite his general clarity about capitalism's pervasiveness and its perversions, Ellis himself often seems swept away by the romantic possibility of a largely uncontaminated indigenous way. Indeed, his retreat into culture and onto the trail are prompted by this search; after a brief stint in Los Angeles trying to make it as a screenwriter, he is told that "anything that was spiritual didn't make money in Hollywood." In other words, his Cherokee-infused tales didn't sell, and so, "I knew the time had come to declare my values or possibly get lost in a game I was starting to play and hated. Just what it was doing to my soul and self-image anyone with eyes half-opened could see. Anyway, I packed up and moved back home, back to the mountains of the old Cherokee Nation. That it took two years before I found the nerve to begin the walk only says, rather sadly, that I was more a prisoner than I realized" (220). Both the return to "the old Cherokee Nation" and the walk are symbolic attempts to purge the profit-mongering element from his soul and self-image. In both cases, indigenous history and identity serve as antidotes to the cruel, corrosive world, "feeding and healing" his evacuated soul (220).

On the trail, he marvels, "I have no time clock to rattle a ball and chain by day and I have no alarm clock to darken my nights with dread. I have no boss looking over my shoulder and no fellow workers to step around. I have no wife to explain myself to and no bill collectors at my door. I'm in my element doing what I do best, feeling *free*" (42; emphasis added). This kind of freedom resembles a "dream come true" because it stands in such stark contrast to the lived reality of working-class America, where time clocks and shift bosses rule the day and one's psyche. Having sold most of what he owned to fund the trip, Ellis purchases himself freedom not just from the daily grind but from the emotional weight of such a life—the "dread" and despair of being chained to necessity and labor. The urge and the euphoria here are sympathetic; but his thoughts take a dark turn when part of his "dream" involves having "no wife" to answer to. For a man whose carnal needs are alive and well, who longs repeatedly throughout the narrative for a good woman to bed down with every night, the statement seems contradictory. But it's not exactly: as we have already seen repeatedly in this chapter, part of the effect of living under the thumb of capitalist dread involves the rearing of a hungry, self-enclosed interiority, a delimited desire that is more about immediate satisfaction of one's needs than nourishing relationships and familial bonds.

What is most disturbing about all this is that as much as Ellis celebrates his freedom from the mechanisms and the people who would make demands on his time and his soul, he shows us — unwittingly, I think — that "freedom" is just another word for the illusory agency of capitalism. Slaves learned this in the decades and generations following emancipation and Reconstruction, when sharecropping and tenant farming reproduced in barely distinguishable forms the conditions and exploitations of slavery in the South. Ellis confronts the prison of subjection, too, in the heady freedom of his walk; yet the recognitions come too deeply embedded in his own narcissistic reveries and the same old structures of capitalist feeling to provide him any unencumbered, critical distance for reflection. Soon after announcing his freedom from the laws of work and money, Ellis employs a curious fiscal metaphor to describe his pure physical satisfaction. Free from the sweat of labor, he declares that he enjoys instead the perspiration of this sustained athletic endeavor: "If I could sell my sweat by the cupful, I'd be a rich man." Such a moment could seem offhandedly cliché, and in a way it is; but the sweat pointedly signifies more to him than simple perspiration. As the wetness rolls down to his mouth, he tastes the salt and "past lovers come to mind. How *they* tasted. How they used their tongues. How drops of sweat dripped from my face onto their lips and breasts." In this tangle of positions and personae, what is primary is his own sweat — his own taste reminds him of the taste of others, but even in those memories his own perspiration is dripping *onto* the women, infusing them with his own substance. In this reverie, at once a nostalgic daydream and a sensuous, self-satisfied moment of physical exertion, he is so tangled in his own narcissism that he becomes oblivious to the irony of his outlook: he has merely replaced the currency of his prewalk prison with a self-absorbed, self-enclosed fantasy of consumption, a delirious appreciation of his own body's "richness." When he pauses to replenish himself, his introspection grows even more markedly erotic: "I had forgotten just how wonderful water can be. I pause a few seconds between mouthfuls to feel the cool run down my throat and let anticipation build for the next drink. I get lost, however, in the sensations and drink almost all the water before I realize it" (43). The heady, self-gratifying sensations of his own substance and the fevered appreciation of being in a natural state overcome him and he devours greedily. In fact, he *over*-consumes — the inevitable effect of a lifetime of deprivation under economies of exclusion and marginality. Such incidents would not seem so distressing and ripe for overreading if we weren't so vividly aware of his aching loneliness and the blinding solipsism that so often attend him throughout the book.

Indeed, his need for individual "human contact" and bodily pleasures throughout the narrative is intense and sometimes uninhibitedly revealing, as when in several remarkable instances he drools loudly and lasciviously over attractive women, generally much younger than his middle-aged self. Transfixed by all the "surrounding young ladies" at a Christian college, he becomes "a bit paranoid" that they might have "an erection detector or a lust meter" and decides, "I've just got to deal with my passion like a real man; I'll suppress it and try to carry on a serious conversation" (69). These excessive moments are only partially self-deprecating and unconvincingly facetious, making him seem more like an ogling teenager than the "real man" he sheepishly impersonates. More importantly (and perhaps in a way that explains their extremity), these effusions stand in hyperbolic counterthrust to the signs of inhuman, unfeeling distance and anonymity that plague him, his culture, and seemingly the entire South. Indeed, his loneliness reflects not just the forlorn Indian hidden behind the mask, he implies, but the whole region — once colorful, sensuous, alive, and fecund, and now deathly homogeneous and anonymous. "Progress" came along and demolished the corner stores and meeting spots, replacing them with Walmart, Kmart, McDonald's, Burger King. Surveying his modernized Appalachian village, he comments in a somewhat antic, exaggerated drawl, "We even got cable TV halfway up the mountains. Yes sir, it's a wonderful Age. Every Southern town is starting to look just like the next one. Best of all, the heart surgery is painless, so they say" (9). Ellis's final remark here is cryptic, and he doesn't pause to explain before he moves on — literally, as these are the thoughts he recalls having just before leaving his cabin to begin his journey. Does the ref-

erence to "heart surgery" imply that fast food French fries will clog your
arteries? Or that industrial advances take their toll on our bodies as well
as the landscape? Or is he simply suggesting, somewhat more philosophi-
cally, that this crude "Age" — capital A to signify the seismic caliber of this
climate and psyche-altering epoch — robs the heart and soul from our existence as human beings, leaving us with diseased valves that require salvation from the very world of progress and advance that has injured it in the
first place? If we take for evidence the rest of the book, and Ellis's occasionally heart-wrenching search for human contact and resuscitation throughout, then it seems decidedly the latter — a walk that functions as heart
surgery of sorts, but one that must necessarily be modern in order to be
effective.

So Ellis's project is a formidable one: to access somehow the secrets and
heart and human core of late-twentieth-century America along the trail, both
Indian and non-Indian, while battling the divisiveness and despair already
in his own heart and rampant in the communities he visits. It is important,
then, that Ellis makes little distinction between the demise of the southern
heart and the Cherokee one under the forces of commerce; in fact, this bitter
reverie of progress and consumerism follows immediately in the text after an
arrowhead-inspired lament: poring over a cache of Indian artifacts he found
near his Alabama cabin, Ellis thinks, "It isn't easy to accept that I will become dust just like those who made them" (8–9). Again, while his statement
seems at first a fairly typical anxiety about human mortality, such moments
inevitably come packaged within larger, ambient laments about the dissolution of both Cherokee and southern cultures more broadly. Those arrowheads
compel him to resist his inevitable dissolution into dust, seeking visibility
and acclamation particularly in the South where his indigeneity makes him a
living specimen usually considered a relic along with those buried artifacts.
Accordingly, then, both the walk itself and the critique of rampant consumerism that occupies him along the way seem tangled in his dual (Cherokee-
southern) identities, and deeply submerged in his flesh and love-hungry soul.
Such a web of impulses and references tells us that capitalist proclivities are
not easily shaken, no matter how much he desires otherwise, and that they
have colonized the southern landscape and the Cherokee heart in distressingly analogous ways. Seeing their plight in coterminous context is vital:
rather than pathologize the Native or non-Native souths for its reaction to

systemic exclusion and deprivation, we need to begin seeing those responses in uncanny and sweeping concert both within and well beyond the region.

Indeed, it is becoming a global phenomenon of sorts to respond privately and self-protectively to a steady diet of deprivation and exhaustion. While Ellis misses and craves human contact in a supremely natural way, this impulse is secondary to his broader desire for autonomy and exclusivity. While Ellis is not nearly this introspective about his needs, he does seem at least tacitly aware that the allure of the dollar has thoroughly colonized and isolated the people he meets all along the trail, including the Cherokees he encounters. For many, economics overwhelms everything, and class becomes a much more potent marker of identity than ethnicity. Early on in his walk, while still in Tahlequah, Oklahoma, Ellis meets a fellow Cherokee, a bartender named James who recalls growing up poor and without government assistance; as a result, he recalls, "I wasn't so much aware of being an Indian when I was a boy as I was of being poor" (31). While the inseparability of the two conditions is obvious to the reader (and perhaps to James himself, although he gives no such indication), what is striking is the degree to which economic struggle completely overwhelms the man's self-awareness. "Of course," he reflects, "all that was a long time ago. Now things are much different. I can't complain about business." One combats economic shame, of course, by seeking a better, lucrative life, as James proudly demonstrates. His "long time ago" impoverishment might indicate forty, fifty, sixty years — but Ellis tells us that James is just "around thirty." How much can have changed in his short lifetime? Certainly not the larger struggle of the Cherokee for resources, visibility, and solvency, which continues unabated for most tribal communities. The only thing that has changed, it seems — despite the inclusive implications of his locution — is James's own state of being. He has bought a bar, which is fairly successful, and it seems to promote his assumption that "things are different" now, at least for him.

The luxury of financial comfort does not bring him closer to his culture; rather, his connections to tribal tradition deteriorate further. When Ellis asks James whether he's going to the powwow that weekend, James replies that he never goes to "those things." He explains, "They're like car clubs. Either you're into them or you're not. I got my own powwow here. I got a business to run" (31). The ease with which he compares the "powwow" to both a "business" and "car club" makes culture uncannily analogous to commerce and fashion; moreover, he casts such activities as external, fleeting things, choices to be made rather than the integral rituals of a culture. Immediately after James finishes speaking, Ellis tacitly endorses the young man's position: "I'm comfortable with James. I like his straightforward manner" (31). On the one hand, James's statement *is* refreshingly "straightforward"; he acknowledges that the reality of contemporary American Indian identity can often be one of performance rather than substance, and that many Natives have opted instead for a more openly "Americanized" culture. And yet, it is the implicit yoking of such choices to the inherently choice-*less* condition of economic struggle that makes the erosion of cultural "authenticity" so much more painful. The slow decline of one's traditional folkways is not in itself a cause for alarm; it happens as a matter of course in the process of change and evolution. But when those cultures have been usurped and overwritten against one's desire or control, and when "Americanization" entails a totalizing consumerization and evacuation, then we have ample reason to worry.

Ellis meets another, older Cherokee along the trail who explicitly criticizes the commercialization of indigenous culture, particularly as it impacts the literal health of the community. As he explains it, there is a whole new breed of Indians who practice traditional medicine for money, making it difficult for those who simply *"do medicine"* in the old way and without regard for profit; the culture peddler is "in great demand" among mainstream Americans, while the latter types endeavor actually to "help people" (36). The distinction is a felt and sympathetic one, until we learn a few pages later of the same man's hypocrisy: he is about to compensate a medicine man for performing a "secret ritual" by giving him "a twist of tobacco and two and one half yards of cloth, along with some good old American cash" (41). Ellis reports this with a distinctly wry tone, as if he is well aware of the irony, or at least of the eventual compromise: when one lives in America, "good old American cash" necessarily interferes with even the most sacred social rituals and exchanges. The principle of bartering is still at work, but it seems increasingly clear that standard U.S. currency is the most useful and coveted payment of all. The old Cherokee man nonetheless clings to the hope that things might be different, that "helping people" rather than exploiting them might still be a value construed in a system apart from capitalism.

Ellis harbors this fantasy, too, but not very successfully. Despite his conviction that abandoning the diurnal workaday sphere will help him recover his own true "value" and the plummeting worth of his culture, he struggles to achieve such transcendence in a world that is thoroughly "tainted" (111). On the one hand, he longs for immersion in the natural world — evinced, as we have seen, in his more-than-physical thirst for the simple, "wonderful" water than he can't stop drinking. But while he guzzles bottled water erotically, he stops short of drinking from a spring where he worries there may be "pesticides and bacteria" (82). In one telling moment, he has a brief "conversation" with a crow using his pocket crow caller. The bird answers, and Ellis remarks with glee: "It may not be a telegram from American Sweepstakes, but, hey, it's contact with another living creature, and I'm not so sure that birds aren't worth more than money" (55). The ecstatic moment again expresses Ellis's certainty that "contact" with other creatures will redeem him from the meaningless, soulless existence he's been living. And while this statement is meant patently to assert the alternative value of such encounters, he executes the affirmation badly in an awkward rush of litotes: being "not so sure" that birds "aren't worth more" than customary currency is a contorted way of making — and unwittingly enfeebling — his point.

Throughout Ellis's journey, the reminders of industry run amok make it difficult to get down to the essence of things, to find real spiritual value amid the clutter and contamination of modern life. While he persists in hunting those vestiges, we grow increasingly dubious that even he believes he will succeed. As he lumbers along the early steps of the return trail, he is vividly aware of himself as a walking symbol, passed briskly and ignored by motorists "as if I'm a sign saying SPEED UP" (23). On the one hand, this moment reads heavily as a critique of modern American "progress" and velocity juxtaposed against the loping, reluctant, antimodern Indian. But at the same time, Ellis seems tacitly aware of this false dichotomy by emphasizing its existence as a "sign," a flat, unreal, mass-produced message heralding civic hegemony — these things with which we silently cooperate in order to keep our ideas of society and ourselves running smoothly, and one with which he resists complete identification. But behind the sign, especially that of the American Indian who serves as just such a silent placeholder and foil for American values and progress, what is there? Ellis's ruminations don't go quite this far, but in another moment he does, perhaps subliminally, express his frustration over the distraction of veneers and masks, even and especially within Native culture: passing through a small Oklahoma town, a waitress asks if he's in town for the Cherokee National Holiday festivities. To himself, he answers, "The dancing and bow-shooting events intrigue me. But it's one-on-one human contact I seek. I want to hear secrets and see emotions. I'm tired of masks, especially my own" (29). Rejecting the group activities in favor of "one-on-one" interaction, Ellis tacitly chooses self-gratification over tribal celebration; and yet what he's rejecting is not community celebration or solidarity per se but rather the "masks" that go along with it, the opaque veneer of cultural performance and traditional pageantry. What he craves is understandably something more intimate and individual, something truer to the "secret" life of his own culture. This admission happens as internal monologue, though, and we never hear what he tells the waitress; we can probably infer that he lies politely, with his "mask" of civility on.

Indeed, while Ellis's hunger for spiritual sustenance drives his quest, we see repeatedly that such retreats conjure a lost world grown achingly remote, supplanted by a cruel order that inspires such nostalgia. In Arkansas, he meets an Apache named Ben Conway who complains, "There's too much greed and violence [in the world today]. Money, money, money . . . man is out of step with where he came from" (99). Their implied understanding is that the white world has introduced this state of greed and violence along with the advent of colonialism on the continent; while this is in many ways true, it is also a dangerous oversimplification that implies that the precolonial indigenous world featured no such ill elements. Ben's wife, a Cherokee, gives voice to this hyperbole: "Indians didn't used to cry, she says. Did you know that? Well, they didn't. The white man taught 'em how to cry. They pushed 'em and kicked 'em till they had to learn tears" (99). She ends her outburst by politely offering Ellis an Oreo cookie. The problem with such moments is that — once again — they help perpetuate a false dichotomy between Indian and non-Indian cultures, rendering the latter the purveyors of ultimate injustice and greed and the former hapless, innocent victims of a foreign economy. While there is no way to dampen the impact of colonial crimes on native soil, there is also little that is productive about claiming the existence of, or promise of a return to, an uncorrupted, precontact innocence. Such presumptions are in large part what makes indigenous culture so attractive to outsiders, and especially to southerners who hunger for a more profitable existence under capitalism — often disguised as a desire to opt out altogether. What Ellis shows repeatedly, if not consciously, is the irrefutable condition of now — the hegemony of acquisition that we all operate under and can hope to evade only in these fervent, culturally centered ways.

Near the end of his walk, Ellis passes by a prison yard and attempts to explain his curious undertaking to the security guard patrolling the property:

> This was an old Indian route, I say. I'm walking it to see what folks are like along it today.
>
> I can see in his eyes that this just doesn't make any sense in today's world. I try to connect it to something he can relate to.
>
> It's my job, I say. I'm a writer working on a book.
>
> Who do you work for? he says, his investigative eyes drilling me with the third degree.
>
> I free-lance, I say. No one hired me for this.
>
> You mean you're walking for *nothing*? he says. (185)

The only way for Ellis to make his project explicable is to cast it in terms of work and profit, still the ruling ideologies of the world; the prison itself must have struck him as a fitting reminder of his own precarious state of "freedom" on the trail, as his exhilarating "freelancing" nonetheless leaves him constantly aware of his dwindling assets. As it did for Hobson's Darko, the jailyard serves as a reminder that this is the world he will inevitably return to, one that imprisons with its logic of profit and loss, an economy outside of which few alternatives and freedoms are intelligible. When the guard asks incredulously whether (and why) he is walking *"for nothing,"* he radically unsettles Ellis's conviction that his walk might have use value beyond the material economy that rules our choices and our minds. And we wonder, along with Ellis, whether the entire walk will be, in the end, "for nothing."

Certainly, he has achieved one of his goals, which was to make the public tune in and remember the trail, for a few sound-bites anyway. Local newspapers and television outlets carry his story all along the route. But his more personal objectives — to declare his "values," to slow down, to reconnect with his heritage — seem considerably harder to attain, precisely because they consistently betray their individual, narcissistic import. We do get a sense of just how self-serving the walk is when, somewhere in Missouri, he decides, "If the walk ends right now, it is a success. In this Modern World which goes a thousand miles an hour, I'm finally catching up with myself" (165). The profession is puzzling — he's only in Missouri! — until we realize that the walk is less a historical re-creation and ceremony than it is a retreat into a usable past for the convalescence of his own soul. Or perhaps he has already seen enough of the corrosive effects of postmodern industry, making his geography of hope an internal map rather than a historical trail. How, then, given the disarming precedents and the despair he experiences along the way, can he maintain that ecstasy of self-possession, "these rare feelings that take me to a higher plane"? The question is mainly rhetorical, as he has already gathered enough evidence at this point to know that the "higher plane" is largely a hallucination with little purchase in a world dominated by what he calls "the Great Machine grinding away as it opens its monstrous mouth in the shopping centers and on oil slicks . . . [and] between those giant teeth . . . people dangling with Visas and Mastercards" (200).

Jerry Ellis's reverse walk along the Trail of Tears ultimately showcases his failed attempt to recover the soul of Cherokee tradition, history, and community undone by the bulldozer of American colonial-capitalism. In the end, his journey provides less a spiritual refinancing than a sober affirmation of survival in the South, as both a Cherokee and a southerner. This realization forces him to confront gravely the dominant, overriding, unifying element of the southern condition: that reliance on "good old American cash" that overwhelms and binds us all together. As his energy wanes and his homesickness mounts, Ellis meets a fellow walker on the trail who reports that he's bound for California in search of gold. Without acknowledging the eerie colonial implications of this pursuit for both southerners and Indians — particularly when a primary motivation for evicting the Cherokee from Georgia was the discovery of gold on Indian land in the state — Ellis instead merely watches the man go on his way. Rather than reflect on the somber irony of the coincidence or its bleak implications of a disturbingly repetitive history, Ellis simply regrets missing out on the treasure hunt: "[I wished] I had given him my address to keep me informed about the gold strike. After all, a fellow walker might want to share his empire. Shoot, I missed the boat again."[64] The sudden colloquialism of his lament ("Shoot") merged with the language of conquest evokes the *southern* claim of dispossession and loss of "empire" more distinctly than the Native one. The "boat" of enrichment and empire is one that southerners simply keep missing together; and in the deepening stratifications of global capitalism, more passengers than ever are being left behind.

Near the end of Ellis's travelogue, he wanders into a truck stop in the Ozarks, where a white trucker overhears Ellis mention his Alabama home. "I'm from Alabama myself," he informs Ellis, who peruses the man and thinks, "He may be as redneck as I am on a bad day, but his hand eases forward with the grace of a gentleman wearing a white glove. Fingers open to a rolled bill." Ellis participates fully in the mystification of class here, by elevating the "redneck" trucker to the status of "gentleman" simply because his attitude toward money suggests one of subtle grace and goodwill rather than parsimony. Dutifully, Ellis refuses the money; and in expected fashion, the trucker wonders why "one Southerner can't help another? Hell, son, it ain't charity. It's a contribution." Ellis takes the "contribution," deciding inwardly that "I need the money this good old boy holds." In the next moment, though, he justifies the gift: "I don't take it for myself, though I can be as greedy as the next guy, as much as I do to honor the look in his eyes." The moment is almost too revealing, as Ellis betrays his own, not atypical tendency toward greed — the underbelly of both gentlemen's relations and rednecks' insecurities; and yet he also uses the weighty word *honor* — as in, "honor my ancestors" — to describe the transaction between southerners.

This fraternity of the dispossessed is neither intuitive nor immediately desirable, of course; but Ellis recognizes it as a primal connection that always haunts him and must finally be recognized. The bond is not forged effortlessly, he admits: "I've had a love-hate relationship with Alabama since I was seventeen and ran away one summer to get out from under the tobacco juice, grits, racism, and my own lack of understanding and tolerance. I can't say I'd kiss every cheek in the state today. But whether I like it or not, and I do, I always feel a bond with another soul from Dixie when I'm hundreds of miles from home" (142). Most striking here is not just the sense of being discriminated against as a racial minority but, in fact, the way in which an environment of prejudice tends to breed more of the same; in the end, Ellis runs from his "own lack of understanding and tolerance" as much as others'. Equally disturbing is the sense that the "bond" he feels with a fellow southerner is a distinctly financial one. Provoked by a sense of homelessness and diaspora — precisely the condition of the Cherokee whose trail he walks — Ellis feels more like a southerner than ever. The mode of this recognition is decidedly compensatory and perversely communal, as the roll of bills changes hands between the white trucker and the Native Alabamian.

The gesture of goodwill seems momentarily to transcend racial difference, but the white man's very effort to distinguish between "charity" and a "contribution" reminds us of how baldly financial transactions can sketch and maintain power relations beneath the veneer of social graces and semantics. Ellis's parting comment both reaffirms their kinship at the same time that it reminds us of the immeasurable gulf between these men and their aspirations: "When you get back to Alabama," he tells the trucker, "tell 'em I'm coming. I may be crawling when I get there, but I'm on the way" (142).

In the end, then, Ellis's narrative is at least as much about a southern homecoming as it is an Indian one, to the convergences as well as the impassable gulf between those experiences and identities. Ultimately, his story bears vivid witness to the dogged experience of industrial-capitalist subjection that suffuses the entire region with a kinship both distinctly material and intractably unequal. While he attempts to keep alive the specter of a precious, lost Cherokee past as a way to recover a more fulfilling spiritual existence, he instead reveals to us the most unsettling truth of being Cherokee in contemporary America: the popular stereotypes and the cultural compromises are often more potent and accessible than the past, which comes shrouded in unprofitable myth and inaccessible wonder. Indeed, one of the most striking aspects of Ellis's narrative is that while he walks along and in honor of the original Trail of Tears, references to the actual Removal are infrequent and vague at best. The effect is at once arresting and sobering: we are reminded by absence of a history so remote and a culture so devastated as to be virtually unrecoverable, replaced by a landscape of Walmarts and Mastercards where southerners from opposite sides of the ethnic divide have cause to shake hands and exchange dollar bills in proxy for souls. Indeed, Ellis's experience along the modern-day trail witnesses an America whose conversion to an economy of human exploitation has become so complete as to be ordinary. In a narrative almost completely devoid of actual historical reminiscences, Ellis seems to be turning our attention instead to the legacies of what that uniquely American spirit of settlement and exploitation has wrought on subsequent, scattered, searching generations that both rebuild and retreat under the dazzling gifts, thefts, and horrors of advanced capitalism.

CHAPTER FOUR

EXCAVATING THE WORLD

Unearthing the Past and Finding the Future on Southern Soil

> We live in a world full of buried things, many of them very painful
> and often horrific . . . and until we acknowledge and come to terms
> with the past we'll keep believing in a dangerous and deadly kind of
> innocence, and we'll keep thinking we can just move on and leave it
> all behind.
>
> —Louis Owens, conversation with John Purdy

> Familiar and strange, old and new, the American South can make it
> seem as if you are always traveling, always exploring, even when you
> are driving distance from your home.
>
> —Belle Boggs, *Southern Living* magazine (January 2011)

> This is history: that every world grows smaller.
>
> —Janet McAdams, "The Polar Journeys" (2007)

What we have seen so far in *Reconstructing the Native South* are the shadows
of a shared history, yet under a common economy of exclusion and erasure,
the result has been antagonism and separatism more often than solidarity.
To produce a meaningful new appraisal of community, both southern and
Native, requires us to deal soberly with the losses and thefts of contact as
well as its bequests. And increasingly throughout these narratives, southeastern Indians have posed the unparalleled gift and promise of choice—to
elect survival over extinction, affiliation over isolation, and cohesion over
fragmentation. These choices are neither simple nor unfettered, and they of-

ten entail finding common ground in places where we have historically feared to tread.

Just what these choices consider and entail in an intrinsically interwoven South are as difficult as they are imperative in awakening us to the deepening struggles of the broader global community. Globalization theory has emerged as the next wave in postcolonial studies, emphasizing the imbrication of cultures and the cosmopolitanism once typical of the metropole and now characterizing formerly isolated geographies like the South and Indian country.[1] Indeed, perhaps the greatest paradox of our time is the way that the world seems to be expanding and contracting all at once. In ways unprecedented in human history, the vastness of the globe is accessible for travel and consumption, people crisscross the earth in restless and constant mobility, and every major metropolis begins to resemble each other's multicultural diversity and skyscraper majesty. At the same time, and not accidentally, the local becomes a more freighted category of identity and belonging, partly because the monotony of globalization makes the formerly strange seem ultimately familiar and parochial. Any place could feel like home; and yet, for many, only one place can truly *be* home. That tension adheres powerfully in southern and Native spaces, where protecting the boundaries and the distinctiveness of individual communities means warding off the totalizing, obliterating forces of global capitalism. As Jerry Ellis and the trucker meet and diverge in a delicate dance of affinity and disavowal at the end of chapter 3, Ellis acknowledges the pull toward home and the difficult embrace with kindred but distinct others — an ambivalence provoked and negotiated by a roll of dollar bills. As our authors repeatedly show, the peoples' struggle against the herculean, sublime enemy of global capitalism is at best a fantasy; the truest kind of sovereignty in our world today belongs to the economic regime that reigns over our bank accounts as well as our languages, cultures, and futures.

Under this sober lens, perhaps the best kind of sovereignty we can hope for is a pragmatic, unified, and regenerative new sense of human community and commonality — one that we choose and define for ourselves. For Native peoples, this iteration of power is not new: Robert Warrior's notion of "intellectual sovereignty" has been applied widely by Native critics, particularly in the service of developing tribal nationalist criticism. On an increasingly global scale, indigenous scholars are engaging in cooperative efforts to liberate and repossess their intellectual traditions and, in the process, recapture the stories long told *about* rather than *by* Native peoples themselves.[2] At their best, such approaches are inclusive and flexible rather than rigidly essentialist or exclusionary; as Sharon Holland suggests, even this supreme gesture of indigenous autonomy must nevertheless be recognized as a vitally conjunctural enterprise fed by multiple influences and actors. Focusing particularly on Afro-Native literatures, Holland stresses "a process of both *emancipation* and *sovereignty*, as we are seeking the history and lives of a people whose experience crossed both the barriers of enslaved bodies and lands."[3] While it may be an unsavory byproduct of protracted colonial processes, the crossing and alteration of multiple communities by and in one another's stories is a reality that needs to be reckoned with. Recognizing the transformative force of this pluralism is something that few studies of southern literature have managed to do; divisiveness and segregation have captured our critical imaginations largely because stories of dreadful racism and acts of cruelty have dominated our historical narratives and emotional sensibilities. Yet the terrible fractures accomplished by such outrages belie the extent to which discrete cultural and racial practices, bloodlines, and experiences have long bled fluidly into one another.

In *Beyond Multiculturalism*, David Hollinger advocates a new "postethnic perspective" that "favors voluntary over involuntary affiliation, balances an appreciation for communities of descent with a determination to make room for new communities, and promotes solidarities of wide scope that incorporate people with different ethnic and racial backgrounds."[4] Perhaps the most productive — if provocative — way to move forward in these similarly segregated communities of thought, discourse, and habits of mind is to turn our gaze and emphasis to a new kind of localism, to choose to see the South that has always been there, one steeped in indigenous culture and character as much as back-country swamp humor or African folklore and rural wit. To do so — to see the South as Native and the Native as South — need not threaten tribal sovereignty as a matter of course. As Stuart Christie has recently argued, pluralism is in fact "the modality . . . through which the contemporary experience — and vitality — of indigenous sovereignty is lived," a position that aims (along with similar efforts by Native critics like Jace Weaver and Chadwick Allen) to forge a workable consensus between tribal nationalist positions on the one hand and assimilationist/constructivist perspectives on the other.[5] Put another way, many contemporary Natives are launching their sovereign projects from positions of inherent hybridity, acknowledging the fallout of long colonial histories that leave little choice but to gather together the pieces of a manifold existence and own and inhabit it fully. Perhaps this is our last best hope for saving not just tribes and regions but humanity altogether from the corrosive pressures and private terrors of global capitalism.

The Archaeology of Hybridity

The most profound revelations about our current state of hybridity come first from the earth and the histories it harbors; put another way, the hybridity of the New South is not a product of contemporary globalization but an ancient fact of existence in a region that has long shared its histories and buried its secrets. As we saw in chapter 1, the repressed Native trauma in the region often resurfaces in the form of violent murder fantasies and revenge narratives that take place in caverns, wells, and mounds. Rather than providing relief, however, these paths into the barren earth yield only the illusion of traditional sustenance or of coeval partnerships; the solutions provided by their authors are too deeply undercut and wounded by the pressures and exclusions of contemporary economic competition and exclusions to be ultimately productive. But we need to return to such excavations here at the end, searching for the other stories and solutions that southern soil offers up. Its first and most fundamental secret is the suppressed reality of Native persistence itself.

Alice Walker's Civil Rights–era novel *Meridian* (1976) centers on a young African American woman (the eponymous Meridian Hill) whose quest for racial justice in Mississippi is persistently destabilized by an incomplete, vacant understanding of herself and her own history.[6] "Something's missing in me! Something's *missing!*" Meridian wonders. "Something the old folks with their hymns and proverbs forgot to put in! What is it? What? What?" (27). As the narrative proceeds, it becomes increasingly clear that what is "missing" may well be an occluded Cherokee heritage; while she never directly acknowledges that this ancestry might explain the sense of absence in her spiritual fabric, the novel provides enough clues to fill in both the genealogical and the regional chart. Yet whether Meridian is Cherokee or not is somewhat beside the point, Walker knows. As a girl named after a ravaged, violent city, Meridian is always already a metonym for a place, and that place has erased the indigenous traces that underlie and complete its topography. Walker makes the erasure literal in an archaeological scene: Meridian's father's farm, allotted to *his* grandfather after emancipation, and yet clearly Indian territory, complete with a Serpent Mound. Meridian remembers a story about her father's grandmother, suggestively named "Feather Mae," who lived on the land and apparently experienced moments of ecstasy on the Indian mound. Meridian feels drawn to Feather Mae's mysticism and herself experiences several moments of transcendence while seated on the mound: "She was a dot, a speck in creation, alone and hidden. She had contact with no other living thing; instead she was surrounded by the dead" (59). This spiritual, out-of-body experience seems the only physical way she can embrace a deeply repressed heritage — *not in her body*. In her daily life as a black woman in the South, her only "tangible connection to the past" and all the buried dead comes in these rare places and moments, ones she experiences briefly only to have snatched away (59). Meridian's father gives away the land that he feels they wrongfully possess.

Indeed, Meridian's father develops an acute empathy for the absent Indians: he plasters his toolshed with settlement maps and photographs of "Indian women and children looking starved and glassy-eyed and doomed" (53), which he gazes at mournfully for hours on end. "That mound is full of dead Indians," he tells his wife. "Our food is made healthy from the iron and calcium from their bones. . . . We were part of it, you know. . . . Their disappearance" (54–55). Prompted not just by compassion but by complicity, Mr. Hill attempts to give back the land to a proxy, an Oklahoma Cherokee named Walter Longknife who happens to wander into the area; but the exchange predictably fails to satisfy his enormous sense of guilt, nor does it do any good for Longknife, who elects to "move on" instead and returns the deed (55). Shortly after, the State of Georgia lays claim to the land, razing its crops and the mound in order to erect "a tourist attraction, a public park. . . . Sacred Serpent Park which, now that it belonged to the public, was of course not open to Colored" (56). All at once, the land serves as a storehouse of regional history and the multiple, amplified, ongoing dispossessions of the South's dispossessed people; and it belongs to the state, seized by the dominant cultural body as a memorial to loss and a celebration of civic order. As Harilaos Stecopoulos has argued, this episode "reminds us that in the modern U.S. South, no response to loss, past or present, can completely escape

Jim Crow. . . . For Meridian's father insists through his compassion for Native Americans that the southland is the site of many lost causes: 'that what had already and forever been lost' was not only antebellum white slaveholding society, but also societies far more crucial to the spiritual and political health of the republic." Indeed, Stecopoulos avers, Walker's novel suggests that "subaltern grief has the capacity to render the South less a touchstone for empire than a potential source of its undoing."[7]

If Walker's novel indeed purveys this message, what good does this "subaltern grief" ultimately do? In these acts of reparation and reclamation, neither the African American nor the Native American figures are able to recover what has been lost; their impoverishment on southern terrain is apparently cyclical and unrelenting. Meridian's connection to her Cherokee past is too remote to be tangible or restorative: with the last name "Hill," this girl named after a city seems destined to identify only with a burial mound and a history that she can never fully inhabit or recover. She spends the rest of the novel slowly trying to disappear: she "valued her body less, attended to it less, because she hated its obstruction" (96–97). She is periodically paralyzed, lets herself be beaten, grows frail, has a baby forcefully ripped from her womb in an abortion without anesthesia, and tries to get rid of all her possessions (114, 31). While Meridian's mother coldly resists her husband's empathy for the Indians and his sentimental desire to return their land, she does in the end voice the cruelest truth in the book: "The answer to everything . . . is we live in America and we're not rich" (56).

While the histories of all those undone, exploited, dispossessed, and discarded by the white South emerge to haunt and undo its tyranny in the late twentieth century, they ultimately hunker back down into the earth again, digging futilely for the riches that have been stolen. In this world, though, what restores and elevates is more concrete than memory: and without access to the material rewards of being "rich" in America, these occluded others seem destined never to be complete or whole. In the short chapter called "Gold" just before the Indian mound episode, Meridian recalls a memory from her youth: "One day when Meridian was seven she found a large chunk of heavy metal. It was so thickly encrusted with dirt that even when she had washed the metal it did not shine through. Yet she knew the metal was there, because it was so heavy. Finally, when she had dried off the water, she took a large file and filed away some of the rust. To her amazement what she had found was a bar of yellow gold. Bullion they called it in the movies" (52). Dirty and encrusted though it is, the gold is something Meridian recognizes and believes in viscerally. A dazzling piece of bullion like one sees "in the movies" comes up out of the earth; elated, she runs inside to show it to her family. One by one, her mother, father, and brothers are "not impressed" (52). She polishes and tends to it for a time, until finally she decides to bury it again "under the magnolia tree that grew in the yard. About once a week she dug it up to look at it. Then she dug it up less and less . . . until finally she forgot to dig it up" (52). Directly preceding the narration of the Serpent Mound in the text, this brief episode serves as a harbinger: even a heavy brick of gold that "could make us rich!" (52) is a sight not to be trusted or believed; eventually, it gets buried and forgotten again under a symbol of the Old South itself, a magnolia tree, because the gold is not meant for them, its allure better "forgotten." How could the excavation of a genealogical and spiritual treasure trove of indigenous ancestry and transcendence prove any more real or fulfilling? What Meridian and her family take away from their glancing connection to the Cherokee past and the glittering brick of gold are not riches per se, but the sober recognition that inestimably precious connections and convergences indissolubly bind and foreclose those who "are not rich" in this land.

Modest though they are, such revelations are critical on the path not to reversing history but to redeeming the future for those who labor to survive under persistently inequitable terms and equations of value. Burial mounds are ubiquitous symbols in Native American literature because they preserve tangibly the bodies and histories of the people who still struggle to find their own gold in the stories the earth harbors. As Annette Trefzer has demonstrated at length in *Disturbing Indians* (2007), literary excavations of such sites correspond with the actual archaeological digs unearthing prehistoric and indigenous pasts throughout the region, especially in New Deal projects of the 1930s. In both the figurative and the literal cases, we see efforts at progress—the preparation of earth for dams and construction, or the modern writer's attempt to capture and narrate a ghostly new century—interrupted repeatedly by the submerged histories that very literally demand to be seen and reckoned with. Increasingly, though, those narratives are converging with a sense of the multiracial expanse of loss and subjection buried by colonial societies that continue to exact and inter its crimes. The most productive of these meditations seem to be the ones with that capacious, forward-looking sweep; they attempt to exhume integrity and solvency in ways that are less private and insular and instead cooperative and pragmatic.

For Karenne Wood, a Virginia Monacan poet, the significance of these excavations has been immense. As director of historical research for her tribe, Wood has been vitally involved in the identification and repatriation of sacred objects and even bodies disinterred from the earth decades earlier and housed in state museums and archives. Working collaboratively with archaeologists, Wood and other Monacan tribe members have played a crucial role in repossessing and remaking the histories long taken and told on their behalf.[8] Throughout her poetry, Wood attests to the enduring significance of locating one's tradition and histories in this profoundly physical way; in doing so, she suggests, modern Indians stand their greatest chance of reconstructing home, identity, and history simultaneously. The titular poem in her 2001 collection *Markings on Earth* remarks on the precious significance of what "little is left us" in these recovered objects, which amount to "nothing really": "Stone / axes, chipped flints, potsherds: we locate our markings on earth. / As the only descendants of a nation . . . / We are left among ruins to save what we can . . . / Weeping for stones we cannot find" (ll. 18, 21–23, 26–27, 31–32). While the poem structures itself around absence and loss, it ends with a signature of hope: "We are safe, for now. The earth and sky remain" (l. 36).

When so little is left, the individual fragments and rare pieces become heavy with meaning because they are immovable components of the place; and from there, the notion of survival — of the people and the earth — can grow. But throughout Wood's work, she is acutely aware that the landscape is only safe "for now," as it suffers the ravages of industrial development, pollution, and greed. In "Oronoco," she tells the story of the tribe's involvement with tobacco cultivation, which seemed at first like "Dark gold . . . / A gift to us, it seemed, this money and land enough for all, until / the earth itself failed us, its richness spent, and the topsoil drifted away" (ll. 3, 9–10). Despite the prayers of the people, the "greed spread like blight, and others / took the money, then the land" (ll. 13–14). Tobacco went south and apple trees were planted in their place, but the people never recovered: "we stood in the orchards at breaktime, smoked our ready- / rolls, coughing a little — we scuffed the ground with our feet when we spoke and did not see each other's eyes" (ll. 16–18). The blight of greed works its way into the people's lungs as surely as it infests the land; and in turn, the people cough rather than speak or breathe freely, and they make new scuffing "markings on earth" to replace the old ones. Above all, the shame of participating in the blight is a force of silence and loneliness: neither poetry nor communion can occur in this environment.

As surely as greed shames and isolates the people, the sweat and struggle of labor is what promises to liberate and rejoin them: and for Wood, the potential for solidarity across racial and ethnic boundaries offers a powerful way to make sense of what the new world has wrought. In "Hard Times," she describes a woman exhausted by generations of hard physical labor and debt; the way Wood paints her, the woman might be an African American sharecropper, gazing at the "fields of rice, cotton, sugarcane, tobacco" in a "printed housedress or sarong / with hair covered or plaited, her face etched / in memories of joy snatched from her / in daylight and auctioned to strangers" (ll. 7, 8–11). Clearly, she selects details that conjure a black woman toiling in southern fields, "auctioned" body and soul to those she labors for; but while the "hard times" of slavery are over, the vestiges of that past continue to bedevil the inheritors of that landscape. The woman has no clear identity because she is identified only by her labor: "Her hands have scrubbed cities of floors, washed / the nameless dead, cooked food for armies, so little of it / hers; hands that failed to protect her or any of her children. / She believes that if she speaks, she might break apart, / the dust of her flying across stooped men / chained by their debt to the fields" (ll. 12–17). Her hands are only as powerful as their accomplishments and failures, and her voice has no place in any of it: anything she utters would send her shattered across the fields where workers in crippled postures are anchored by debt to the land. The woman "will not speak" of the hard times she has endured because, like the choking tobacco, the dust of labor and fear constitutes her very voice; so the poet speaks for her, gives testimony to her endurance in the verses of this poem. Because someone needs to speak for the voiceless, she seems to say, and because the common struggle of these "sisters" of undisclosed races gives her the knowledge and intuition she needs to articulate their story: "The stars that connect us / gather like sisters around her. We hear, *They were hard times*, / across the continuous land of our women, until as sun / rises above the droning flies and the garrulous chickens, / a voice speaks in our old language, which we do not know. / We sift through a history with dust on our hands, / the empty rocker creaking in the breeze" (ll. 19–25). There will be no rest — the rocker is "empty" and the "dust" of history and labor remain — but the women find strength in digging together for a lost language and past that will hold them. In the process, the speaker is able to find a common voice in the "continuous land" where the chatter of stars, animals, and insects will not let them forget or be silent.

For Wood, these connections between women, workers, and the indigenous run consistently throughout her poems, which are rooted firmly in local terrain at the same time that they reach for global resonances and connections. In "Returning," which is dedicated *"after Derek Walcott,"* she invokes the black Caribbean poet in order to narrate the process of reclaiming a past and even a language that you no longer know or understand. Implicitly, she draws on Walcott's notion of the "phantom Africa," much like the postcolonial idea of the phantom limb, to make sense of a cultural aporia: How do you reclaim a land that you cannot remember owning?[9] Wood's poem surveys a Virginia landscape that "You never forget" — the hills, mountains, granite, animals, and even buildings. Midway through the poem, the speaker asks: *"Can you genuinely claim these, / and do they reclaim you?"* (ll. 13–14). At this point, the details shift abruptly from physical features of the landscape to the people with "red-rimmed eyes," "stained hands," "thin voices," "brittle . . . joints" and root cellars filled with carefully stacked and prepared provisions (ll. 14, 15, 16–17). It is "the land you never forget" that claims her explicitly in the end, but it is effectively the collection of work-weary kin and their warehouse of survival supplies that endorse the homecoming: *"yes, they reclaim you in a way you need not understand"* (ll. 22–23).

While the kind of faith that Wood endorses here is as ephemeral as the gold that Meridian finds and places her trust in, the ownership of tradition is potentially more viable because it works in reverse: the land and its people reclaim her, rather than the other way around. What is more, the notion of a broader human community of the oppressed joins her, invited by her opening homage to Walcott; increasingly, the working class and the racially oppressed together become vital allies in the effort to preserve a history that few know or "understand" in the contemporary world. Perhaps one of the most vocal and sentient mouthpieces for this composite indigenous working class is Allison Adelle Hedge Coke, a Cherokee and Huron writer who grew up partly in North Carolina. Like Wood, Hedge Coke also locates in such solidarity the means of shoring up a present wracked by change, greed, and isolation. In *Blood Run* (2006), she recounts her work aiding in the preservation of Indian burial mounds. And most notably in *Off-Season City Pipe*, her 2005 collection of poetry, Hedge Coke makes especially clear just what such recovered historical sites mean to the contemporary workers laboring in the fields of their ancestors.

In "Change: For the Sharecropper I Left Behind in '79," Hedge Coke clearly draws on her experience as a young fieldworker in North Carolina, married to an abusive husband. The details of her failing relationship and her work in an altered and poisonous landscape merge consistently throughout the poem. Early on, the couple labors "simultaneously, / as married to the fields as we were to each other" (ll. 43–44). Yet they are persistently plagued by thirst, racing one another to the jugs of water that leave them unsatisfied; and the chemicals sprayed over the crops assault the young couple with "raw, oozing hives that / covered ninety-eight percent of our bodies" (ll. 17–18). The tobacco they pick, like the dark gold in Wood's memory, is collected and sold to Philip Morris and Winston-Salem, "before the encroachment of / big business in the Reagan era / and the slow murder of method / from a hundred years before" (ll. 95–98). The young couple and their bodies are painful witnesses and casualties of the "slow murder" in their midst, which transforms the work they do as utterly as it assaults their skin. Their marriage suffers, too: after "they came and changed things," she remembers, "you left me for a fancy white girl / and I waited on the land / until you brought her back / in that brand-new white Trans Am, / purchased from our crop" (ll. 127–31). A direct result of the mechanical advances in tobacco processing, the profits from their land go to a "white" Trans Am (its very name implying the "beyond" or "across" an abbreviated *America*) for a "fancy white girl" — nothing for the speaker herself, who waits on the land for the return of her husband and for a love she will never get back. Finally, she leaves him for a place of her own, alone near "empty fields" with "no running water of any kind," and hunts her own meat; as for her ex-husband, she says, "I heard you remarried / and went into automated farming / and kept up with America" (ll. 143, 151, 156–58).

Hedge Coke's speaker goes backward, away from progress and betrayal and movement, in order to find her own stability and peace. In one sense, the solution is a fantasy of escape and reversal. She imagines herself and her husband in a time "Before all of this new age, new way, / I was a sharecropper in Willow Springs, North Carolina / as were you and we were proud to be Tsa la gi / wishing for winter so we could make camp / at Qualla Boundary and the Oconaluftee River / would be free of tourists and filled with snow / . . . home again / with our people" (ll. 110–18). Importantly, that memory of a blissful homecoming "free of tourists" and shame is a composite one: not just Indians but "Europeans, / working now shoulder to shoulder with descendants / of their slaves they brought from Africa. . . . / then the tobacco was sacred to all of us and we / prayed whenever we smoked and did not smoke for pleasure and / I was content and free" (ll. 119–21, 123–26). Those days are gone, and so apparently is the sense of community shared with the other workers, their shoulders differently colored but bent to a common purpose and joined by sacred principles and pleasures. Knowing that such worlds are lost, replaced by the divisions and antagonisms and betrayals of progress and competition, the speaker "turned away, away from the change / and corruption. . . . / Away, so that I could always hold this concise image / of before that time and it / floods my memory" (ll. 165–66, 168–70).

The long blank spaces between words throughout Hedge Coke's poem testifies to the gaping, primal absences and losses that can no longer be recovered or narrated. What quenches and satisfies in the end is the flood of "memory," which preserves as a fossil the "concise" promise of a fullness, harmony, purity, and solidarity that satiate like nothing else. Memory is not always real, we know, and its essence can never be regained. But as Hedge Coke reminds us, it may be the most important thing we can recover from the occluded graves of the southern landscape in order to move forward. Moving on may mean moving "away," as it has for so many southeastern Indians, Hedge Coke included; but it might also entail *returning* with the knowledge that the lessons of the South are multiple and mobile, linking its people to the oppressed across the nation and the globe. "Memory is what compels us to act in the world," Hedge Coke explains in her memoir, *Rock, Ghost, Willow, Deer* (2004). "And congenital memory, that of belonging by nature to landscapes, runs the deepest of all the rivers of the earth" (xiv). What these vibrant new poets in the New Native South uncover is a memory that runs deep and long in the land, one that cuts new channels, which might carry us together, out and away from its betrayals without ever leaving home.

Let That Other Story Go: Going Global, Going Feral

The Cherokee-Appalachian poet Marilou Awiakta, raised on the atomic frontier in Oak Ridge, Tennessee, has spent several decades attempting to convince readers that the power of such rooted, multivocal representation is the best weapon we have in a world of poisonous essentialisms, competitive antagonisms, and the very real and feasible threat of nuclear annihilation. She refers commonly to what she deems her "three heritages: Cherokee, Appalachian, and scientific"; all three contribute vitally to both her identity and her work, which draws its power from her ability to harmonize her multiple affiliations. In her best-known work *Selu*, a smooth amalgamation of nonfiction essays and poetry, Awiakta's indomitable optimism is a force to be reckoned with, as she embraces the possibilities of hybridity, inclusion, and truly cross-cultural relationships with unquestioning good faith. The result is not, as many might fear, an evasion of history but in fact a courageous confrontation with it. The contemporary insistence on boundaried essentialisms, however well intentioned or politically obligatory, are not stolen rights but colonial fictions. That revelation comes easy and often (if not painlessly) in the vitally imbricated world of the South — a true "hybrid mess" in all the ways Womack fears, but an essential and an accurate mess it is, and one we need to own. Peering further beyond the borders of the South, to other regions of the United States and to other nations entirely, offers a still more vital perspective on the continuities of colonial and capital processes, ones magnified by the South's particular histories but by no means exceptional to it.

Awiakta's awakening to such connections happens when she is living in Léon, France, where her husband in stationed at a reconnaissance Air Force base. While there, Awiakta works as a translator and social liaison officer on behalf of the U.S. military during the NATO withdrawal. Quickly, she feels at home: "The French spoke in images. They were realists. And their concept of time was familiar, too: the past informing the present, influencing the future. They burnished the raw edges of life with their sense of ceremony, style, art and ironic humor. Appalachian mountain people think this way, the Cherokee, the Europeans (primarily Celts) and the Africans, who came much later." They fondly remember Benjamin Franklin as a "philosopher in a coonskin hat! *Formidable!*," which prompts Awiakta to recall how "In the same century, many French in the American South came to know the Cherokee leader and master diplomat, Attakullakulla . . . [whose] wily diplomacy, especially in negotiating treaties, is still legendary" (31). What seems most important about her French peers is not their kindredness, but rather the way they prompt her to take pride in her multiple heritages and neighbors: both Franklin and Attakullakulla, and the Cherokee as well as the European and African. Indeed, she reflects that "Living in France made me think deeply about who I was, about the value of my heritage, and about the necessity of working out harmonies with peoples from different cultures. By the time I returned to America, I knew that I was a Cherokee/Appalachian poet. I was determined to sing my song" (31). These "harmonies" don't simply happen naturally or of their own accord; they demand "working out" and, often, a remote global perspective to see their "necessity." Perhaps living where she did in France, "on a northern route used by invading armies eighty-seven times since the days of Julius Caesar," gives her a keen, knowing vantage on the vast and enduring paths of empire that run through southern and subjugated territories on their way to northern prosperity. Awiakta signals her camaraderie with such communities through the act of "song" and writing, and in doing so expressly as a hybrid-hyphenated writer with plural influences and commitments.

A distinct benefit of this widened perspective is a revivified appreciation for the tribalographic imprint on the settler mind accomplished by early indigenous cultures. Later in *Selu*, Awiakta recounts how Native stories and values traveled throughout the rapidly settling American continent and back to Europe, delivering the seeds of egalitarian government and sustainable economies; often contingents of Natives, particularly the great leaders of the southeastern dynasties like Attakullakulla, would travel to remote locations to negotiate treaties and convey cultural wisdom along the way. This "loquacious human vine twined around the explorers and philosophers who were inspired by the new form of government discovered among the Indians"; explorers and philosophers from Columbus to Montaigne, Voltaire, Shakespeare, Hobbes, Locke, Bentham, and Rousseau "consume[d] the air" of these lessons and evinced the fruits of such thought in their writings (360–61). Reading deeply in history and letters confirms that vast tracts not just of land but of knowledge were absorbed from the Native presence in the New World, but to what end? Certainly the most principled tenets of democracy

and egalitarianism have failed to come to fruition in the American capitalist state; but Awiakta is not dwelling on missed opportunities or misuses of
indigenous wisdom. Rather, when she surveys the landscape of Washington,
D.C., she sees a country that indomitably bears the traces of its multiple,
unseen influences: the Washington Monument looks much like "the great
white prong of a deer antler"; and "many have called [the Statue of Liberty]
an Indian because of her flowing robe and the headdress with its sheaf of
feathers" (326). What we see — or don't see — in the shapes and symbols
of our nation are products of our individual will and imagination, Awiakta
avers. Seeing through to the indigenous presences on the country's façade
constitutes a way forward, "the guiding messages for the twenty-first century" (326) — a recognition that jars us into assuming responsibility for the
national space that we inhabit and narrate together, a portrait and a reality
that we may still have the power to control and revise if only we can learn to
see its complexities clearly.

In that process, writing may prove as political as any legislative act; while
poems rarely effect judicial change, they present vital correctives to the very
foundations and supremacy of Western law and order. Awiakta recalls the
1970s controversy over the flooding of sacred Cherokee land at Chota in order
to build the Tellico Dam. "All I can do is write," she knew — so "what good
is it to sling a poem at a dam?"[10] Unsure of her potential to have an impact
on the situation, Awiakta nonetheless submitted an editorial in the form of
a poem to an underground newspaper in Memphis called *The Dixie Flyer*. In
"The Covenant" (reprinted in *Selu*), she retells the story of Tsali, a Cherokee
traditionalist who resisted Removal violently and was fatally punished for it.
The twist in the story is that he is captured and killed because of the direct
assistance of a fellow Cherokee, Will Thomas, who betrays Tsali in exchange
for the safety of his remnant band of Eastern Cherokee. Tsali's story has
been passed down through the generations in widely varying permutations,
yet in each version, he is consistently portrayed as a veritable martyr for his
people: he bravely accepts his own execution in order that a large contingent
of Cherokees be permitted to remain in their homelands. Awiakta resurrects
this tale implicitly to remind the public of the people's sacrifices and long tenancy in the very land about to be flooded and dammed, terrain that included
"Chota, holy city and ancient capital of the nation; Tuskegee, birthplace of
Sequoyah, inventor of the Cherokee syllabary; Tenase, for which Tennessee

was named; and many other towns, as well as the sacred burial mounds. None of the sites is more than 20 percent excavated. All will be lost — if the waters rise" (47).

The poem does not work: the project goes forward, the dam authorized by a sudden congressional fiat that "showed staggering contempt for democracy" (57). Yet while Awiakta's retelling of the Tsali story, among other voices in defense of Chota, fails to be heard in a meaningful way, what is perhaps more important in the end is the manner in which she speaks. That is, she writes a poem not about the dam itself but about the losses and betrayal the site represents. This is not just Cherokee knowledge; in fact, "Most Tennesseans grown up knowing this story; they feel it in their bones" (45). In the end, the legacy of Tsali and the frail preservation of democracy are common, congenital stories for the southerners among whom she lives. The site upon which Chota sits is less than 20 percent excavated: who knows what else lies beneath the mounds and the sacred sites, what further archaeological evidence of community and contact, of intimacy and betrayal? When federal marshals were ordered in to evict the final three residents at Tellico, a television crew arrived to record what Awiakta tellingly calls "the removal" all over again. These families, not Natives now but white folks undeniably rooted to the place, are forcibly ejected from homes on the brink of final devastation: "Thomas Burel Moser's house was bulldozed into a giant hole that had been dug for it. Moser told the nation, 'It's a hell of a country, ain't it?' Jean Ritchie said that what TVA had done was 'stealin'.' When Nellie McCall was asked where she would go now, tears welled in her eyes and she could not answer" (53). Clearly detailed to evoke the Cherokees' removal from the same soil, the eviction of Tellico's new generation of non-Native residents admits how small and redundant our common histories have become. Before we have adequately excavated the historical ground on which we sit, we are in peril of being bulldozed straight back into the earth.

Above all, Awiakta's writing reminds us that what is truly crucial is remaining aboveground, surveying the terrain of our shared losses and treachery, and finding somehow a common purpose in resisting these overwhelming economic incursions — perhaps the only real democratic force in a nation seemingly absent of quotidian agency and choice. But what, finally, can be the usefulness of claiming space within the boundaries of regions or nation-

states drawn in blood and patrolled by avarice? What do these Native southerners have to offer to indigenous allies who necessarily locate sovereignty
in spaces categorically distinct from American borders and states? Do such
sacred territories even exist anywhere beyond our most fervent, backward-
looking imaginations and projections of possibility and desire? Alabama
Creek poet Janet McAdams seems to provide a compelling answer to such
a conundrum in her second collection of poetry, *Feral* (2007). In her own
words, the book is "about wildness, about what gets tamed and what cannot
be tamed, only destroyed . . . that one key to our destruction is something
crucial that white culture has forgotten, this simple fact: that we are animals,
children to them, siblings, kin, and they to us."[11]

What McAdams's gorgeously rendered poems offer is a powerful commentary on what it truly means to be human: a state of natural, ineffable grace
and wildness that we have persistently corroded in the supposedly civilizing processes of colonial-capitalist existence. Her poems draw variously on
historical episodes of arctic exploration, feral children, royal courts, and the
persistent despair of humans shuttling between worlds known and discovered, between states of nature and the brute constructions of society. By
excavating our relationships to the earth and uncovering the awful tragedies
of our attempts to understand, tame, control and ravage it, ourselves and
each other, she suggests that we might eventually arrive at a new kind of
peace and communion. In "The Collectors," she sketches the myriad ways
we convert bodies and bones into artifacts and commodities: when we dig
into the past, we are searching not for the essence of ourselves but for a
usable history that feeds, fulfills, enriches in some way. You find "a tooth
hollowed out / rattling in the canvas glove you pull on for gardening. Let /
your feet find the path of broken shells, / bits of ivory, the fingerbones of
Sioux children, / the broken skull of Osceola, stolen for a talisman, / teeth
without their gold fillings, bits of skin . . . / Oh, sweet adventure with pirates and map, a trunk / so stuffed with gold it will blind the one / who
cracks it open" (ll. 3–8, 11–13). As we protect our bodies with gloves against
the wildness that we prune and tame, we inevitably bump up against the
remains of those whose lands and bodies have been pilfered, "hollowed out"
for the privilege of planting such ordered gardens. Settlement ("map") is
equated with theft ("pirates"), an elision perpetuated in our archaeological
and historical explorations: all these graves have already been robbed of their

riches, our moral and historical vision "blinded" by the quest for a dazzling treasure.

For the "collectors" of imperial histories, that treasure chest is filled with the rewards of empire and the quiet extinction of its casualties. But what would those unearthed fingerbones and skulls of the indigenous say if they could speak? McAdams's voice eloquently suggests some possibilities, ones audible for all of us if we listen closely enough. Osceola's skull speaks volumes: a fierce fighter on behalf of the Florida Seminoles in the Second Seminole War (1835–42), Osceola was of mixed Indian, Scottish, English, and African American descent; he purportedly married a black woman and vehemently opposed chattel slavery. His identity and commitments typify both the early mixture of peoples in the South and their suffering on behalf of the colonial forces that divided and enslaved them along violent lines of demarcation. Osceola was eventually imprisoned, gawked at by tourists, and painted by George Catlin; after his death, a U.S. army doctor had his head embalmed, and it (along with the rest of his body) has circulated among numerous private hands and museums.[12] "Crudely put," says Florida Museum of Natural History curator Jerald T. Milanich, "parts of Osceola are everywhere."[13] Osceola's story is brutally poetic, a testimony of how not just tribes but actual bodies are enclosed, plundered and riven by the fault lines of imperial violence, racial essentialism, and historical memory.

Over and over again, McAdams's poems interrogate the conjoined artifacts exhumed from the South's unquiet earth: what stories do they tell, separately and together? And what difference does it make to those of us now, who would hear and honor them? "Ghost Ranch," a poem late in the collection, returns to an archaeological site: ostensibly referring to the real-life Ghost Ranch in Abiquiú, New Mexico, a retreat and educational center in New Mexico and a favorite landscape for the painter Georgia O'Keefe, the setting functions also as a metaphor for the western landscape as one teeming mass grave:

> Light picks this landscape down to bone.
> It's Boxing Day. The orange jumpsuits
> six miles back pick trash while they do time.
> The guards in their blue suits are white.
> Someone has cut the Indian prisoners' hair.

The mesa's one short hard haul straight up.
Gray feather in the crack I work my fingers
into and tug and work them out again.
The flat on top for miles and miles —
so much land. You find a pile of bones

and hold the pelvis up to frame a ragged disc
of sky. Not the real sky, I thought that day,
but blue enough to tell this story. You say
the feather's from a dove and spot an eagle
circling high across the canyon, but I am not

so sure. We touch and circle and touch and circle
until we only circle: cloth against cloth, skin
not quite meeting, the way fences touch at the corners
of nations. Last night you slept so quietly,
I put a hand to your back to make sure

you were breathing, the other over your shoulder
and flat against the skin between breast
and solar plexus because breath may not be
a sure enough measure. We hover
over the animal that carved itself

this place to rest, past molecule, atom,
the stinging energy that drums the universe
into being. Don't say you never felt it.
Even the stone was pulsing. Take my hand
if you can bear it, but let the other story go. (ll. 1–30)

Against the backdrop of a holiday (Boxing Day) that signifies specifically as a *non*-U.S. tradition, the poem immediately triggers an awareness of how national borders instantiate identity and practice; moreover, as a holiday with charitable origins ("boxing" gifts for the needy, or giving servants the day off along with a box of presents), Boxing Day has now become a thoroughly commercial occasion associated with department store sales and returns, thus announcing the globalization of market forces. This, McAdams seems to declare, is the "bone" revealed by the light-struck landscape, the message announced by this earth: concomitant revelations come in the visage of jump-suited convicts picking trash while doing time — a clear metaphor for the scant refuse afforded the marginalized in the prison house of a global economy and history (the place where one "does time"). McAdams carefully delineates the identity of the jailers (white) and the jailed (Indian), whose hair was cut in prisons, in boarding schools, and in the confines of a world that equates conformity with control.

From this allegorical opening that seems to capture all time and history in one agonized present moment, the speaker and a companion begin to excavate the stone mesa. What they discover ultimately is not evidence or artifact, not knowledge of another species that they might contain and control. The speaker's distrust of the "real" extends to the very sky; this earth we have constructed for our own needs and fears is now utterly beyond knowing. Carving lines to separate nations and races also posits impassable barriers between human spirits yearning for connection: the lovers here can only "circle," separated by cloth and skin; when they connect, it is like "the way fences touch at the corners / of nations." The drive to segregate and control, to own and to name, makes it impossible for human beings to inhabit and nurture themselves, much less one another. In a later moment in bed, trying desperately to "measure" and confirm her lover's presence and weight and life, a memory of the exhumed pelvis bone intercedes — and in fact, it becomes a fluid metaphor for the present moment, for the way they "hover" together over this "animal that carved itself this place to rest." Their ability to understand in the animal what they might constitute together, away from history's gaze, finds a "place to rest" in their own bed.

But how do we forget history? The final lines of the poem hint at a troubled past, a hurt that must be forgotten in order to go on: "Take my hand / if you can bear it, but let the other story go." The "story" of what lies in the earth, the pelvis bone of a narrative seeking only peace and quiet now, is the one we must abandon. Some manner of healing, or at least of true connection, is what comes next. McAdams's final poem in the collection seems to promise that the attempt itself is worth everything: "Earth My Body Is Trying to Remember" narrates the lonely journey back to "The land they took us from" after "They chipped away at us, / hammered us out like gold." This land is the South, surely, but it goes by another, earlier name, too — one we may just "remember," after all, if we can manage to stop searching in only the likely, visible, cordoned-off spaces. Going forward, the gold we can heft and hold in our hands is the kind the speaker offers to her lover, the story that tethers us here in the present and, vitally, to one another.

Homecoming: Remaking the World

At the end of these forward-moving, inclusive journeys, it may be time again to listen to the non-Native voices whose bones and brains have been cultivated on indigenous terrain, among Indian neighbors and shared experiences of loss and hunger in the contemporary South. Belle Boggs, an emerging writer from Virginia, may be the ideal voice to begin those conversations. In 2010 Boggs's masterful collection of short stories, *Mattaponi Queen*, won the prestigious Bread Loaf Writers' Conference Bakeless Prize. Percival Everett, the African American author and critic who judged the nominees, praised Boggs's stories for their "rare glimpse of Indian and reservation life in Virginia. There is not a lot of literature from eastern tribes," he adds. "I write this in order to point out that none of this is why these stories are so good. . . . These stories are good because they are true, true in that way that only good fiction can be." Unlike stories that have "no sense of place or the world," Boggs's tales are immersed deeply and fully in both "place" and "world" all at once.[14] That place belongs to the Mattaponi Indians as completely as their black and white neighbors; and in the seamless world of these stories, Boggs unveils a region of dynamically mixed racial and ethnic groups that have long coexisted. Set near King's County, Virginia, these stories weave in and out of the lives of interconnected individuals and families both on and off the reservation. The trick is that she rarely offers clarity on any one character's racial identity, and when she does, it hardly seems to matter.

In "Imperial Chrysanthemum" and "Election Day," for instance, a black woman named Loretta is employed as part-time caretaker and driver for an elderly white lady called Cutie Young. But just as names fail to properly capture a person — as Loretta wonders why people call the old woman "Cutie," since "She's mean and stubborn and takes a long time in the toilet" — so, too, Boggs seems to say, will racial signifiers miss the mark of a person's true essence (29).[15] Rather, what does serve to mark and polarize most distinctly — and viciously — is class: as Loretta drives Cutie from pawn shop to pawn shop in search of her stolen silver, Cutie gasps at the sight of a new development of cheap ranch houses: "Her eyes pop open like she was stuck by a pin. 'White trash,' she pronounces, the *sh* like gnashing her teeth" (32). Her rage at the sight seems extreme, but in fact it deftly reminds us of the often illogical, self-defensive mechanisms of class antagonism: having recently been dispossessed of a forty-thousand-dollar prized possession, Cutie is wounded at the plain visage of scrounging poor folks who might take away what is hers, just as "they knocked down all the trees to build" those flimsy houses (32). The mere sight explicitly revives her own sense of dispossession: "Stole Mother's silver," she says abruptly, unexpectedly. We later learn that Cutie owns several parcels of land throughout town and is considered a "founder" of this town on the margins of Indian land, a fact that renders her privileged outrage deeply ironic. The most vicious irony of all, though, is that Loretta knows who really did take the silver — a "no-good" relative of hers hired to do some painting at Cutie's house (30). But Cutie suspects neither the African American worker nor Loretta herself, even when the police obviously do, because Loretta "would not know what to do with silver asparagus tongs or cucumber forks" and "has a pension" besides (32, 33). Boggs is savvy enough to let us squirm in the wriggle of these contradictions: on the one hand, we are often tempted to see Cutie covering her real fondness and respect for her black nurse beneath a veneer of dismissive elitism, echoing the ironic and destructive affection for a mammy figure. Certainly, her inability to accuse or suspect Loretta or her kin of the theft, as a racist surely would, seems evidence of some kind of progress. Or does it? And does Loretta's knowledge of the thief's identity — which she pointedly never reveals to Cutie — confirm the cloaked racism underneath it all anyway?

Boggs puts her reader consistently in the uncomfortable position of asking such questions and realizing that they teeter on complicated and superficial assumptions and categories. Often, only the subtlest cues — a hairstyle, an outfit, a turn of phrase — will prompt us to label a character one race or another. And then we must deal with the consequences of our profiling: in "Homecoming," a boy named Marcus comes back to King's County to live with his grandmother after his entire family gets arrested and imprisoned for drug dealing up in New York City. Marcus is a "good boy," though, who studies hard and runs track and "cried so little" as a baby that his mother would "forget all about him" (131). In Virginia, he is recruited for the football team and quickly becomes popular; soon, he is encouraged to take steroids to get bigger and stronger, and not long after that, friends convince him to begin dealing drugs himself. Throughout the story, superficial details like his "baggy jeans," references to rap artists, and former home in "Bed-Stuy" — Brooklyn's largely black neighborhood—seem to indicate that he is African American (136). None of these things *necessarily* mean Marcus is black, though; we simply collect the evidence suggesting that he is, which becomes problematic when he gets caught selling Ecstasy to his classmates and ends up in a juvenile detention facility. Boggs clearly wants us to confront our easy, internalized racism in such plot turns; but more important, she wants us to acknowledge that race has become a signifier and a fiction that we interpret according to the language and the code—rather than the actual people—that we know. What if we were compelled to read differently? she seems to ask. How might our lives, and theirs, change then?

The question haunts Marcus, who escapes the hegemony of his own identity in both a semantic and a disastrously consequential way. Long assumed to simply be a "good boy," the events of the story—which feature him being steadily reinterpreted and miscast by those around him — finally prompt him to abandon the notion of "goodness" altogether: "*Good:* it's a word [Granny] still hangs on to. It means nothing to Marcus now. It's a lie, something you tell little kids about but you know they'll figure out the truth later, like Santa Claus and college. Nobody's good, Marcus thinks, but some people are tolerable" (171). Marcus's sober awakening to the fiction of his own decency seems like an excuse; and indeed, it is underwritten by his delinquent father's long-ago apologia: there's simply "no sense in fighting it" (170). For Jerome, this phrase describes the ineluctable gravity of his errant life, and for a long time, Marcus simply saw it as an excuse for his father's inability to "fight" the trouble and temptations that would get him sent back to jail repeatedly and seemingly permanently; but now he sees it as "the truth," and it becomes the trajectory of Marcus's own world, too, despite his best efforts and great promise. Boggs doesn't ask us to see this as mere fatalism, though, or as the internalized cynicism of an oppressed race, where being "good" in the first place might simply be a relative assessment in a world of persistent transgression. Surely, it is partly that; but Marcus's fate is less a result of his own self-assessment than what the rest of the world expects him to be and represent. His friends egg him on into dealing drugs simply because he looks and seems the type—his New York past and mystique function as "a marketing maneuver," and they want to benefit from proximity to the se-ductive menace he represents (152). Marcus's docile nature does not exactly announce "thug"; but his vulnerability lies in his utter lack of alternatives or connections: "Marcus thought about what he had at stake. Not much, he guessed. . . . He envied Wally, with his big muscles and his nice house and all he had to lose" (152). Alone in the world with only his grandmother to care for him, Marcus is prey to his overwhelming desire for what others have: "big muscles" and "nice houses," vanity and status, are all tangled up together. For Marcus, though, who struggles to increase both his weight and his wal-let's contents—he "had put on five pounds and saved two hundred dollars, but it wasn't enough" (144)—the process is achingly futile and masochis-tic. Startled by his first hit in football practice, Marcus thinks, "This is what I've been running from? . . . This was nothing; it was better than nothing. It felt *good*. He wanted to be hit again and again and again" (138). His reaction seems perverse until we realize that the simple feeling of pain is pleasurable because it is something: it is "better than nothing," a reminder that he, too, has something to lose.

The pedagogy of this world continues to teach him to assess himself through the eyes and standards of others, and through the matrix of pos-session and fullness that signifies one's strength and status. School was once the path that kept him away from the den where his mother dealt drugs; now it becomes a detour into self-amplification, as he carries the envelope containing not homework but his first course of steroids, tucked "under his arm like a school assignment" (146). Marcus is right: there really is no use in resisting what society encourages and directs him to expect and learn about himself at every turn. And what, exactly, is the lesson? To be both strong and vulnerable, it seems: to take up space in the world and to have posses-sion over one's physical territory. The problem, of course, is that his body is simply not meant to carry so much weight around, and the effort of trying becomes unbearable. Inured to the tyranny of being judged and steered by others, Marcus longs to see himself through an unbiased lens. Thus, what he craves repeatedly throughout the story are photographs: of himself with his beautiful Homecoming date; of his ever-strengthening form on the football field—verifications of his good looks, his physical strength, perhaps his es-sential self. Yet these mirrors of proof are, importantly, never to be had: just as Boggs denies us a full, certain view of Marcus's racial identity, Marcus is never able to grasp these images of himself *for* himself. The story in fact closes with Marcus on the eve of departing for juvenile hall; his boss Skinny — a Mattaponi Indian who is not skinny at all — has prepared him a huge going-away feast to be shared along with the viewing of "two whole rolls" of pictures from the big Homecoming game. "A lot of the shots are blurry and dark," the story ends, "but he and Marcus are going to look at every one of them, they're going to take their time, and when Marcus goes home again, he'll have his own set to keep" (171). We're reminded that the images will be "blurry and dark," no more distinct and revealing than anything the story has given us or Marcus so far, and that the darkness of his entire existence will haunt him well after the narrative ends. And end the story does, well before Marcus sees the photos; his anticipation remains an unfulfilled hope, a poised expectancy that he will bring "home . . . to keep" a record of his life and potency, however hazy or dim.

In myriad ways like this, Boggs's collection serves as a stunning and important reminder about the crucial importance and responsibilities of representation in this incubator of racial, class, and ethnic anxiety; and at the heart of this knowledge, the Mattaponi Indian repeatedly emerges as both the represented and the artist. It can't be a mistake that a full-blooded Indian and a (probably) African American youth, whose relationship has become more like father and son than boss and employee, recognize the importance of bonding over a shared meal while savoring the pictographic evidence of Marcus's crowning triumph. Skinny's greatest gift to Marcus is his ability to empathize with that desire to see oneself unfiltered, in a moment of victory and virility, freed from the expectations and imaginings of those around them. Indeed, throughout Boggs's stories, Indians consistently serve as the most effective and illustrative reminders and teachers, local examples of what happens when control over one's representation and image have been long appropriated by others. Skinny, then, is Marcus's most apt ally and teacher, a partnership that ultimately means more than the sanguine transcendence over their circumstances, which never happens for either man. The goal of Boggs's stories seems more modest: they are as much about troubling society's fictions as they are about the artist's power to either reproduce or reinvent those mythologies.

Several of Boggs's characters are identified precisely as Indian, perhaps to ensure that they do not simply continue to blend into the backdrop of the rural South; but the full run of these genealogies and their enormous impact on fellow members of the community are large, impressionistic, unbounded notions that run throughout the collection. Everywhere in this rural Virginia world, the presence of the Indian sits at the very heart of southern experience. As artist, Boggs seems to claim the responsibility of depicting these relations, just as she bequeaths a similar sense of duty to one of her characters, the young half-Indian painter Ronnie. Ronnie is an art school dropout who returns to the reservation when her new husband returns home an amputee after a brief tour of duty in Iraq. While staying with her father, Bruce, a white man who lives on the reservation next door to Skinny, Ronnie's emotional catharsis and search for purpose results in a project of painting all the full-blood Indians in the area: "They're all about Pocahontas, in one way or another. I'm painting scenes from her life, using the natural parts of the river as the background, and then I'm also painting her descendants, so that means people on the reservation as it is now" (76). The challenge, she finds, is rendering the "people" and the "reservation as it is now" as sharply as the historical backdrop — not just the river, but the overwhelming past and mythology of Pocahontas that threatens always to subsume and overwrite the present world. While completing her painting of Skinny, she realizes that "she'd rendered every detail [of his house], down to the very grain of the cedar siding. So much detail you could forget to see the man in the foreground, shoulders slumped, beer cans at his feet, a worried look on his face" (82).

Ronnie's painting is a sober reminder of all the difficult ways that representation must confront a new reality born of historical haunting and fetishistic reproduction. By representing the geographical space as a devouring backdrop, Boggs makes clear that the southern environment, with all its repressed colonial traumas, is what harbors the power to consistently overwhelm its indigenous subjects. Leaving one of his many doctors' appointments in Richmond, Skinny walks out into the busy street where the "cars and buses and frowning businesspeople went about their business like he wasn't there" (92). A writer who chooses words with painstaking and sparing rigor wouldn't simply repeat "business" twice here without purpose: the "business" of the place, the sweeping economics of it, rush past Skinny and render him invisible, insignificant. Similar to posing for Ronnie, in Richmond too he just "sat there, hands resting on his knees, like someone having his picture made" (92). The story ends thus, freighted with the knowledge that the "business" of the South inevitably echoes and informs the business of the artist, directing her gaze away from the subject and back to the objects that surround him, the material markers of one's existence. On the one hand, this is a perfect approximation of the industry of southern literature and its often complicit negotiation of capitalism's blindspots and exclusions. On the other hand, what Ronnie is able to depict in vigilant detail is not a tawdry set piece but a vital construction: her painting captures this Mattaponi man's home, a house he built himself, carefully and slowly by hand, three small buildings modeled "on the idea of a teepee" yet ultimately looking "more like duck blinds than like teepees, but their size and close grouping suggested readiness, temporary shelter for someone on the move, just the way teepees had for Powhatan's tribe. He built them that way out of necessity—the steeply sloping cliff would not support a regular house's foundation—but over the years he'd found ways of adding small measures of comfort" (69–70). Skinny's teepeelike abode is not historical reenactment per se but a supremely necessary, natural blending into the contours of the earth that his family has always inhabited, and a settlement that grows more pragmatic and comfortable as the years pass. The construction is difficult, unstable, and imperiled; but it is also a crucial defiance of what a "regular house" and a standard, "normal" Western lifestyle would demand. In this way, the backdrop of his existence is a vital part of the frame, and an important antidote to the kind of "picture being made" of him in places like Richmond, or similar metropolitan zones with the power to expunge and render him an impermanent, mobile feature of a historical imaginary always "on the move" and receding out of view.

This seems Boggs's project, too, as she places her Indian characters within a world that acknowledges them comfortably and naturally, and one that refuses to be represented in crude lines and distinctions. In many ways, Skinny serves as a community anchor for the variously wounded and searching characters within the world of these stories. He is full-blooded Indian, we are told, but he is no shamanistic throwback: a recovering junkie, he is dying now of a drug-resistant strain of hepatitis C that he overmedicates with Percocet and Budweiser. Nonetheless, he is a good neighbor, a caring boss, and an earnest if unsuccessful father. He tunes in regularly to the Food Network and cooks extravagant meals that he shares with his friends and family, even when he is so ill that he can hardly stomach plain soup and crackers himself. Simply put, Skinny's role—like so many Indians before him—is to feed a vast, insatiable hunger in those around him, a spiritual craving that they all share. Skinny, "who was not skinny at all," shares this ontological vacancy but cannot fill it with food; the feasts are a symbol, though, an enduring acknowledgment that a chasm of loneliness and desire for community run through these differently dispossessed individuals. And the explicitly global influences of his cuisine — he watches Paula Deen, Rachael Ray, Emeril, and Mario Vitale, though *Molto Mario* is his favorite — bespeak the full and potentially nourishing hybridity of the surrounding community and the meals he might offer, at the same time that they warn of a stylized, packaged, commercial version of such multicultural satisfaction. His own children fail to eat a meal he tenderly prepares for them — they stop at a fast-food joint instead — in the same way that they refuse the gifts of tradition and heritage he wants to pass down to them: "He imagined taking the moccasins out at the mall or handing them across the table at the Olive Garden. . . . He imagined [his daughter] brushing their dirt from her hands" (70–71). His relationship with his children is no longer a tie forged in blood and tradition but in materialism: "Apart from when he was buying them something, Skinny sometimes thought they acted like they hardly knew him anymore" (70). Skinny's culinary pluralism feeds Bruce, Ronnie, Marcus and his friends — a multiracial cast of dinner guests — but fails to connect him to his own progeny in his attempts to pass down traditional knowledge and gifts.

In striking ways, Boggs seems repeatedly to aver that a new genealogy has taken over southern communities, and it is one that emphasizes neighborly, kindred, and commercial relations over mere blood and ancestry. This hybridization has been accomplished both by nefarious histories, as we have seen in the destructive racial polarities and essentialisms of a segregated culture, as well as by material forces, which sunder genealogical ties and replace them with more encompassing bonds of market interests and relations. Boggs signals the death of pure, inviolate culture in what is surely the most insistent theme of her collection: that of abandonment and absence. Rampant throughout each story are instances of wives fleeing their husbands, children being raised without mothers, a young soldier losing his arm. Like the injured limb, family members are simply amputated from the lives of these characters routinely and briskly, and the remaining daughters and husbands go on with a combination of cheerful fortitude and tamped-down rage. Boggs emphasizes the materiality of such loss most strikingly in the story "Good News for a Hard Time." The young artist Ronnie recalls her mother disappearing when Ronnie was just ten years old; it was not dysfunction that destroyed the family so much as the seductive market for indigenous pageantry: "Disney had flown [her mother] out to their studios in Glendale as an animator's model for the movie *Pocahontas.* . . . . She was tanning leather in a teepee in Colonial Williamsburg when an agent came by on vacation. Of course, she never came back, which was what Ronnie had feared would happen all along. Two years later all the kids were wearing plastic Halloween costumes with big-eyed, anglicized drawings of her mother on them, and Bruce had wept, handing out candy at the Central Garage hayride, while Ronnie had wanted to scream" (14). While she never returns or even calls, Ronnie's beautiful mother reappears in the community in the form of a "plastic," mass-produced cartoon. Ronnie can never understand her father's inability to be angry at their abandonment; but perhaps Boggs is telling us that their loss is vitally different. As a white man who fell in love with a dazzling Indian princess, he can only weep for a tragic absence he never fully possessed; for Ronnie, there is simply ire for what seems like a barren choice, a selling out, and an irreversible betrayal. Like the loss of her mother, the absence of her husband's limb is quickly quantified: "Everyone [in the vet hospital] was talking about how much money they were going to get — so much for a leg, so much for a hand, an arm below the elbow, to the shoulder — and how they had no regrets" (15). The fact that Jeremy's accident occurs during a U.S. military campaign merely heightens the sense that national and regional pressures and obligations underwrite these catastrophic physical and psychic losses, ones that devour holes in families and bodies and offer recompense only in plastic costumes and commercial prosthetics.

Given the insistence with which this theme resurfaces in nearly every story in her collection, Boggs seems intent on conveying a sense of foreclosed hope for the future of families disrupted by pointedly American and southern stereotypes, markets, and conflicts. What emerges throughout is the frail hope that we might remake new genealogies and communities in ways that are truly regenerative and inclusive, jettisoning the poisonous essentialisms and exchanges of the past. Boggs's deft handling of these complicated racial narratives and identities helps: no one in her world is exactly what he or she seems, as neither names nor stereotypes track with the unfolding realities of these characters. The blurry darkness of it all, like the photographs Marcus looks forward to possessing, becomes in itself a feeble hope, something better than the harsh glare of imposed boundaries and possibilities. This slim hope is what links the otherwise relentlessly bleak stories throughout the collection, and it is an optimism forged expressly through human partnerships that defy easy categorization or expectation. The Indian Skinny sits down daily to dinner with a black youth or his white neighbor, people closer to him than his own estranged children. Cutie and Loretta get on in an easy comfort forged by necessity: Cutie looks forward to Loretta's reliable presence, and Loretta needs what Cutie pays her in order to make her payments on the boat *Mattaponi Queen*, which gives its name to the title of the collection. The boat represents escape, a vehicle that "can't tell you anything you don't want to know. All it says is get away, get away" (44). It is an economic relationship, to be sure, but Loretta's fungible reward is the purchase of a kind of social freedom and autonomy that she has never known.

The younger generations in these stories move toward an unmediated sense of solidarity as well: upon entering the Homecoming dance, Marcus's girlfriend Tasha assures him that the blaring country music won't last long: "I rigged it so they play one song for them, one for us," she promises. Wally, her brother, is the one to respond teasingly, "And what do you mean by them and us?" Tasha simply "rolled her eyes" (161). She rolls her eyes presumably because the answer is so obvious, but Wally's question invites both her and us to scrutinize the simplicity of boundary-making based on superficial factors like musical preference. Moreover, we really don't have any idea whether Tasha and Wally are even the same race as Marcus: they are all friends and conspirators, but Tasha and Wally have more in the way of privilege, as "their mama owned a popular restaurant on Route 30 and they lived in a brick split-level house with a neat green lawn and a lawn jockey painted white" (144). The family's economic status might tempt us to read them as white, but Boggs never allows for such easy elisions between race and class. In the literary geography of the South, the "lawn jockey" has a precise location: as the central symbol (and source for the title) of the short story "The Artificial Nigger" by Flannery O'Connor, one of Boggs's professed favorite writers, it functions as a property marker in a white Atlanta neighborhood and an accidental vehicle of grace. O'Connor's protagonists, an old white man from the country and his grandson, come upon it after a long day of exploring the city and quarreling: "They stood gazing at the artificial Negro as if they were faced with some great mystery, some monument to another's victory that brought them together in their common defeat. They could both feel it dissolving their differences like an action of mercy." The "differences" between the two white men are not racial, nor is their "common defeat" anything like the black trauma behind the lawn jockey's visage; but the "artificial" monument to a regional and racial victory awakens them to the need for solidarity unto themselves. More insidiously, the moment sends them fleeing back to the comfort of their rural home, away from both the city's racism and its other races, which remain a confounding "mystery." Boggs's countryside is different, and differently mysterious: the lawn jockey "painted white" on Tasha and Wally's grass is either a gesture at political correctness or a subversive reversal of a poisonous racial legacy. Either way, the borders between "us" and "them" have revealed themselves as blurry and artificial at best, and the need for a harmony of difference triumphs above all.

We might be tempted to read such a sly postracial vision cynically, as the work of a well-meaning white liberal who wants desperately to move past divisions that cannot be erased so simply. Boggs is not nearly that sanguine or naïve: her efforts stem not from a delusion that racial antagonisms and anxieties no longer exist, but from a conviction that there are greater forces and traumas now connecting rather than fracturing us. Partly, this is a deeply historical revelation, a reminder that whatever histories have shattered the ground on which southerners move and live, the fault lines have been created and traversed in complicated synergies. The title of her collection itself conjures this notion by referring not just to Loretta's coveted *Mattaponi Queen*, a vessel of freedom with a price tag, but inherently to the Mattaponi River itself: a waterway formed by the mingling of three separate streams. The confluence poses a fitting metaphor for the way that red, black, and white communities have long lived in fluid, if not always peaceful, cohesion in rural Virginia. As the previous chapters here have demonstrated, the tyranny of space and geography and its imagined communities and borders, *especially* in southern studies, can blind us to the intricately mixed and coeval societies that have been forged there. For the Mattaponi Indians whose land houses all of those streams and who nonetheless are most fully obscured, the awakening process is especially critical.

The fact that Ronnie is pregnant throughout "Good News for a Hard Time" is just that: good news for a hard time, a way to compensate for the devastating loss of her husband's arm and, even more, for the haunting absence of her mother and all that her disappearance emblematizes. At the end of the story, Bruce's instinct is to turn back to the river, hosting a shad feast to celebrate the news and also to soften Jeremy's somber homecoming from the veterans' hospital. Ronnie contemplates the vital importance of the shad to her people, a tradition begun by old-time Indians and continuing until the present day: "It was a fishy fish, and no one much liked it . . . but for a certain kind of person, and Ronnie guessed she was one, it was something that had to be eaten" (26). Even when distasteful or ugly, what matters is continuing to cultivate and consume history and tradition — not Wendy's hamburgers or Pocahontas-themed Happy Meals. Skinny mixes these traditional ingredients and recipes with outside influences and ingredients to create meals that sustain: "*homemade*," Ronnie describes his cooking in a later story, not manufactured and empty, like the cookies another Mattaponi neighbor tries to feed her out of a "enormous Aunt Jemima cookie jar. Blackface and everything, polka-dotted kerchief, big gummy smile" (80). In this explicitly southern, history-haunted, trenchantly racist space, it is the "homemade" cookie that adapts to a changing world, imperfect and flawed yet true, and the one that has the potential to sustain.

The shad, and the celebration of Ronnie's pregnancy, thus form a symbol of sustenance and survivability in the region that the Mattaponi Indians have long called home even as the place has steadily endeavored to unhome and erase them. Coming near her father's house for the shad feast, Ronnie "thought about how far each shad she'd eaten in her life had traveled to spawn, from the salty bay to the fresh waters of the Mattaponi, the same place it had been spawned. She wondered if, to the shad, it had all been worth it, if after spawning it looked around at the shallow, mud-bottomed river and thought its tiny thoughts, *Oh, yeah, I remember this*" (26). Like the shad, Ronnie returns to the place where she had been "spawned" in order to birth her own new life and child; and implicitly throughout the story, she, too, wonders "if it had all been worth it." But the full collection of stories, which are filled with "tiny" moments of grace and joy, suggests that is worth it all and then some. To arrive back at the "same place" where you were born, the muddy soil of your ancestors, seems the ineluctable gravity of these narratives, even as so many characters need and desire first to run, to get away. The homecoming is not always easy or comfortable, but there is something eminently sustaining in the ability to say, "I remember this." What these characters remember is not pageant or performance but humble, hybrid beginnings: in that mud-bottomed stream are the vestiges of other waterways, the fluid commingling of the Mattaponi's multiple sources.

Boggs in fact opens the entire collection with a very short story, more like a vignette, that establishes the centrality of this titular theme throughout: in "Deer Season," a third-person omniscient narrator ranges through a school half-deserted by the local boys who quit attending in order to hunt with their fathers. In the quiet space vacated by the hunters, off in pursuit of the deer who are perennially figured as kindred stand-ins for the Indian, an art class carries on. The assignment is to draw a still life of an object, and the teacher has brought in several examples excavated from her own property: "a beautiful little hand-blown glass bottle, an arrowhead, a Confederate belt buckle, a bone toothbrush without any bristles. How did you find those things anyway? her husband wanted to know. I dug around a little, she said, remembering descending the sloping sides into the hole's cooler air, brushing away the layers and layers of leaves and scraping the damp clay away with her fingers. Next time you'll likely find a copperhead, he said, meanness in his voice" (5).

Held in not just the symbolic river but in the very striations of earth are the reminders of a shared past — a Confederate artifact and a Native weapon lying together in the same earth — and it becomes the artist's task to resurrect them. But the challenge of doing so is formidable. The art teacher's husband is not wrong: poisonous discoveries lie in wait for those who "dig around" in the South's deeply buried, layered, and collective traumas; this is not mere archaeology, we know, but grave digging. Still, there is beauty and handicraft here, too, in the delicate glass bottle — an empty container that suggests possibility, perhaps perpetually unrequited hope. This, if anything, seems the dominant mood of Boggs's collection, and perhaps of all the voices and stories being unearthed in the contemporary Native South: "empty" vessels filled with desperately beautiful anticipation lie alongside incongruous and counterproductive fossils of antagonistic histories and objects, like the bone toothbrush, used to cleanse and purify them. So what do we do with these relics once we have recovered them? The art teacher places them on the windowsill in her classroom, just above the heating vents, where their "images bend and waver in the warm, billowing air." They are potential objects for the still-life assignment, but the images refuse to stay still or unchanged. Moreover, "no one has chosen to draw them; even the girl who forgot [to bring in] something to draw dug around in her book bag until she found something of her own — a pencil, nervously bitten during last week's trigonometry test . . . at least it is hers and not someone else's. Those are her tooth marks, after all; she bought the pencil herself at Walgreen's. She has made no mark on the glass bottle, the arrowhead, the belt buckle, or the toothbrush, nor does she know where they came from. Better to leave them on the windowsill, mysterious and wavering and fragile-looking" (6).

In the anxious spaces of global capitalism and the tyranny of individualism and narcissism, we devour and reproduce what is "ours," the things we have purchased, the objects we mark with our own bodies and lives. In such a world, our archaeological digs are shallow, extending into our own bags and purses and pockets; and our historical memory is equally depthless, our known worlds small and contained. There is no question that the full, deep history of the Native South remains a "fragile," "wavering," "mysterious," and painful thing, and perhaps it moves and bends too much to ever be represented in its essential form. But the important thing is simply to keep digging deeper, and to try to locate both the awful and the beautiful stories that unearth themselves along the way — and with that, to remake the world.

THE SOUTH IN THE INDIAN
AND THE INDIAN IN THE SOUTH

Storytelling is, at its essence, how human beings create tribe.
—Daniel Alarcón, Interview

In a 2005 *New York Times Magazine* article titled "The Newest Indians," journalist Jack Hitt describes his visit to the annual powwow of a Cherokee tribe of northeast Alabama near Jasper. The event was newsworthy because it featured a tribe that has existed as an organization only since 1997; and to Hitt, these Indians do not "look as much like Indians as they do regular Alabama white folks. In fact, every Indian at the powwow looked white." During the middle of a particularly impressive dance solo, Hitt finds himself distracted by "another handsome teenage boy with light brown hair, the head grass dancer, who didn't seem to have made the full transition to Indian yet. His outfit was a painstaking interplay of beads and feathers and a series of striking variations of white and red shapes sewn onto his vest, which for some reason caught my eye and seduced me into leaving the bleacher seats in order to wander closer to the rail, elbowing my way out in front of even small children to peer more carefully and to make absolutely sure that the tiny red rectangles were—yes, indeed, no doubt about it—little Confederate battle flags."[1]

Hitt's article goes on to document the rise of newly discovered Indian groups like the northeast Alabama clan and, along with it, "a new kind of ethnic unease that can be felt throughout Indian country." The explosion of such tribes particularly throughout the South — Hitt reports over six hundred such groups in Alabama alone — is a testament to how long Native southern experience has been both overlooked and transformed in the shadows of the region's Lost Cause. Finally, in the twenty-first century, many tribal groups are regaining visibility and viability, but contending with the vestiges of colonial transformation and the demand for indigenous authenticity continues to plague contemporary Native communities. What the journalist fails to consider, not incomprehensibly, is that perhaps the Confederate battle flag sewn onto Indian regalia is an appropriate rather than an incongruous emblem of the southeastern Native experience. Doubtless, there is a shocking and distasteful element to such a revelation; but the ossified, separatist symbols and codes of regional and cultural identity are what prompt our too-easy assumptions and interpretations. In order to begin seeing more accurately the sober vestiges of tribal community vibrantly resurgent on southern soil, the old, superficial codes and tropes of identity and belonging need at long last to be reviewed and revised.

Both southern and Native communities have been irrevocably altered and revivified by the narratives that each attempts to tell about the other and in turn about themselves — stories and motives that have far more in common than they at first suggest. Indeed, Native and non-Native southerners have been defiantly making their own stories and worlds in parallel streams for as long as they have coexisted geographically; the time has come to see them occupying the same space, both material and discursive. What emerges in the intersection between Native and southern narratives is, I believe, a disarming new chronicle of region, tribe, and world that will have dynamic implications for future analysis and more productive affiliations, both within literary studies and on the ground. Forging comparative solidarities rather than polarized binaries is neither an easy nor a necessarily transcendent maneuver, particularly in the face of overwhelming economic competition and cultural transformation. But if we expect to survive the terrific and unparalleled pressures exacted by global capitalism, we need new strategies and partnerships now more than ever.

Until now, the pressures of the southern context and the material demands of economic survival have not been conducive to these conjunctural conversations and stories; instead, they have tended to address insular needs and basic hungers for knowledge and survival. As Louis Owens commented on his own fictional creations, "Some are stories I've told myself to fill in the empty places in memory and received history. Some are just stories, inventions, the kinds of fictions we create to make sense of the otherwise uninhabitable world we must, of necessity, inhabit."[2] In the centuries of contact, Removal, occlusion, and erasure in the South, these fictions have constructed safe territories in an "otherwise uninhabitable world," and they contain enduring power to shore up our senses of self and community. While these are often compensatory fictions that can do as much harm as good, stories do inherently contain the capacity to locate the intersections and patterns of meaning that lead to revelatory truths. In the dark shadows of southern history, Owens knows, "Language must be the surest way, as we remain here telling ourselves stories in the dark, spinning webs of language against ever-encroaching myriad history like Faulkner, or writing ourselves into pages that read themselves out in the ending of our various selves like García Márquez, or laying a terrifying balm of language over the abyss of history like Cormac McCarthy — or writing back toward the center like N. Scott Momaday, Leslie Silko, James Welch, Gerald Vizenor, Thomas King, Louise Erdrich, and so many others. . . . At the center [of all these stories], of course, is the hybrid monster of self, the ultimate cannibal to which all stories lead" (xiii, xiv). It is no accident that Owens mentions two southern writers (Faulkner and McCarthy) and a South American (García Márquez) alongside the major voices in Native American literature, in a passage that waxes unmistakably Faulknerian in its style and scope. That "hybrid monster of self" we are always creating in our stories emerges ineluctably from these rich, diverse, intimate springs that nurture and create us, eventuating in tales that feed the hungry "cannibal" at the center of all of history's terrorized, searching victims. Often, these are not the directions that seem most likely or concordant with the "prevailing assumptions" either in the field or on the ground; but sometimes we need simply to rely on the voice of the people themselves, speaking together in unlikely and unexpected conjunctions, to point us in the direction of new revelations, innovative partnerships, and renewed hope for the future of the world we make together.

As Mark Fisher suggests, the "very oppressive pervasiveness of capitalist realism means that even glimmers of alternative political and economic possibilities can have a disproportionately great effect. . . . From a situation in which nothing can happen, suddenly anything is possible again."[3] Throughout

Reconstructing the Native South, the Native and non-Native Souths together offer a bleak, composite account of domination, hunger, erasure, and greed; the space they occupy together is bloody historical terrain and persistently embattled contemporary ground, striated by racial hostility and competitive anxiety. Yet the undeniable resonances within and between these eruptions suggest the kind of resemblance that can only be forged in a common lot; and understanding and deconstructing the material bases of such opposition and suppression are vital to combating the monstrous economic forces that continually reach new heights of domination and dehumanization. In the remarkable landscape of contemporary Native literature, Gordon Henry Jr. finds in just this kind of transcendent possibility a conduit for "the imagined sovereignty of more interesting ways of telling what we know and who we are, in our own terms and language."[4] Perhaps stepping away from everything we *thought* we knew can be the best way to return to ourselves, to "who we are" and what we need. This is a pursuit uniquely suited to the inheritors of the contemporary South and its multiple voices just beginning to unearth their stories, their secrets, and a stunning new kind of pragmatic sovereignty. In times when racial and class antagonism and economic disparities and anxieties are growing worse rather than better, this is perhaps the kind of narrative that might save us.

Just as writers have the exquisite power to render and remake worlds, we critics, too, have the capacity to influence the contours and directions of both the literature and the lives we examine. In *Reasoning Together*, Craig Womack emphasizes the crucial importance of Native critics "who are willing to think for themselves instead of accepting the prevailing assumptions, critics who realize that their statements have both philosophical ramifications and the potential to affect the real world in both positive and negative ways. Simply put, we are still at a point in the discipline when we need to lay a lot more historical groundwork in order to map our way through these philosophical dilemmas. Historical specificity, in my view, is a correct direction — not the only direction, but a useful one" (39). The notions of historical specificity and correlation have especially potent ramifications on southern soil, where maps of shared trauma and rebuilding have given way to common vocabularies, cruel thefts, and undeniably entangled communities. Our best hopes for moving past the antagonisms born from such histories begins with a sober assessment of their reality and legacy; and from there, partnerships between tribal and local governments, between Native and non-Native neighbors, seem the most pragmatic way to move forward in a cultural landscape that measures sovereignty in dollars, and one that is fed rather than fought by competitive antagonisms.

In the end, these are mobile gifts that suggest vast new geographies of affiliation and community. The unique experience of southeastern Indians prompts likely parallels with indigenous neighbors to the north, particularly New England, where the Native population, exceeding one hundred thousand before European contact, was swiftly and drastically reduced until "survivors huddled in 'enclaves'" where "they became invisible in history books. . . . Nowhere did Indian extinction seem more assured than in New England"—except, perhaps, in the South.[5] Like their southeastern neighbors, though, New England tribes have rebuilt sovereignty and visibility literally from the ground up; it's time our scholarly narratives caught up. But there are other horizons and allies—particularly global ones—and potent new enemies here to consider, too. Perhaps the spirit of community and resistance, and the stubborn commitment to survive at all costs, constitutes the greatest gift of the Indian's vast stolen treasures; there is terrific irony and grave redundancy in such a notion, to be sure, but in the face of formidable new obstacles and faceless, systemic enemies, perhaps this kind of expectant reterritorialization is our last best hope.

"Your one job as an Indian person," Jessie Doe Baird (Wampanoag) recently said, "is to be able to lay on your deathbed and say, 'I left something for my community that wasn't here when I came, and I left my community in a better place than I found it.'"[6] For the Wampanoags of Massachusetts, Baird will leave the gift of a resuscitated Native language, a triumph for which she recently won a MacArthur "genius" grant. For not just the U.S. South but a broader human community, southeastern Natives will leave a reconstructed terrain of unnoticed relations, stories of the power and the danger of intercultural contact, and injunctions to face the sublime new threats of the present economic age rather than the nagging ghosts of an effacing past. In the new millennium, resituating the American Indian experience at the heart of global crisis represents the real hope and fruition of relational regionalism, pan-tribal nationalism, or true *human* sovereignty, in perhaps the only way that promises survival of this "hybrid mess" of a human community we own and inhabit together. Where we go from here is boundless.

NOTES

1. Janet McAdams, "From *Betty Creek*," 253.

2. Janet McAdams, "From *Betty Creek*," 254.

3. As Mark M. Smith notes, "questions concerning the economic and social character of antebellum southern slavery still inform modern historical debates which have raged with increasing volume and occasional acrimony in the twentieth century" (1). Eugene Genovese, a prolific Marxist historian of the South, himself famously vacillated from the position that slaveholders were anticapitalist figures with an "aversion to profit" to a partial admission that planters desired a return on their investments but were neither fully integrated into the market economy nor very successful at negotiating it (M. Smith 13). In *Time on the Cross*, their groundbreaking statistical analysis of slavery's profitability, Robert Fogel and Stanley Engerman exhaustively argued that the plantation was categorically a business enterprise, organized and geared for revenue and participation in both local and national economies. Smith suggests that the Old South may well have constituted "a society where plantation capitalism and conventional capitalism articulated" cohesively (94). Most (but not all) scholars now agree that the South's plantation system clearly embodied the characteristics of a protocapitalist economy even without pure market relations.

4. David S. Williams, "Lost Cause Religion."

5. Blain Roberts and Ethan J. Kytle, "Dancing around History."

6. Robert Behre, "NAACP to Protest Secession Event."

7. Quoted in Katharine Q. Seelye, "Celebrating Secession without the Slaves."

8. See, for example, David Harvey, *Spaces of Global Capitalism* (2006).

9. Edward Ball, "Gone with the Myths."

10. Rupert Vance was among the first to identify the system of interregional dependency as a colonial economy in *Human Geography of the South* (1935). Howard Odum, in his 1936 sociological study, *Southern Regions of the United States*, called the South "essentially colonial in its economy." These observations were corroborated by the

1938 federal *Report on Economic Conditions of the South* incited by President Roosevelt's infamous and belated lament that "the South presents right now the Nation's No. 1 economic problem. . . . For we have an economic unbalance in the Nation as a whole, due to this very condition of the South" (1); Roosevelt's letter is reprinted at the start of the United States Emergency Council's *Report*. New Deal programs, particularly the Agricultural Adjustment Act of 1933, were instituted federally in an attempt to excite the region's stagnant economy and crop prices. A separate body of literature arose that viewed the colonial state of North-South relations as a situation of deliberate manipulation and advantage taking; see, for example, Webb, *Divided We Stand*. For more on the South's post-Reconstruction economic colonialism, see Gavin Wright, *Old South, New South Revolutions in the Southern Economy since the Civil War*; C. Vann Woodward, "The Colonial Economy" in *Origins of the New South*; Morton Rothstein, "New South and the International Economy."

11. James Ronald Kennedy and Walter Donald Kennedy, *The South Was Right!*, 9.

12. For more on the long genealogy of "Lost Cause" rhetoric, begin with Edward A. Pollard's *The Lost Cause: A New Southern History of the War of the Confederates* (1866) and Jefferson Davis's 1881 *The Rise and Fall of the Confederate Government*. More recent works by historians include William C. Davis, *The Cause Lost: Myths and Realities of the Confederacy* (2003); David Goldfield, *Still Fighting the Civil War: The American South and Southern History* (2004); and Charles Reagan Wilson's *Baptized in Blood: The Religion of the Lost Cause, 1865–1920* (1983). Moreover, historians have begun to question whether the Lost Cause ideology was as fluidly accepted as we assume, or whether its proponents were well aware of its construction as a salve for emotional and economic loss (and not as a *de facto* defense of slavery). These include Gary W. Gallagher and Alan T. Nolan, eds., *The Myth of the Lost Cause and Civil War History* (2010) and Gaines Foster, *Ghosts of the Confederacy: Defeat, the Lost Cause and the Emergence of the New South, 1865–1913* (1988).

13. Patrick J. Buchanan, "The New Intolerance."

14. See, for instance, Robert F. Berkhofer, *The White Man's Indian* (1979). According to Homi Bhabha, such stereotypes function within colonial societies as a primary means of control and suppression, a way of identifying the Other and keeping him in his purported place. See Bhabha, "The Other Question," 75–84.

15. Gidley and Gidley, "The Native-American South," 167.

16. John H. Peterson Jr., "Introduction," 4.

17. As of 2010, the following southeastern tribes have federal recognition (by state): Alabama: Poarch Band of Creek Indians; Florida: Seminole Tribe and Miccosukee Tribe of Indians; Louisiana: Coushatta Tribe, Jena Band of Choctaw Indians, Tunica-Biloxi Indian Tribe, and Chitimacha Tribe; Mississippi: Mississippi Band of Choctaw

Indians; North Carolina: Eastern Band of Cherokee Indians; South Carolina: Catawba Indian Nation.

18. Loretta Leach, "Varnertown in the 1950s," 213.

19. Hobson, McAdams, and Walkiewicz, eds., "Introduction: The South Seldom Seen," 1. For similar examples throughout the Southeast, see also Jack D. Forbes, *Black Africans and Native Americans* (1990).

20. This phenomenon has occupied social historians like Gidley and Gidley, Michael Green, Malinda Maynor Lowery, Joel Martin, and Theda Perdue as well as a few literary critics such as Eric Gary Anderson, Sharon Holland, Kirstin Squint, Annette Trefzer, and myself.

21. Tom Mould, *Choctaw Prophecy*, xxii–iii.

22. Excellent new work on the global South includes *The American South in a Global World* (ed. Peacock, Watson, and Matthews) and *Globalization and the American South* (ed. Cobb and Stueck).

23. Peacock, Watson, and Matthews, *The American South in a Global World*, 2–3.

24. Christina Snyder, *Slavery in Indian Country*, 8.

25. Patricia Yaeger, "Ghosts and Shattered Bodies," 107.

26. Yaeger, "Ghosts and Shattered Bodies," 95, 101, 104.

27. Quoted in Arnold Krupat, *The Turn to the Native*, 25.

28. See Janice Acoose et al., eds., *Reasoning Together: The Native Critics Collective* (2008); Elizabeth Cook-Lynn, "The American Indian Fiction Writer: Cosmopolitanism, Nationalism, the Third World, and First Nation Sovereignty"; Cook-Lynn, "American Indian Intellectualism and the New Indian Story"; Jace Weaver, Craig S. Womack, and Robert Warrior, eds., *American Indian Literary Nationalism* (2006); Robert Allen Warrior, *Tribal Secrets* (1995); Robert Warrior, *The People and the Word* (2005); Jace Weaver, *That the People Might Live* (1997); Craig Womack, *Red on Red* (1999).

29. Acoose et al., *Reasoning Together*, 37.

30. Shari M. Huhndorf, *Mapping the Americas* (2009).

31. Chadwick Allen, *Blood Narrative* (2002).

32. See, for example, Renya K. Ramirez, *Native Hubs* (2007).

33. Tol Foster, "Relations and Regionality," 271, 270.

34. Foster, "Relations and Regionality," 273.

35. Paul Lai and Lindsey Claire Smith, "Introduction," 411, 407–8.

36. Douglas Reichert Powell, *Critical Regionalism: Connecting Politics and Culture in the American Landscape* (2007), 7, 24–25.

37. Timothy R. Mahoney and Wendy J. Katz, eds., *Regionalism and the Humanities* (2008), ix.

38. Edward Said, *Orientalism* (1979).

39. Leigh Anne Duck, *The Nation's Region* (2006).

40. Scott Romine, *The Real South*, 9.

41. Paul Chaat Smith, *Everything You Know about Indians Is Wrong*, 6.

42. Appending a "post" to the word "colonial" at all is itself a provocative maneuver, as Anne McClintock observed early on and most Native scholars have agreed: the colonial subjugation of American Indian peoples is too far from finished to be "post" anything yet. My reference to a postcolonial world, however, does not detract from the potential of tribal sovereignty, which remains a compelling political goal and reality even for southeastern tribes; instead, it urges us toward recognition of the common crisis experienced by all Americans in the encompassing crisis of late capitalism.

CHAPTER ONE. Reconstructing Loss

1. Annette Trefzer, *Disturbing Indians*, 182.

2. Trefzer, *Disturbing Indians*, 182.

3. Colonial agitators famously conducted the Boston Tea Party in 1773 while disguised as Mohawks; during the same period, Maine's Liberty Settlers dressed as vicious "White Indians" to help intimidate wealthy speculators to lower land prices. For more on these and other examples, see Bernard Bailyn's *Ideological Origins of the American Revolution* (1992), Philip Deloria's *Playing Indian* (1998), Alan Trachtenberg's *Shades of Hiawatha* (2004), and Alan Taylor's *Liberty Men and Great Proprietors* (1990).

4. Joel Martin, "'My Grandmother Was a Cherokee Princess,'" 140.

5. Theda Perdue and Michael Green, *The Columbia Guide to American Indians of the Southeast*, 147.

6. In Twelve Southerners, *I'll Take My Stand* (1930): Ransom, 20; Fletcher, 99–100; Nixon, 183.

7. *I'll Take My Stand*: Ransom, 8; Owsley, 71

8. *I'll Take My Stand*: Ransom, 23; Nixon, 193.

9. *I'll Take My Stand*: Nixon, 183.

10. William Alexander Percy, *Lanterns on the Levee: Recollections of a Planter's Son*, 16 (emphasis added).

11. Martin, "'My Grandmother Was a Cherokee Princess,'" 138

12. Renée Bergland, *The National Uncanny*, 4.

13. Fiedler, *Return of the Vanishing American*, 13.

14. David Treuer, *Native American Fiction*, 14.

15. Treuer, *Native American Fiction*, 16.

16. In *Collected Stories of William Faulkner*: "Red Leaves," "A Justice," "A Courtship,"

and "Lo!", as well as "Mountain Victory" and "A Bear Hunt"; and in *Go Down, Moses: "*The Old People," "The Bear," and "Delta Autumn."

17. Thomas S. Hines, *William Faulkner and the Tangible Past*, 149 n.4.

18. Frederick L. Gwynn and Joseph L. Blotner, *Faulkner in the University*, 9.

19. Quoted in Theresa M. Towner and James B. Carothers, *Reading Faulkner: Collected Stories: Glossary and Commentary*, 163.

20. See Robert Dale Parker, "Red Slippers and Cottonmouth Moccasins: White Anxieties in Faulkner's Indian Stories," 81–100.

21. Duane Gage, "William Faulkner's Indians," 27.

22. Tom Mould, *Choctaw Prophecy*, xxii–xxiii.

23. From Joseph Blotner, ed., *Selected Letters of William Faulkner*, 46–47.

24. Faulkner was apparently aware that "du homme" was an incorrect aberration of the French "de l'homme"; when his editor Malcolm Cowley inquired about the error, Faulkner responded, "I know it's *de l'homme*. I made it incorrect mainly because I decided no one would care especially. That is, it seemed righter to me that Ikke., knowing little of French or English either, should have an easy transition to the apt name he gave himself in English, than that the French should be consistent." See Malcolm Cowley, *The Faulkner-Cowley File*, 43.

25. Annette Trefzer offers a reading of Faulkner's Indian characters as a critique of colonialism; yet she, too, finds that he ultimately reverses such efforts by reinscribing the hegemonic logic of white paternalism and hierarchy. See Trefzer, "Postcolonial Displacements in Faulkner's Indian Stories of the 1930s," 68–88.

26. See Lewis M. Dabney, *The Indians of Yoknapatawpha* (1974); Elmo Howell, "William Faulkner's Chickasaw Legacy"; Trefzer, *Disturbing Indians* (2007); Don H. Doyle, *Faulkner's County* (2001); Gene Moore, ed., special issue on "Faulkner's Indians," *The Faulkner Journal* 18: 1&2 (Fall 2002/Spring 2003), 81–100.

27. Faulkner, *Go Down, Moses*, 180.

28. Treuer, *Native American Fiction*, 25.

29. An earlier and fuller version of my reading of Carter's novel appears in Melanie Benson, "The Native Screen: American Indians in Contemporary Southern Film."

30. "Asa Carter," in "George Wallace: Settin' the Woods on Fire."

31. Whether or not Carter had any distant Native ancestry in his family tree has been disputed, but it is at least certain that he was not raised in the culture. For more on Carter's biography, see Dan T. Carter's *The Politics of Rage* (1995) and "Southern History, American Fiction" in *Rewriting the South: History and Fiction* (1993); Diane McWhorter's *Carry Me Home* (2001); Calvin Reid in *Publisher's Weekly*; and Allen Barra, "The Education of Little Fraud."

32. Dan T. Carter, *The Politics of Rage*, 11, 109.

33. Barra, "Little Fraud."

34. In addition to *Little Tree*, Carter also wrote a number of popular westerns, including a "biography" of the Apache Geronimo called *Watch for Me on the Mountain* (1978) and republished in 1980 as *Cry, Geronimo!* Perhaps his most well-known western was *The Rebel Outlaw: Josey Wales* (1973), with Clint Eastwood playing (in the 1976 film adaptation) the protagonist Josey Wales, whose ecological sagacity includes statements like "don't piss down my back and tell me it's raining."

35. A handful of critics have uncovered and discussed the novel's underlying racism and white supremacist messages; see especially Eileen Elizabeth O'Connor Antalek, *Deforrestation Begins with a Little Tree* (1994) and Shari M. Huhndorf, *Going Native* (2001). When Oprah learned the truth about Carter's biography, she stated: "'I no longer — even though I had been moved by the story — felt the same about this book,' she said in 1994. 'There's a part of me that said, "Well, OK, if a person has two sides of them and can write this wonderful story and also write the segregation forever speech, maybe that's OK." But I couldn't — I couldn't live with that'"; yet the book remained on her virtual bookshelf of recommended reads (apparently due to an archival error) until late 2007 and, even then, remained a "wonderful story" in her memory. See Hillel Italie, "The Education of Oprah Winfrey."

36. Italie, "The Education of Oprah Winfrey."

37. Roger Ebert, for example, suggested that Carter's apparent empathy for Native American experience might constitute his "redemption" for his prior bigotry. See Roger Ebert, "Review of *The Education of Little Tree*." For a Native American response more aligned with Alexie's, see Daniel Heath Justice, "A Lingering Miseducation."

38. Elisabeth Keating, editorial review of *The Education of Little Tree*.

39. JumpStart Media Group, LLC, "Humanitas Prize."

40. Andrew L. Urban, "Education of Little Tree."

41. Michael Marker, "*The Education of Little Tree*."

42. My own essay (from which much of this reading is derived) is the single exception. See Melanie R. Benson, "Southern and Western Native Americans in Barry Hannah's Fiction."

43. Situating Hannah in this context may seem antithetical to recent critical work by Michael Kreyling, Martyn Bone, Matthew Guinn, and others, which places him in a *post*-southern context, one in which provincial conceptions of regional identification no longer apply. To be sure, while Hannah publicly "adores" the South, he certainly does not glorify or romanticize it. Instead, his novels are filled with extreme, racist, often grotesque characters and situations. He depicts a region still very much battling the demons of its historical transgressions, imprisoned, like the protagonist of *Ray*, "in so many centuries. Everybody is still alive" (41). Besieged by memories of both the

Civil War and the conflict in Vietnam, Ray Forrest's fragile mental state demonstrates that not only the South but the entire country remains haunted by the specter of imperialism. Guinn traces *Ray*'s even bleaker connections between the war in Vietnam and the De Soto expedition that "discovered" the Mississippi River and inaugurated the displacement and slaughter of the southeastern Indians. But Hannah's representation of unquiet *Indian* histories and spirits is more telling and troubling than Guinn allows because Hannah does not seem to acknowledge them as victims of the South's own nightmarish origins.

44. Martin, "'My Grandmother Was a Cherokee Princess,'" 136.

45. Martin, "'My Grandmother Was a Cherokee Princess,'" 140.

46. James D. Lilley and Brian Oberkirch, "An Interview with Barry Hannah."

47. Daniel Williams, "Interview with Barry Hannah," 266.

48. I am drawing here on Fredric Jameson's *The Political Unconscious* (1981), which advocates the "unmasking of cultural artifacts [like novels] as socially symbolic acts" with appreciable political significance, import, and influence (20). See also Lucy Maddox's *Removals* (1991), in which Maddox argues that nineteenth-century U.S. writers inevitably participated discursively in the effects of Removal.

49. Michael Spikes, "Lee Durkee's *Rides of the Midway* and Barry Hannah's *Geronimo Rex*," 411.

50. For instance, the founder of Harry's Hedermansever College (modeled on Hannah's own alma mater, Mississippi College) is suggestively named "President Hannah," née "Captain Hannah" of Civil War fame (125–26).

51. John Griffin Jones, ed., "Interview with Barry Hannah," 148.

52. The South's role in racial slavery is also alluded to here. In fact, the image of Geronimo in a cage closely resembles a scene in letter 9 of Crèvecœur's *Letters from an American Farmer*, in which John visits Charleston and witnesses the horrific treatment of a Negro slave, suspended in a cage and ravaged by birds and insects, left there to die "a living spectre" as punishment for killing an overseer (243–45).

53. The song was a hit, and it resulted in Murphey's eventual adoption into the Lakota Nation by the Dull Knife family. "Geronimo's Cadillac" has since been recorded by other singers such as Hoyt Axton, Mary McCaslin, and Cher. See Murphey's official website: www.michaelmartinmurphey.com/bio.htm.

54. Stephen Metcalf, "Yokely-Dokely America."

55. Melanie R. Benson, "Contemporary Crises of Value," in *Disturbing Calculations* (2008), especially 157–63.

56. Walker Percy, *The Last Gentleman*, 11.

57. Dorothy Allison, *Bastard Out of Carolina*, 207.

58. Quentin Tarantino, writer and director, *Inglourious Basterds* (2009); quoted

from "Memorable Quotes" page of *The Internet Movie Database*, imdb.com (accessed September 28, 2010).

59. Gidley and Gidley, "The Native-American South," 167.

60. Martin, "'My Grandmother Was a Cherokee Princess,'" 144. It is important here to note that the Indian Removal Act passed by the Jackson administration in 1830 — effecting within a mere decade the migration of over seventy thousand Indians from the Southeast's Five Civilized Tribes to lands west of the Mississippi — occurred prior to the Civil War and was instrumental in solidifying the South's cohesion: "The antebellum white South, devoted to slavery at all costs, was expanded, empowered, and consolidated by Indian Removal" (Martin 134).

61. Barry Hannah, *Captain Maximus* (New York: Penguin, 1986); subsequent references from the text will be cited parenthetically. The blurb on the back cover of the first Penguin edition states, "In this bold collection Barry Hannah blends the events of his own life and the 'life' that literary notoriety has attributed to him."

62. Arnold Krupat, *Red Matters*, 103.

63. "hanta," in Cyrus Byington, *A Dictionary of the Choctaw Language*, 136.

64. Louis Owens, *Nightland* (1996). Subsequent references from this text will be cited parenthetically.

65. Linda Lizut Helstern, "Re-Storying the West: Race, Gender, and Genre in *Nightland*," 119.

66. Jacquelyn Kilpatrick, "Introduction," 6.

67. Patrice Hollrah, "Decolonizing the Choctaws." See also Kirstin Squint, who suggests that Howe's books are "artistic productions that use decolonization tactics" ("Choctawan Aesthetics" 213).

68. Quoted in Hollrah, "Decolonizing the Choctaws," 73.

69. LeAnne Howe, *Shell Shaker* (2001), 42–43.

70. Howe, *Shell Shaker*, 200.

71. Howe, *Shell Shaker*, 72; Faulkner, *Requiem for a Nun*, act 1, scene 3.

72. Howe, *Shell Shaker*, 73.

73. Howe, *Shell Shaker*, 204.

74. Howe, *Shell Shaker*, 197.

75. See Howe's comments on tribalography in Squint's "Choctaw Aesthetics," 216–17. See also Howe's "My Mothers, My Uncles, Myself," 212–28.

76. Howe in "Choctaw Aesthetics," 216.

77. David Anderson, "Down Memory Lane," 108.

78. Eric Gary Anderson, "The Presence of Early Native Studies."

79. Keith Basso, *Wisdom Sits in Places*, 32.

80. Diane Glancy, *Pushing the Bear: A Novel of the Trail of Tears* (1996), 239. Subsequent references to this text will be cited parenthetically.

81. Glancy, *Pushing the Bear*, 176.

82. Glancy, *Pushing the Bear*, 237.

83. Amy J. Elias, "Fragments that Rune Up the Shores," 205.

84. Jennifer Andrews, "A Conversation with Diane Glancy," 651.

85. Gwynn and Blotner, eds., *Faulkner in the University*, 1.

86. Michael Kreyling, *Inventing Southern Literature*, xiv–xvi.

87. Janet McAdams, "News from the Imaginary Front," in *The Island of Lost Luggage*, 16.

CHAPTER TWO. Red, Black, and Southern

1. The following reading of Julie Dash's novel appears in an earlier, condensed form in my article "The Native Screen: American Indians in Contemporary Southern Film."

2. Marjorie Baumgarten, "Daughters of the Dust."

3. "Daughters of the Dust," *Kirkus Reviews*.

4. "Julie Dash Discusses *Daughters of the Dust*."

5. Ed Guerrero, *Framing Blackness*, 175.

6. Dash quoted in Scott MacDonald, *The Garden in the Machine*, 302.

7. MacDonald, *The Garden in the Machine*, 302.

8. Dash even named her production company "Geechee Girls."

9. Julie Dash, *Daughters of the Dust*, 31. Subsequent references from this novel will be cited parenthetically.

10. James F. Brooks, ed., *Confounding the Color Line*, 5.

11. See Jack D. Forbes, *Africans and Native Americans* (1993); Ivan Van Sertima, *They Came Before Columbus* (1976), and *African Presence in Early America* (1992).

12. Jack D. Forbes, "The Evolution of the Term Mulatto."

13. For a comprehensive and concise overview of Indian slavery in America, see Jonathan Brennan, "Introduction," *When Brer Rabbit Meets Coyote*, 3–10.

14. For example, as Stephen Webre explains in "The Problem of Indian Slavery in Spanish Louisiana, 1769–1803," Spanish law forbade Indian slavery but it was never enforced in French Louisiana where the practice abounded; after 1790, several Indian slaves sued successfully for their freedom, but when the United States purchased the region in 1803, it instituted codes that abolished slaves' civil rights.

15. For early instances of Natives and African resistance to European colonialism (particularly in the Caribbean, and later in Florida), see Jan Carew, "United We

Stand!"; and for specific instances of Afro-Indian alliance and intermixing during and after slavery, see Walton L. Brown, "The Forgotten Heritage."

16. See, for example, Carolyn T. Gassaway, "Black Indians in the Seminole Wars."

17. This effort has been broadly multidisciplinary in nature, covering historical, sociological, anthropological, and literary terrain. Foundational critics in this movement include Jack Forbes, James F. Brooks, Sharon Holland, Tiya Miles, Claudio Saunt, Christina Snyder, Jonathan Brennan, and others.

18. Brennan, *When Brer Rabbit Meets Coyote*, 17.

19. Mary Ellison, "Black Perceptions and Red Images," 45.

20. Barbara S. Tracy, "Transcultural Transformation: African American and Native American Relations" (PhD diss., 2009).

21. See especially Sharon Holland, Barbara S. Tracy, and Christa Davis Acampora and Angela L. Cotten.

22. Brennan, "Introduction," *When Brer Rabbit Meets Coyote*, 34–48.

23. *Turning South Again* (2001) is Houston A. Baker Jr.'s influential book, which explains the persistent racism in U.S. society by exploring its ideological roots in southern society and its continued influence on national thinking at large.

24. Toni Morrison, *A Mercy* (2008). Subsequent references to this text will be cited parenthetically.

25. Michele Norris, "Toni Morrison Finds 'A Mercy' in Servitude."

26. Patrick Minges, *Black Indian Slave Narratives*, xviii.

27. Craig Womack, "Tribal Paradise Lost but Where Did It Go?" 20.

28. Laura L. Lovett, "'African and Cherokee by Choice,'" 196.

29. Lovett, "'African and Cherokee by Choice,'" 193.

30. Honorée Fanonne Jeffers, "Hawk Hoof Tea," ll. 1–6, 22–30.

31. Jeffers, "Hawk Hoof Tea," l. 20.

32. Jeffers, "Hawk Hoof Tea," ll. 31–32.

33. Zora Neale Hurston, *Dust Tracks on a Road*, 235.

34. Hurston, *Dust Tracks on a Road*, 235.

35. Melville J. Herskovits, *The Anthropometry of the American Negro*, 15.

36. "Mardi Gras Indians: Tradition and History."

37. Alice Walker, *Living by the Word*, 82.

38. Alice Walker, *The Way Forward Is with a Broken Heart*, 35–37.

39. Forbes, *Black Africans and Native Americans*, 5.

40. Claudio Saunt, *Black, White, and Indian*, 4.

41. Tracy, "Transcultural Transformation," front matter/abstract (unnumbered).

42. Ron Welburn, "A Most Secret Identity," 292.

43. The literature on Indian slavery (both in the South and later in Indian Territory)

is voluminous: major works include Daniel Littlefield, Theda Perdue, and most recently, Tiya Miles, Celia Naylor and Christina Snyder.

44. Snyder, *Slavery in Indian Country*, 5. For a similar perspective on the pre-racial character of Indian slavery, see Kathryn E. Holland Braun's essay on early-eighteenth-century Creek slavery, "The Creek Indians, Blacks, and Slavery." Jack Forbes further describes the process by which colonial "envelopment" gives way to a race-caste society among the indigenous in "Envelopment, Proletarianization and Inferiorization."

45. Sharon P. Holland, "'If You Know I Have a History, You Will Respect Me,'" 335.

46. See Gerald Vizenor, *Crossbloods*, vii.

47. Scott Richard Lyons, *X-Marks: Native Signatures of Assent*, 1.

48. See Nancy Shoemaker, "How Indians Got to Be Red."

49. See James H. Merrell, "Racial Education of the Catawba Indians."

50. See Theda Perdue, "Cherokee Planters, Black Slaves, and African Colonization."

51. Susan Greenbaum discusses the ways that southern policies for racial identification appear on the federal level as well, complicating many tribes' (such as the Lumbee's) bids for recognition. See her "What's in a Label? Identity Problems of Southern Indian Tribes."

52. While their focus is largely on Indian and black relations outside of the South after Removal, Donald A. Grinde Jr. and Quintard Taylor detail the rising animosity between Freedmen settlers and Natives whose battles over land rights engendered fierce racial hostility and precipitated the adoption of segregation laws in Indian Territory. See their "Red vs. Black: Conflict and Accommodation in the Post-Civil War Indian Territory."

53. The status of Freedmen in the Cherokee Nation has long been a source of division and dissension within. For an account of Indian and Freedmen's dispute over land cession moneys in the 1880s, see Gary R. Kremer, "For Justice and a Fee."

54. Jane Dysart, among others, describes the intense pressure to assimilate into the southern biracial economy (usually by passing as white) and thereby evading the stigma of primitivism in "Another Road to Disappearance."

55. Craig Womack, "Tribal Paradise Lost," 27.

56. Louis Owens, *The Sharpest Sight* (1992). Subsequent page references from this text will be cited parenthetically.

57. For major examples of Native literary texts that feature Indian soldiers fighting in U.S. wars with profoundly mixed, vexed, and often tragic responses and results, see N. Scott Momaday's *House Made of Dawn;* Leslie Marmon Silko's *Ceremony;* and for a more recent, nonfictional/autobiographical, and southern example, see Delano Cummings, *Moon Dash Warrior*.

58. Louis Owens, *Mixedblood Messages*, 5–6.

59. In his frequent autobiographical writings, Owens divulges numerous details, events, and even names that match exactly those given to Cole's story in both *The Sharpest Sight* (1992) and *Bone Game* (1994).

60. Malinda Maynor Lowery, *Lumbee Indians in the Jim Crow South*, 13.

61. Theda Perdue, "Native Americans, African Americans, and Jim Crow," 30.

62. See, for example, historian Katherine M. B. Osburn, "The 'Identified Full-Bloods' in Mississippi."

63. Theda Perdue, "Native Americans, African Americans, and Jim Crow," 33.

64. Dawn Karima Pettigrew, *The Way We Make Sense*, 91. Subsequent references from this novel will be cited parenthetically.

65. Ralph Ellison, *Invisible Man*, 16.

66. Quoted in Roy Hurst, "Stepin Fetchit, Hollywood's First Black Film Star."

CHAPTER THREE. Reckoning the Future

1. In *Genocide of the Mind* (2003), an anthology of new Native American writing compiled by MariJo Moore (herself a North Carolina Cherokee). Lucci-Cooper, "To Carry the Fire Home," 3. Subsequent references from this text cited parenthetically.

2. Lucci-Cooper, "To Carry the Fire Home," 5.

3. Lucci-Cooper, "To Carry the Fire Home," 5.

4. See Melanie R. Benson, *Disturbing Calculations* (2008).

5. See Andre Gunder Frank, "The Development of Underdevelopment." For a fuller examination of the variety of dependency models emerging during the mid-twentieth century, advocating finally a reinvigorated approach to the power (versus the impotence) of these "southern" peripheries, see Tony Smith, "The Underdevelopment of Development Literature."

6. For a thorough overview of the development of this line of critical thought, see Colleen O'Neill's "Rethinking Modernity and the Discourse of Development," 6.

7. Kathryn Lucci-Cooper, "Finding Carrie," 376–77.

8. Andrew Nelson Lytle, "The Hind Tit," 234.

9. Lucci-Cooper, "Finding Carrie," 376.

10. Rosalind Krauss, "The Cultural Logic of the Late Capitalist Museum," 11.

11. Lucci-Cooper, "To Carry the Fire Home," 7.

12. Chief Phillip Martin with Lynne Jeter and Kendall Blanchard, *Chief*, 27.

13. Jessica R. Cattelino, *High Stakes*, 3–4.

14. Lynn Hotaling, "Tribal Council Approves Wal-Mart Lease."

15. See, for example, Partha Chatterjee, *Nationalist Thought and the Colonial World*, 30.

16. Richard D. Starnes, ed., "Introduction," *Southern Journeys*, 7.

17. Terry Eagleton, "Culture and Barbarism."

18. Alexis Celeste Bunten, "More Like Ourselves: Indigenous Capitalism through Tourism."

19. John L. and Jean Comaroff, *Ethnicity, Inc.*, 20.

20. Comaroff, *Ethnicity, Inc.*, 20.

21. Mickey Duvall, "Cherokee Retail and Business Update."

22. Douglas C. Wilms, "Cherokee Land Use in Georgia Before Removal," 1.

23. Akiva Friedland, "Progress in the Land of the Cherokees? Living and Dying by Tourism," 118.

24. Friedland, "Progress," 118.

25. Friedland, "Progress," 118.

26. Friedland, "Progress," 121.

27. Henry Lambert, quoted in Starnes, "Creating a 'Variety Vacationland,'" *Southern Journeys*, 146.

28. Friedland, "Progress," 121–22.

29. Quoted in James A. Schaap, "The Growth of the Native American Gaming Industry," 368. The full report referenced by Schaap is Jonathan Taylor and Joseph Kalt, *American Indians on Reservations*.

30. Starnes, "Creating a 'Variety Vacationland,'" 147.

31. http://www.nc-cherokee.com

32. http://www.cherokee-nc.com/index.php

33. See Martin, "'My Grandmother Was a Cherokee Princess,'" 144. For data on racial prejudice in response to preferential treatment and affirmative action–type policies more generally, see James H. Kuklinski et al., "Racial Prejudice and Attitudes toward Affirmative Action." As Eve Darian-Smith argues in *New Capitalists* (2004), largely as a result of tremendous economic development on reservations with gaming enterprises, Native Americans "are now receiving greater visibility in mainstream society. This visibility, upheld on the legal grounds that Native American sovereignty exists and can now be used to legally justify certain segregated privileges denied ordinary American citizens, helps to create a new sense of injustice by many non-Indians who now claim they are being unfairly treated" (8).

34. Alexandra Harmon, *Rich Indians*, 3.

35. Martin, *Chief*, 21.

36. Martin, *Chief*, 151.

37. Lucci-Cooper, "Finding Carrie," 381.

38. Lucci-Cooper, "Finding Carrie," 382, 381.

39. Jack Amariglio, Joseph W. Childers, and Stephen E. Cullenberg, *Sublime Economy*, 8.

40. Slavoj Žižek, *Violence*, 1–2.

41. Antonio Hardt and Michael Negri, *Commonwealth*, 7.

42. I am paraphrasing here the phenomenon described at greater length in the chapter "Capitalist Sovereignty" in Antonio Hardt and Michael Negri's *Empire*, 325–50.

43. "Yazoo Dusk," part of an unfinished novel, is published in Owens's collection of essays and vignettes, *I Hear the Train: Reflections, Inventions, Refractions* (2001), 160–175. Quoted material here is cited from the story's reprinting in Hobson et al., eds., *The People Who Stayed*, 217–29.

44. Owens, *I Hear the Train*, xiv.

45. These events are related in Louis Owens's *Bone Game*, 68–70.

46. Treaty with the Choctaw, 1830, Article XIV, *Indian Affairs: Laws and Treaties*, vol. 2. Ed. Charles J. Kappler (Washington, D.C.: Government Printing Office, 1904).

47. The removal of the Cherokees split the tribe and resulted in the assassination of two members of the Ridge family and Elias Boudinot by fellow Cherokees (John Ross's faction) in 1839.

48. Mark Fisher, *Capitalist Realism*, 34.

49. Hobson, *The Last of the Ofos*, ix.

50. The subhead above is a reference to the title of a short story by Sherman Alexie called "What You Pawn I Will Redeem," in which a homeless Spokane Indian attempts to reclaim his grandmother's powwow regalia from a city pawn shop.

51. Jerry Z. Muller, *The Mind and the Market*, 396–97.

52. Fisher, *Capitalist Realism*, 7, 3.

53. Fisher, *Capitalist Realism*, 71.

54. Chip Livingston, "Pond," 243.

55. Louis Owens, "Finding Gene."

56. Pamela Masotti, "Jukebox," 128.

57. Masotti, "Jukebox," 132.

58. Pettigrew, *The Way We Make Sense*, 16. Subsequent references to this novel will be cited parenthetically.

59. See George R. Stewart, *Names on the Land*, 191.

60. Pettigrew, *The Marriage of Saints*, 11.

61. From a souvenir view book of the exposition, *Blue Book: A Complete Souvenir View Book Illustrating the Panama-Pacific International Exposition*, 48.

62. Subsequent references from this text will be cited parenthetically.

63. For example, in late June 2009 a Cherokee Nation news release reported that a group of Oklahoma Cherokee called the "Removal Riders" had just traveled to Rome, Georgia, where they planned to begin their 900-plus-mile bike ride back to Tahlequah along the removal route. The ride reenacts a similar event (the "Remember the Removal" ride) held in 1984. See Cherokee Nation News, "Remember the Removal Riders Will Retrace Ancestors' Footsteps through History."

64. Ellis, *Walking the Trail*, 141.

CHAPTER FOUR. Excavating the World

1. Foundational works in globalization theory include Aijaz Ahmad, *In Theory: Classes, Nations, Literatures* (1992); Fredric Jameson, "Postmodernism; or, The Cultural Logic of Late Capitalism"; Fredric Jameson and Miyoshi Masao, eds., *The Cultures of Globalization* (1998).

2. See Robert Warrior, "Intellectual Sovereignty and the Struggle for an American Indian Future," 18–19.

3. Sharon Holland, "'If You Know I Have a History, You Will Respect Me,'" 337.

4. David A. Hollinger, *Beyond Multiculturalism*, 3.

5. Stuart Christie, *Plural Sovereignties and Contemporary Indigenous Literature*, 2.

6. Subsequent references to this novel will be cited parenthetically. A more detailed reading of *Meridian* and the protagonist's occluded Native ancestry appears in chapter 4 of my *Disturbing Calculations*, 129–63.

7. Harilaos Stecopoulos, *Reconstructing the World*, 167.

8. A report on one such collaboration, co-written by Karenne Wood and Jeffrey L. Hantman and titled "Writing Collaborative History," appears in *Archaeology Magazine*.

9. Derek Walcott, *Omeros*, 72.

10. Marilou Awiakta, *Selu*, 3.

11. Janet McAdams, "From *Betty Creek*: Writing the Indigenous Deep South," 255.

12. See Patricia R. Wickman, *Osceola's Legacy* (2006).

13. Jerald T. Milanich, "Osceola's Head."

14. Percival Everett, preface to Belle Boggs, *Mattaponi Queen*, ix.

15. Belle Boggs, *Mattaponi Queen* (2010). All subsequent references from this work will be cited parenthetically.

CONCLUSION. The South in the Indian and the Indian in the South

1. Jack Hitt, "The Newest Indians."

2. Louis Owens, *I Hear the Train*, xi. Subsequent reference cited parenthetically.

3. Fisher, *Capitalist Realism*, 81.

4. Gordon D. Henry Jr., "Allegories of Engagement," 20.

5. Colin Calloway, ed., *After King Philip's War*, 2, 8.

6. Laura Collins-Hughes, "'Genius Grant' a Boost to Linguist as She Revives a Native Language."

BIBLIOGRAPHY

Acampora, Christa Davis, and Angela L. Cotton. *Unmaking Race, Remaking Soul: Transformative Aesthetics and the Practice of Freedom*. Albany: State University of New York Press, 2007.

Acoose, Janice, et al., eds. *Reasoning Together: The Native Critics Collective*. Norman: University of Oklahoma Press, 2008.

Ahmad, Aijaz. *In Theory: Classes, Nations, Literatures*. London: Verso, 1992.

Alexie, Sherman. *Indian Killer*. New York: Atlantic Monthly Press, 1996.

———. "What You Pawn I Will Redeem." *New Yorker*, April 21, 2003, 168–75.

Allen, Chadwick. *Blood Narrative: Indigenous Identity in American Indian and Maori Literary and Activist Texts*. Durham, N.C.: Duke University Press, 2002.

Allison, Dorothy. *Bastard Out of Carolina*. New York: Penguin, 1992.

Amariglio, Jack, Joseph W. Childers, and Stephen E. Cullenberg. *Sublime Economy: On the Intersection of Art and Economics*. New York: Routledge, 2009.

Anderson, David. "Down Memory Lane: Nostalgia for the Old South in Post–Civil War Plantation Reminiscences." *Journal of Southern History* 71, no. 1 (February 2005): 105–36.

Anderson, Eric Gary. "The Presence of Early Native Studies: A Response to Stephanie Fitzgerald and Hilary E. Wyss." *American Literary History* 22, no. 2 (Summer 2010): 280–88.

Andrews, Jennifer. "A Conversation with Diane Glancy." *American Indian Quarterly* 26, no. 4 (2002): 651.

Antalek, Eileen Elizabeth O'Connor. *Deforrestation Begins with a Little Tree: Uncovering the Polemic of Asa Carter in His Novels as Forrest Carter*. MA thesis, Clark University, 1994.

"Asa Carter." In "George Wallace: Settin' the Woods on Fire." *The American Experience*. PBS, 2000. http://www.pbs.org/wgbh/amex/wallace/peopleevents/pande01.html (accessed June 18, 2008).

Awiakta, Marilou. *Selu: Seeking the Corn-Mother's Wisdom*. Golden, Colo.: Fulcrum, 1993.

Bailyn, Bernard. *The Ideological Origins of the American Revolution*. Cambridge: Belknap/Harvard University Press, 1992.

Baker, Houston A., Jr. *Turning South Again: Re-Thinking Modernism / Re-reading Booker T.* Durham, N.C.: Duke University Press, 2001.

Ball, Edward. "Gone with the Myths." *New York Times*, Opinion Pages, December 18, 2010. http://www.nytimes.com/2010/12/19/opinion/19Ball.html?scp=6&sq =secession%20ball&st=cse (accessed January 13, 2011).

Barra, Allen. "The Education of Little Fraud." *Salon.com*. Salon.com Books. December 20, 2001. http://archive.salon.com/books/feature/2001/12/20/carter (accessed June 21, 2008).

Basso, Keith. *Wisdom Sits in Places: Landscape and Language among the Western Apache*. Albuquerque: University of New Mexico Press, 1996.

Baumgarten, Marjorie. "Daughters of the Dust." *Austin Chronicle*, February 14, 1992. http://www.austinchronicle.com/gyrobase/Calendar/Film?Film=oid%3A139192 (accessed November 23, 2008).

Behre, Robert. "NAACP to Protest Secession Event." *Charleston Post and Courier*, December 3, 2010. http://www.postandcourier.com/news/2010/dec/03/naacp-to -protest-secession-event (accessed December 14, 2010).

Benson, Melanie R. *Disturbing Calculations: The Economics of Identity in Postcolonial Southern Literature, 1912–2002*. Athens: University of Georgia Press, 2008.

———. "The Native Screen: American Indians in Contemporary Southern Film." In *American Cinema and the Southern Imaginary*, ed. Kathryn McKee and Deborah Barker. Athens: University of Georgia Press, 2011.

———. "Southern and Western Native Americans in Barry Hannah's Fiction." In *Perspectives on Barry Hannah*, ed. Martyn Bone, 139–60. Oxford: University Press of Mississippi, 2006.

Berardi, Franco. *The Soul at Work: From Alienation to Autonomy*. Cambridge: MIT Press, 2009.

Bergland, Renée. *The National Uncanny: Indian Ghosts and American Subjects*. Hanover, N.H.: University Press of New England, 2000.

Berkhofer, Robert F. *The White Man's Indian: Images of the American Indian from Columbus to the Present*. New York: Vintage, 1979.

Bhabha, Homi. "The Other Question." In *The Location of Culture*, 66–84. New York: Routledge, 1994.

Boggs, Belle. *Mattaponi Queen*. Minneapolis: Graywolf Press, 2010.

Bone, Martyn. "'All the Confederate Dead . . . All of Faulkner the Great': Faulkner,

Hannah, Neo-Confederate Narrative and Postsouthern Parody." *Mississippi Quarterly* 45, no. 2 (Spring 2001) 197–211.

———. *The Postsouthern Sense of Place in Contemporary Fiction.* Baton Rouge: Louisiana State University Press, 2005.

Braun, Kathryn E. Holland. "The Creek Indians, Blacks, and Slavery." *Journal of Southern History* 57, no. 4 (1991): 601–36.

Brennan, Jonathan, ed. *When Brer Rabbit Meets Coyote: African-Native American Literature.* Urbana: University of Illinois Press, 2003.

Brooks, James F., ed. *Confounding the Color Line: The Indian-Black Experience in North America.* Lincoln: University of Nebraska Press, 2002.

Brown, Walton L. "The Forgotten Heritage: African-Amerindian Relations in America." *Proteus* 9, no. 1 (1992): 11–17.

Buchanan, Patrick J. "The New Intolerance." *Patrick J. Buchanan: Right from the Start*, April 9, 2010. http://buchanan.org/blog/the-new-intolerance-3878 (accessed September 23, 2010).

Bunten, Alexis Celeste. "More Like Ourselves: Indigenous Capitalism through Tourism." *American Indian Quarterly* 34, no. 3 (Summer 2010): 285–311.

Calloway, Colin, ed. *After King Philip's War: Presence and Persistence in Indian New England.* Hanover, N.H.: University Press of New England, 1997.

Carew, Jan. "United We Stand! Joint Struggles of Native Americans and African Americans in the Columbian Era." *Monthly Review* 44, no. 3 (1992): 103–27.

Carter, Dan T. *The Politics of Rage.* New York: Simon & Schuster, 1995.

———. "Southern History, American Fiction: The Secret Life of Southwestern Novelist Forrest Carter." In *Rewriting the South: History and Fiction*, ed. Lothar Honnighausen and Valeria Gennaro Lerda, 286–304. Transatlantic Perspectives 3. Tübingen: Francke, 1993.

Carter, Forrest. *Cry Geronimo.* New York: Random House, 1980.

———. *The Education of Little Tree.* New York: Delacorte Press, 1976.

———. *The Rebel Outlaw: Josey Wales.* Frankfort, Ky.: Whippoorwill Press, 1973.

———. *Watch for Me on the Mountain.* New York: Delacorte Press, 1978.

Cattelino, Jessica R. *High Stakes: Florida Seminole Gaming and Sovereignty.* Durham, N.C.: Duke University Press, 2008.

Chatterjee, Partha. *Nationalist Thought and the Colonial World: A Derivative Discourse.* London: Zed, 1986.

Cherokee Nation News. "Remember the Removal Riders Will Retrace Ancestors' Footsteps through History." http://www.cherokee.org/NewsRoom/FullStory/2925/Page/Default.aspx (accessed June 25, 2009).

Christie, Stuart. *Plural Sovereignties and Contemporary Indigenous Literature*. New York: Palgrave Macmillan, 2009.

Cobb, James C., and William Stueck, eds. *Globalization and the American South*. Athens: University of Georgia Press, 2005.

Cohn, Deborah N. *History and Memory in the Two Souths: Recent Southern and Spanish American Fiction*. Nashville: Vanderbilt University Press, 1999.

Collins-Hughes, Laura. "'Genius Grant' a Boost to Linguist as She Revives a Native Language." *Boston Globe*, September 28, 2010. http://www.boston.com/lifestyle/ articles/2010/09/28/reviving_wampanoag_earns_linguist_a_genius_grant (accessed September 28, 2010).

Comaroff, John L. and Jean. *Ethnicity, Inc*. Chicago: University of Chicago Press, 2009.

Cook-Lynn, Elizabeth. "The American Indian Fiction Writer: Cosmopolitanism, Nationalism, the Third World, and First Nation Sovereignty." *Wicazo Sa Review* 9, no. 2 (Autumn 1993): 26–36.

———. "American Indian Intellectualism and the New Indian Story." *American Indian Quarterly* 20, no. 1 (1996): 57–76.

Cummings, Delano. *Moon Dash Warrior: The Story of an American Indian in Vietnam, a Marine from the Land of the Lumbee*. Livermore, Maine: Signal Tree, 1998.

Dabney, Lewis M. *The Indians of Yoknapatawpha: A Study in Literature and History*. Baton Rouge: Louisiana State University Press, 1974.

Darian-Smith, Eve. *New Capitalists: Law, Politics, and Identity Surrounding Casino Gambling on Native American Land*. Belmont, Calif.: Wadsworth, 2004.

Dash, Julie. *Daughters of the Dust: A Novel*. New York: Plume, 1999.

Daughters of the Dust. Written and directed by Julie Dash. American Playhouse, 1991.

"Daughters of the Dust." *Kirkus Reviews*, August 1, 1997. LexisNexis Academic (accessed August 21, 2010).

Davis, Jefferson. *The Rise and Fall of the Confederate Government*. New York: D. Appleton and Co., 1881.

Davis, William C. *The Cause Lost: Myths and Realities of the Confederacy*. Lawrence: University Press of Kansas, 2003.

Deloria, Philip. *Playing Indian*. New Haven: Yale University Press, 1998.

Dippie, Brian. *The Vanishing American: White Attitudes and U.S. Indian Policy*. Middletown, Conn.: Wesleyan University Press, 1982.

Doyle, Don H. *Faulkner's County: The Historical Roots of Yoknapatawpha*. Chapel Hill: University of North Carolina Press, 2001.

Duck, Leigh Anne. *The Nation's Region: Southern Modernism, Segregation, and U.S. Nationalism*. Athens: University of Georgia Press, 2006.

Duvall, Mickey. "Cherokee Retail and Business Update." *Cherokee One Feather,* April 19, 2010. http://www.nc-cherokee.com/theonefeather/2010/04/19/cherokee -retail-and-business-update (accessed January 22, 2011).

Dysart, Jane. "Another Road to Disappearance: Assimilation of Creek Indians in Pensacola, Florida, during the Nineteenth Century." *Florida Historical Quarterly* 61, no. 1 (1982): 37–48.

Eagleton, Terry. "Culture and Barbarism: Metaphysics in a Time of Terrorism." *Commonweal,* March 27, 2009. http://www.commonwealmagazine.org/culture -barbarism-0 (accessed March 2, 2010).

Ebert, Roger. "Review of *The Education of Little Tree.*" Rogerebert.com. *Chicago Sun Times* (January 20, 1998) http://rogerebert.suntimes.com/apps/pbcs.dll /article?aid=/19980120/reviews/801200301/1023 (accessed July 5, 2008).

Elias, Amy J. "Fragments that Rune Up the Shores: *Pushing the Bear,* Coyote Aesthetics, and Recovered History." *Modern Fiction Studies* 5, no. 1 (1999): 185–211.

Ellis, Jerry. *Walking the Trail: One Man's Journey Along the Cherokee Trail of Tears.* Lincoln: University of Nebraska Press, 1991.

Ellison, Mary. "Black Perceptions and Red Images: Indian and Black Literary Links." *Phylon* 44, no. 1 (1983): 44–55.

Ellison, Ralph. *Invisible Man.* 1952. Reprint; New York: Random House, 1995.

Everett, Percival. Preface to *Mattaponi Queen,* by Belle Boggs, ix. Minneapolis: Graywolf Press, 2010.

Faulkner, William. *Absalom, Absalom!* 1936. Reprint; New York: Vintage, 1990.

———. *Collected Stories.* New York: Vintage, 1995.

———. *Go Down, Moses.* 1942. Reprint; New York: Vintage, 1990.

———. *Selected Letters of William Faulkner.* Ed. Joseph Blotner. New York: Random House, 1977.

Fiedler, Leslie A. *The Return of the Vanishing American.* New York: Stein and Day, 1968.

Fisher, Mark. *Capitalist Realism: Is There No Alternative?* UK: Zero Books, 2009.

Fogel, Robert William, and Stanley L. Engerman. *Time on the Cross: The Economics of American Negro Slavery.* 1974. Reprint; New York: W. W. Norton, 1995.

Forbes, Jack D. *Africans and Native Americans: The Language of Race and the Evolution of Black-Red Peoples.* Urbana: University of Illinois Press, 1993.

———. *Black Africans and Native Americans.* London: Basil Blackwell, 1990.

———. "Envelopment, Proletarianization and Inferiorization: Aspects of Colonialism's Impact upon Native Americans and Other People of Color in Eastern North America." *Journal of Ethnic Studies* 18, no. 4 (1991): 95–122.

———. "The Evolution of the Term *Mulatto:* A Chapter in Black-Native American Relations." *Journal of Ethnic Studies* 10, no. 2 (1982): 45–66.

Foster, Gaines. *Ghosts of the Confederacy: Defeat, the Lost Cause and the Emergence of the New South, 1865–1913*. Cambridge: Oxford University Press, 1988.

Foster, Tol. "Relations and Regionality." In *Reasoning Together: The Native Critics Collective*, ed. Janice Acoose et al., 265–302. Norman: University of Oklahoma Press, 2008.

Frank, Andre Gunder. "The Development of Underdevelopment." In *Dependence and Underdevelopment*, ed. James D. Cockcroft, Andre Gunder Frank, and Dale Johnson. Garden City, N.Y.: Anchor Books, 1972.

Frazier, Charles. *Thirteen Moons*. New York: Random House, 2006.

Friedland, Akiva. "Progress in the Land of the Cherokees? Living and Dying by Tourism." Issue on "Race: Past Present and Future." *Oxford American Magazine* 64 (March 2009): 118–23.

Gage, Duane. "William Faulkner's Indians." *American Indian Quarterly* 1, no. 1 (Spring 1974): 27–33.

Gallagher, Gary W., and Alan T. Nolan, eds. *The Myth of the Lost Cause and Civil War History*. Bloomington: Indiana University Press, 2010.

Gassaway, Carolyn T. "Black Indians in the Seminole Wars." *South Florida History* 27, no. 1 (1998–99): 10–17.

Gidley, Mick, and Ben Gidley. "The Native-American South." In *A Companion to the Literature and Culture of the American South*, ed. Richard Gray and Owen Robinson, 166–84. Malden, U.K.: Blackwell, 2004.

Glancy, Diane. *Pushing the Bear: A Novel of the Trail of Tears*. New York: Harcourt, 1996.

Goldfield, David. *Still Fighting the Civil War: The American South and Southern History*. Baton Rouge: Louisiana State University Press, 2004.

Greenbaum, Susan. "What's in a Label? Identity Problems of Southern Indian Tribes." *Journal of Ethnic Studies* 19, no. 2 (1991): 107–26.

Greeson, Jennifer Rae. *Our South: Geographic Fantasy and the Rise of National Literature*. Cambridge: Harvard University Press, 2010.

Grinde, Donald A., Jr., and Quintard Taylor. "Red vs. Black: Conflict and Accommodation in the Post–Civil War Indian Territory." *American Indian Quarterly* 8, no. 3 (1984): 211–29.

Guerrero, Ed. *Framing Blackness: The African American Image in Film*. Philadelphia: Temple University Press, 1993.

Guinn, Matthew. *After Southern Modernism: Fiction of the Contemporary South*. Jackson: University Press of Mississippi, 2000.

Gwynn, Frederick L., and Joseph L. Blotner. *Faulkner in the University*. 1959. Reprint; Charlottesville: University Press of Virginia, 1995.

Handley, George B. *Postslavery Literatures in the Americas: Family Portraits in Black and White*. Charlottesville: University Press of Virginia, 2000.

Hannah, Barry. *Geronimo Rex*. New York: Penguin, 1972.

———. *Never Die*. Boston: Houghton Mifflin, 1991.

———. *Ray*. New York: Penguin, 1980.

———. "Ride, Fly, Penetrate, Loiter." In *Captain Maximus*. New York: Penguin, 1986.

"hanta." In *A Dictionary of the Choctaw Language*, ed. Cyrus Byington. n.p.: Dyson Press, 2009. 136.

Hantman, Jeffrey L., and Karenne Wood. "Writing Collaborative History." *Archaeology Magazine* 53, no. 5 (Sept/Oct 2000): 56–59.

Hardt, Antonio, and Michael Negri. *Commonwealth*. New York: Harvard University Press, 2009.

———. *Empire*. Cambridge: Harvard University Press, 2001. Harmon, Alexandra. *Rich Indians: Native People and the Problem of Wealth in American History*. Chapel Hill: University of North Carolina Press, 2010.

Harvey, David. *Spaces of Global Capitalism: Toward a Theory of Uneven Geographical Development*. New York: Verso, 2006.

Hedge Coke, Allison Adelle. *Blood Run*. Cambridge, UK: Salt Publishing, 2006.

———. *Off-Season City Pipe*. Minneapolis: Coffee House Press, 2005.

———. *Rock, Ghost, Willow, Deer*. Lincoln: University of Nebraska Press, 2004.

Helstern, Linda Lizut. "Re-Storying the West: Race, Gender, and Genre in *Nightland*." In *Louis Owens: Literary Reflections on His Life and Work*, ed. Jacquelyn Kilpatrick, 119–38. Norman: University of Oklahoma Press, 2004.

Henry, Gordon D., Jr. "Allegories of Engagement." In *North American Indian Writing, Storytelling, and Critique*, ed. Gordon D. Henry Jr., Nieves Pascual Soler, and Silvia Martinex-Falquina. East Lansing: Michigan State University Press, 2009.

Herman, Matthew D. *Politics and Aesthetics in Contemporary Native American Literature*. New York: Routledge, 2009.

Herskovits, Melville J. *The Anthropometry of the American Negro*. New York: AMS Press, 1930.

Hines, Thomas S. *William Faulkner and the Tangible Past: The Architecture of Yoknapatawpha*. Berkeley: University of California Press, 2006.

Hitt, Jack. "The Newest Indians." *New York Times Magazine*, August 21, 2005. http://www.nytimes.com/2005/08/21/magazine/21native.html?pagewanted=1&_r=2 (accessed September 25, 2010).

Hobson, Geary. *The Last of the Ofos*. Tucson: University of Arizona Press, 2000.

Hobson, Geary, Janet McAdams, and Kathryn Walkiewicz, eds. "Introduction: The

South Seldom Seen." In *The People Who Stayed: Southeastern Indian Writing after Removal*, 1–20. Norman: University of Oklahoma Press, 2010.

Holland, Sharon P. "'If You Know I Have a History, You Will Respect Me': A Perspective on Afro-Native American Literature." *Callaloo* 17, no. 1 (Winter 1994): 334–50.

Hollinger, David A. *Beyond Multiculturalism*. New York: Basic Books, 2000.

Hollrah, Patrice. "Decolonizing the Choctaws: Teaching LeAnne Howe's 'Shell Shaker.'" *American Indian Quarterly* 28, no. 1/2 (Winter/Spring 2004): 73–85.

Hosmer, Brian, and Colleen O'Neill, eds. *Native Pathways: American Indian Culture and Economic Development in the Twentieth Century*. Boulder: University Press of Colorado, 2004.

Hotaling, Lynn. "Tribal Council Approves Wal-Mart Lease." *Sylva Herald and Ruralite*, May 20, 2009. http://www.thesylvaheraldblog.com/?p=920 (accessed June 16, 2009).

Howe, LeAnne. "My Mothers, My Uncles, Myself." In *Here First: Autobiographical Essays by Native American Writers*, ed. Arnold Krupat and Brian Swann, 212–28. New York: Random House, 2000.

———. *Shell Shaker*. San Francisco: Aunt Lute Books, 2001.

Howell, Elmo. "William Faulkner's Chickasaw Legacy: A Note on 'Red Leaves.'" *Arizona Quarterly* 26, no. 4 (Winter 1970): 293–303.

Huhndorf, Shari M. *Going Native: Indians in the American Cultural Imagination*. Ithaca: Cornell University Press, 2001.

———. *Mapping the Americas: The Transnational Politics of Contemporary Native Culture*. Ithaca: Cornell University Press, 2009.

"Humanitas Prize." Humanitasprize.org. 2007. JumpStart Media Group, LLC. http://www.humanitasprize.org (accessed November 24, 2008).

Hurst, Roy. "Stepin Fetchit, Hollywood's First Black Film Star." NPR, March 6, 2006. http://www.npr.org/templates/story/story.php?storyId=5245089 (accessed September 20, 2010).

Hurston, Zora Neale. *Dust Tracks on a Road*. Urbana: University of Illinois Press, 1984.

Italie, Hillel. "The Education of Oprah Winfrey." *Reznet: Reporting from Native America*. University of Montana School of Journalism, 2008. http://www.reznetnews.org/article/ap/education-oprah-winfrey (accessed July 6, 2008).

Jameson, Fredric. *The Political Unconscious: Narrative as a Socially Symbolic Act*. Ithaca: Cornell University Press, 1981.

———. "Postmodernism; or, The Cultural Logic of Late Capitalism." *New Left Review* 146 (1984): 59–92.

Jameson, Fredric, and Miyoshi Masao, eds. *The Cultures of Globalization*. Durham, N.C.: Duke University Press, 1998.

Jeffers, Honorée Fanonne. "Hawk Hoof Tea." In *The People Who Stayed: Southeastern Indian Writing after Removal*, ed. Geary Hobson et al., 230–31. Norman: University of Oklahoma Press, 2010.

Jones, John Griffin, ed. "Interview with Barry Hannah." In *Mississippi Writers Talking*, 131–66. Jackson: University Press of Mississippi, 1982.

Jones, Stephen Graham. "Discovering America." In *Native Storiers*, ed. Gerald Vizenor, 41–44. Lincoln: University of Nebraska Press, 2009.

"Julie Dash Discusses *Daughters of the Dust*." African American Literature Book Club (December 19, 1997). http://aalbc.com/authors/juliedashchattext.htm (accessed August 21, 2010).

Justice, Daniel Heath. "A Lingering Miseducation: Confronting the Legacy of *Little Tree*." *Studies in American Indian Literature* 12, no. 1 (2000): 20–36.

Kappler, Charles J. "Treaty with the Choctaw, 1830, Article XIV." *Indian Affairs: Laws and Treaties*, vol. 2. Washington, D.C.: Government Printing Office, 1904. http://digital.library.okstate.edu/kappler/vol2/treaties/cho0310.htm (accessed September 6, 2010).

Keating, Elisabeth. Editorial review of *The Education of Little Tree*. Amazon.com. http://www.amazon.com/Education-Little-Tree-James-Cromwell (accessed July 6, 2008).

Kennedy, James Ronald, and Walter Donald Kennedy. *The South Was Right!* 1991. Reprint; Gretna, La.: Pelican Publishing, 1994.

Kilpatrick, Jacquelyn. Introduction to *Louis Owens: Literary Reflections on His Life and Work*, 3–17. Norman: University of Oklahoma Press, 2004.

Krauss, Rosalind. "The Cultural Logic of the Late Capitalist Museum." *October* 54 (Autumn 1990): 3–17.

Kremer, Gary R. "For Justice and a Fee: James Milton Turner and the Cherokee Freedmen." *Chronicles of Oklahoma* 58, no. 4 (1980–81): 376–91.

Kreyling, Michael. "Fee, Fie, Faux Faulkner: Parody and Postmodernism in Southern Literature." *Southern Review* 29 (Winter 1993): 1–15.

———. *Inventing Southern Literature*. Jackson: University Press of Mississippi, 1998.

Krupat, Arnold. *Red Matters: Native American Studies*. Philadelphia: University of Pennsylvania Press, 2002.

———. *The Turn to the Native*. Lincoln: University of Nebraska Press, 1996.

Kuklinski, James H., et al. "Racial Prejudice and Attitudes toward Affirmative Action." *American Journal of Political Science* 41, no. 2 (April 1997): 402–19.

Lai, Paul, and Lindsey Claire Smith. "Introduction." *American Quarterly* 62, no. 3 (September 2010): 407–36.

Leach, Loretta. "Varnertown in the 1950s." In *The People Who Stayed: Southeastern Indian Writing after Removal*, ed. Geary Hobson et al., 213. Norman: University of Oklahoma Press, 2010.

Lilley, James D., and Brian Oberkirch. "An Interview with Barry Hannah." *Mississippi Review* 25, no. 3 (1997): 19–43.

Livingston, Chip. "Pond." In *The People Who Stayed: Southeastern Indian Writing after Removal*, ed. Geary Hobson et al., 238–44. Norman: University of Oklahoma Press, 2010.

Lovett, Laura L. "'African and Cherokee by Choice': Race and Resistance under Legalized Segregation." In *Confounding the Color Line: The Indian-Black Experience in North America*, ed. James F. Brooks, 192–222. Lincoln: University of Nebraska Press, 2002.

Lowery, Malinda Maynor. *Lumbee Indians in the Jim Crow South*. Chapel Hill: University of North Carolina Press, 2009.

Lucci-Cooper, Kathryn. "Finding Carrie: Reaffirming Identity through Blood, Beads, and Bones." In *Eating Fire, Tasting Blood: An Anthology of the American Indian Holocaust*, ed. MariJo Moore, 374–85. New York: Thunder's Mouth Press, 2006.

———. "To Carry the Fire Home." In *Genocide of the Mind*, ed. MariJo Moore, 3–12. New York: Thunder's Mouth Press, 2003.

Lyons, Scott Richard. *X-Marks: Native Signatures of Assent*. Minneapolis: University of Minnesota Press, 2010.

Lytle, Andrew Nelson. "The Hind Tit." In *I'll Take My Stand: The South and the Agrarian Tradition*. Twelve Southerners. Baton Rouge: Louisiana State University Press, 1977.

Maddox, Lucy. *Removals: Nineteenth Century American Literature and the Politics of Indian Affairs*. New York: Oxford University Press, 1991.

MacDonald, Scott. *The Garden in the Machine: A Field Guide to Independent Films about Place*. Berkeley: University of California Press, 2001.

Madsen, Deborah L., ed. *Native Authenticity: Transnational Perspectives on Native American Literary Studies*. Albany: State University of New York Press, 2010.

Mahoney, Timothy R., and Wendy J. Katz, eds. *Regionalism and the Humanities*. Lincoln: University of Nebraska Press, 2008.

"Mardi Gras Indians: Tradition and History." *Mardi Gras New Orleans*. http://www.mardigrasneworleans.com/mardigrasindians.html (accessed August 22, 2010).

Marker, Michael. "*The Education of Little Tree*: What It Really Reveals about Public Schools." *Phi Delta Kappan* 74, no. 3 (Nov. 1992): 226–27.

Martin, Joel W. "'My Grandmother Was a Cherokee Princess': Representations of
Indians in Southern History." In *Dressing in Feathers: The Construction of the Indian
in American Popular Culture*, ed. S. Elizabeth Bird, 129–47. Boulder: Westview
Press, 1996.

Martin, Chief Phillip, with Lynne Jeter and Kendall Blanchard. *Chief: The
Autobiography of Chief Phillip Martin, Longtime Tribal Leader, Mississippi Band of
Choctaw Indians*. Brandon, Miss.: Quail Ridge Press, 2009.

Masotti, Pamela. "Jukebox." In *The People Who Stayed: Southeastern Indian Writing
after Removal*, ed. Geary Hobson et al., 127–32. Norman: University of Oklahoma
Press, 2010.

McAdams, Janet. *Feral*. Cambridge, UK: Salt Publishing, 2007.

———. "From *Betty Creek*: Writing the Indigenous Deep South." In *The People Who
Stayed: Southeastern Indian Writing after Removal*, ed. Geary Hobson et al., 251–56.
Norman: University of Oklahoma Press, 2010.

———. "News from the Imaginary Front." In *The Island of Lost Luggage*. Tucson:
University of Arizona Press, 2000.

McClintock, Anne. "The Angel of Progress: Pitfalls of the Term 'Post-colonialism.'"
Social Text (1992): 1–15.

McPherson, Tara. *Reconstructing Dixie: Race, Gender, and Nostalgia in the Imagined
South*. Durham, N.C.: Duke University Press, 2003.

McWhorter, Diane. *Carry Me Home: The Climactic Battle of the Civil Rights Revolution*.
New York: Simon & Schuster, 2001.

Merrell, James H. "Racial Education of the Catawba Indians." *Journal of Southern
History* 50, no. 3 (1984): 363–84.

Metcalf, Stephen. "Yokely-Dokely America: The Disgracefulness of Charles Frazier."
Slate Magazine, October 12, 2006. http://www.slate.com/id/2151424 (accessed
January 20, 2011).

Michaels, Walter Benn. *Our America: Nativism, Modernism, and Pluralism*. Durham,
N.C.: Duke University Press, 1995.

Milanich, Jerald T. "Osceola's Head." *Archaeology* 57, no. 1 (January/February 2004):
48–53.

Miles, Tiya. *The House on Diamond Hill: A Cherokee Plantation Story*. Chapel Hill:
University of North Carolina Press, 2010.

———. *Ties That Bind: The Story of an Afro-Cherokee Family in Slavery and Freedom*.
Berkeley: University of California Press, 2005.

Miles, Tiya, and Sharon Holland, eds. *Crossing Waters, Crossing Worlds: The
African Diaspora in Indian Country*. Durham, N.C.: Duke University Press,
2006.

Minges, Patrick. *Black Indian Slave Narratives*. Winston-Salem, N.C.: John F. Blair, 2004.

Momaday, N. Scott. *House Made of Dawn*. New York: Harper & Row, 1968.

Moore, Gene, ed. Special Issue on "Faulkner's Indians." *Faulkner Journal* 18, nos. 1&2 (Fall 2002/Spring 2003).

Morrison, Toni. *A Mercy*. London: Chatto & Windus, 2008.

——. *Playing in the Dark: Whiteness and the Literary Imagination*. Cambridge: Harvard University Press, 1992.

Mould, Tom. *Choctaw Prophecy: A Legacy of the Future*. Tuscaloosa: University of Alabama Press, 2003.

Muller, Jerry Z. *The Mind and the Market: Capitalism in Western Thought*. New York: Anchor Books, 2003.

Norris, Michele. "Toni Morrison Finds 'A Mercy' in Servitude." *All Things Considered*. NPR, October 27, 2008. http://www.npr.org/templates/story/story .php?storyId=95961382 (accessed August 19, 2010).

Odum, Howard. *Southern Regions of the United States*. Chapel Hill: University of North Carolina Press, 1936.

O'Neill, Colleen. "Rethinking Modernity and the Discourse of Development." In *Native Pathways: American Indian Culture and Economic Development in the Twentieth Century*, ed. Brian Hosmer and Colleen O'Neill, 1–26. Boulder: University Press of Colorado, 2004.

Osburn, Katherine M. B. "The 'Identified Full-Bloods' in Mississippi: Race and Choctaw Identity, 1898–1918." *Ethnohistory* 56 (Summer 2009): 423–47.

Owens, Louis. *Bone Game*. Norman: University of Oklahoma Press, 1993.

——. "Finding Gene." *Weber Journal* 16, no. 2 (Winter 1999). http://weberjournal .weber.edu/archive/archive%20C%20Vol.%2016.2-18.1/Vol.%2016.2/louisowens .html (accessed September 22, 2010).

——. *I Hear the Train: Reflections, Inventions, Refractions*. Norman: University of Oklahoma Press, 2001.

——. *Mixedblood Messages: Literature, Film, Family, Place*. Norman: University of Oklahoma Press, 1998

——. *Nightland*. Norman: University of Oklahoma Press, 1996.

——. *The Sharpest Sight*. Norman: University of Oklahoma Press, 1992.

——. "Yazoo Dusk." In *The People Who Stayed: Southeastern Indian Writing after Removal*, ed. Geary Hobson et al., 217–29. Norman: University of Oklahoma Press, 2010.

Panama-Pacific International Exposition Co. *Blue Book: A Complete Souvenir View*

Book Illustrating the Panama-Pacific International Exposition. San Francisco: Panama-Pacific International Exposition Co., 1915.

Parker, Robert Dale. "Red Slippers and Cottonmouth Moccasins: White Anxieties in Faulkner's Indian Stories." In Special Issue on "Faulkner's Indians." *Faulkner Journal* 18, nos. 1&2 (Fall 2002/Spring 2003): 81–100.

Peacock, James L., Harry L. Watson, and Carrie R. Matthews, eds. *The American South in a Global World.* Chapel Hill: University of North Carolina Press, 2005.

Percy, Walker. *The Last Gentleman.* New York: Picador, 1966.

Percy, William Alexander. *Lanterns on the Levee: Recollections of a Planter's Son.* Baton Rouge: Louisiana State University Press, 1974.

Perdue, Theda. "Cherokee Planters, Black Slaves, and African Colonization." *Chronicles of Oklahoma* 60, no. 3 (1982): 322–31.

———. "Native Americans, African Americans, and Jim Crow." In *IndiVisible: African-Native Lives in the Americas,* ed. Gabrielle Tayac, 21–33. Washington, D.C.: Smithsonian Books, 2009.

Perdue, Theda, and Michael Green. *The Columbia Guide to American Indians of the Southeast.* New York: Columbia University Press, 2001.

Peterson, John H., Jr. Introduction to "Setting the Stage: The Original Mississippians." In *Ethnic Heritage in Mississippi,* ed. Barbara Carpenter. Jackson: Mississippi Humanities Council, 1992.

Pettigrew, Dawn Karima. *The Marriage of Saints.* Norman: University of Oklahoma Press, 2006.

———. *The Way We Make Sense.* San Francisco: Aunt Lute Books, 2002.

Pollard, Edward A. *The Lost Cause: A New Southern History of the War of the Confederates.* 1866. Reprint; Whitefish, Mont.: Kessinger, 2010.

Powell, Douglas Reichert. *Critical Regionalism: Connecting Politics and Culture in the American Landscape.* Chapel Hill: University of North Carolina Press, 2007.

Pulitano, Elvira. *Toward a Native American Critical Theory.* Lincoln: University of Nebraska Press, 2003.

Ramirez, Renya K. *Native Hubs: Culture, Community, and Belonging in Silicon Valley and Beyond.* Durham, N.C.: Duke University Press, 2007.

Reid, Calvin. "Widow of 'Little Tree' Author Admits He Changed Identity." *Publishers Weekly,* 25 Oct. 1991, 16+.

Roberts, Blain, and Ethan J. Kytle. "Dancing Around History." *New York Times,* Opinionator/Opinion Pages, December 21, 2010. http://opinionator.blogs .nytimes.com/2010/12/21/dancing-around-history/?scp=4&sq=secession%20 ball&st=cse (accessed January 12, 2011).

Romine, Scott. *The Real South*. Baton Rouge: Louisiana State University Press, 2008.

Rothstein, Morton. "The New South and the International Economy." *Agricultural History* 57 (Oct. 1983): 385–402.

Said, Edward. *Orientalism*. New York: Vintage Books, 1979.

Saunt, Claudio. *Black, White, and Indian: Race and the Un-Making of an American Family*. New York: Oxford University Press, 2006.

———. *A New Order of Things: Power, Property, and the Transformation of the Creek Indians, 1733–1816*. New York: Cambridge University Press, 1999.

Schaap, James A. "The Growth of the Native American Gaming Industry: What Has the Past Provided, and What Does the Future Hold?" *American Indian Quarterly* 34, no. 3 (Summer 2010): 365–89.

Seelye, Katharine Q. "Celebrating Secession without the Slaves." *New York Times*, November 29, 2010. http://www.nytimes.com/2010/11/30/us/30confed.html (accessed January 23, 2011).

Shoemaker, Nancy. "How Indians Got to Be Red." *American Historical Review* 102, no. 3 (1997): 625–44.

Silko, Leslie Marmon. *Ceremony*. New York: Viking Press, 1977.

Smith, Jonathan, and Deborah Cohn, eds. *Look Away! The U.S. South in New World Studies*. Durham, N.C.: Duke University Press, 2004.

Smith, Mark M. *Debating Slavery: Economy and Society in the Antebellum American South*. New York: Cambridge University Press, 1998.

Smith, Paul Chaat. *Everything You Know about Indians Is Wrong*. Minneapolis: University of Minnesota Press, 2009.

Smith, Tony. "The Underdevelopment of Development Literature: The Case of Dependency Theory." *World Politics* 13, no. 2 (Jan. 1979): 247–88.

Snyder, Christina. *Slavery in Indian Country: The Changing Face of Captivity in Early America*. Cambridge: Harvard University Press, 2010.

Spikes, Michael. "Lee Durkee's *Rides of the Midway* and Barry Hannah's *Geronimo Rex*." *Mississippi Quarterly* 55, no. 3 (Summer 2002): 403–17.

Squint, Kirstin. "Choctawan Aesthetics, Spirituality, and Gender Relations: An Interview with LeAnne Howe." *MELUS: Multiethnic Literature of the U.S.* 35, no. 3 (Fall 2010): 211–24.

Starnes, Richard D., ed. *Southern Journeys: Tourism, History, and Culture in the Modern South*. Tuscaloosa: University of Alabama Press, 2003.

Stecopoulos, Harilaos. *Reconstructing the World: Southern Fictions and U.S. Imperialisms, 1898–1976*. Ithaca: Cornell University Press, 2008.

Stewart, George R. *Names on the Land: A Historical Account of Place-Naming in the United States*. New York: Houghton Mifflin, 1967.

Tarantino, Quentin, dir. *Inglourious Basterds*. Universal Pictures, 2009.

Taylor, Alan. *Liberty Men and Great Proprietors: The Revolutionary Settlement on the Maine Frontier, 1760–1820*. Chapel Hill: University of North Carolina Press, 1990.

Taylor, Dale Marie. "We Wait" and "Warrior Woman." In *The People Who Stayed: Southeastern Indian Writing after Removal*, ed. Geary Hobson et al. Norman: University of Oklahoma Press, 2010.

Taylor, Jonathan, and Joseph Kalt. *American Indians on Reservations: A Databook of Socioeconomic Change between the 1990 and 2000 Censuses*. Harvard Project on American Indian Economic Development. Cambridge, Mass.: Harvard University, January 2005.

Towner, Theresa M., and James B. Carothers. *Reading Faulkner. Collected Stories: Glossary and Commentary*. Jackson: University Press of Mississippi, 2006.

Trachtenberg, Alan. *Shades of Hiawatha: Staging Indians, Making Americans, 1880–1930*. New York: Farrar, Straus & Giroux, 2004.

Tracy, Barbara S. "Transcultural Transformation: African American and Native American Relations." PhD diss., University of Nebraska–Lincoln, 2009. http://digitalcommons.unl.edu/cgi/viewcontent.cgi?article=1016&context=englishdiss (accessed August 12, 2010).

Trefzer, Annette. *Disturbing Indians: The Archaeology of Southern Fiction*. Tuscaloosa: University of Alabama Press, 2007.

———. "Postcolonial Displacements in Faulkner's Indian Stories of the 1930s." In *Faulkner in the Twenty-First Century*, ed. Robert Hamblin and Ann Abadie, 68–88. Jackson: University Press of Mississippi, 2003.

Treuer, David. *Native American Fiction: A User's Manual*. Saint Paul: Graywolf Press, 2006.

Twelve Southerners. *I'll Take My Stand*. 1930. Reprint; Baton Rouge: Louisiana State University Press, 1978.

United States Emergency Council. *Report on Economic Conditions of the South*. 1938. Reprint; New York: Da Capo Press, 1972.

Urban, Andrew L. "Education of Little Tree." *Urban Cinefile*. http://www.urbancinefile.com.au/home/view.asp?a=1564&s=Video_files (accessed November 23, 2008).

Vance, Rupert B. *Human Geography of the South: A Study in Regional Resources and Human Adequacy*. 1935. Reprint; New York: Russell and Russell, 1968.

Van Sertima, Ivan. *African Presence in Early America*. New Brunswick, N.J.: Transaction Publishers, 1992.

———. *They Came Before Columbus*. New York: Random House, 1976.

Vest, Jennifer Lisa. "Traditional." In *The People Who Stayed: Southeastern Indian*

Writing after Removal, ed. Geary Hobson et al. Norman: University of Oklahoma Press, 2010.

Vizenor, Gerald. *Crossbloods: Bone Courts, Bingo and Other Reports*. Minneapolis: University of Minnesota Press, 1990.

Walcott, Derek. *Omeros*. New York: Noonday Press, 1992.

Walker, Alice. *Horses Make a Landscape Look More Beautiful*. 1979. Reprint; Orlando, Fla.: Mariner Books, 1986.

———. *Living by the Word*. New York: Harvest Books, 1989.

———. *Meridian*. New York: Washington Square, 1976.

———. *The Way Forward Is with a Broken Heart*. New York: Random House, 2000.

Warrior, Robert. "Intellectual Sovereignty and the Struggle for an American Indian Future." *Wicazo Sa Review* 8, no. 1 (Spring 1992): 1–20.

———. *The People and the Word: Reading Native Nonfiction*. Minneapolis: University of Minnesota Press, 2005.

———. *Tribal Secrets: Recovering American Indian Intellectual Traditions*. Minneapolis: University of Minnesota Press, 1995.

Weaver, Jace. *That the People Might Live: Native American Literatures and Native American Community*. New York: Oxford University Press, 1997.

Weaver, Jace, Craig S. Womack, and Robert Warrior, eds. *American Indian Literary Nationalism*. Albuquerque: University of New Mexico Press, 2006.

Webb, Walter Prescott. *Divided We Stand: The Crisis of a Frontierless Democracy*. New York: Farrar and Rinehart, 1937.

Webre, Steven. "The Problem of Indian Slavery in Spanish Louisiana, 1769–1803." *Louisiana History* 25, no. 2 (1984): 117–35.

Welburn, Ron. "A Most Secret Identity: Native American Assimilation and Identity Resistance in African America." In *Confounding the Color Line: The Indian-Black Experience in North America*, ed. James F. Brooks, 292–320. Lincoln: University of Nebraska Press, 2002.

Wickman, Patricia R. *Osceola's Legacy*. Tuscaloosa: University of Alabama Press, 2006.

Williams, Daniel. "Interview with Barry Hannah: February 6, 2001." *Mississippi Quarterly* 45, no. 2 (Spring 2001): 261–68.

Williams, David S. "Lost Cause Religion." *New Georgia Encyclopedia*, May 16, 2005. http://www.georgiaencyclopedia.org/nge/Article.jsp?id=h-2723 (accessed December 2, 2010).

Wilms, Douglas C. "Cherokee Land Use in Georgia Before Removal." In *Cherokee Removal: Before and After*, ed. William L. Andrews. Athens: University of Georgia Press, 1992.

Wilson, Charles Reagan. *Baptized in Blood: The Religion of the Lost Cause, 1865–1920*. Athens: University of Georgia Press, 1983.

Womack, Craig. *Red on Red: Native American Literary Separatism*. Minneapolis: University of Minnesota Press, 1999.

———. "Tribal Paradise Lost but Where Did It Go? Native Absence in Toni Morrison's *Paradise*." *Studies in American Indian Literatures* 21, no. 4 (Winter 2009): 20–52.

Wood, Karenne. *Markings on Earth*. Tucson: University of Arizona Press, 2001.

Woodward, C. Vann. *Origins of the New South, 1877–1913*. Baton Rouge: Louisiana State University Press, 1971.

Wright, Gavin. *Old South, New South Revolutions in the Southern Economy Since the Civil War*. New York: Basic, 1986.

Wyatt-Brown, Bertram. *Southern Honor: Ethics and Behavior in the Old South*. New York: Oxford University Press, 1989.

Yaeger, Patricia. "Ghosts and Shattered Bodies, or What Does It Mean to Still Be Haunted by Southern Literature?" *South Central Review* 22, no. 1 (Spring 2005): 87–108.

Žižek, Slavoj. *Violence*. New York: Picador, 2008.

INDEX

THE NEW SOUTHERN STUDIES